The Early Life of
Georges Clemenceau

The Early Life of
Georges Clemenceau
1841-1893

JACK D. ELLIS

THE REGENTS PRESS OF KANSAS

LAWRENCE

© Copyright 1980 by The Regents Press of Kansas
Printed in the United States of America

Library of Congress Cataloging in Publication Data

Ellis, Jack D.
The early life of Georges Clemenceau, 1841–1893.
Bibliography: p.
Includes index.
1. Clémenceau, Georges Eugène Benjamin, 1841–1929—
Childhood and youth.
2. Clémenceau, Georges Eugène Benjamin, 1841–1929—
Political career before 1893.
3 Statesmen—France—Biography.
I. Title.
DC342.8.C6E45   944.081'092'4   [B]   79-19118
ISBN 0-7006-0196-1

TO

DME

Contents

Contents

Preface

GEORGES CLEMENCEAU'S REPUTATION as *Père-la-Victoire* during World War I had already earned him acclaim as one of the giants of his age by the time of his death in 1929. Biographies that appeared shortly afterwards magnified his legendary status and were for the most part products of disciples and admirers— Jean Martet, Gustave Geffroy, Léon Daudet, Georges Suarez, and Gen. Jean Jules Henri Mordacq. Except for Ernest Judet's scathing portrait of his old enemy in *Le Véritable Clemenceau*, which had appeared in 1920, such works set the pattern for much of the writing on Clemenceau in France ever since. The most important figure in this school in recent times is Georges Wormser, whose *La République de Clemenceau* was published in 1961. Wormser was once private secretary to Clemenceau and a friend of Clemenceau's son, Michel; while his study provides important insight and information for scholars, it is less a critical biography than a tribute to the man he once served.

Two further French biographies appeared in 1968—one by the popular writer Philippe Erlanger and the other by Gaston Monnerville, who was then president of the Senate. Monnerville's work is the better of the two, despite the fact that its analysis is marred by a tendency toward patriotic hero worship. For years the standard English biographies were the relatively short works by Geoffrey Bruun (1943) and John Hampden Jackson (1948). Then, in 1974, there appeared a new full-length study by the British historian David Robin Watson. Based on an exhaustive search of all available sources, Professor Watson's book is a generally balanced political biography that ranks as the most scholarly treatment to date of Clemenceau's entire career.

Nevertheless, work remains to be done on this controversial

figure. The complexity of his character and the sheer length of
his career, which stretched over half a century and which
touched on almost every political crisis of his time, mean that
both detail and perspective are lost in a single-volume treatment.
My focus is on Clemenceau's years in the wilderness, when he
was out of power, rather than on his better-known activities
after the turn of the century, which have been ably treated by
Watson and others. His later career and especially his wartime
leadership have tended to obscure or distort his early life, a
period when his attitudes were significantly different from those
with which the world now associates him. Many of the same
Frenchmen who praised the old man of World War I as the
savior of France had once condemned him as the *enfant terrible*
of the Republic. In the pre-1893 period he was a fighter for
left-wing causes, not the hero of the nationalists. He was the
champion of workers and trade unions, not the strikebreaker
of 1906. He was the archenemy of Jules Ferry's colonial designs,
not the man who as prime minister presided over the conquest
of Morocco. For many historians, his actions during his early
life have remained an enigma. Guy Chapman's comments in
his study of the first decades of the Third Republic typify the
traditional view: "Clemenceau's reputation rests on his work in
1918, which veils the fact that had the Father of Victory died
in 1914, it would be very different. During much of his early
parliamentary career his activities were pernicious and often
devoid of political understanding."[1]

I hope that the present volume will provide a better understanding of Clemenceau's first political career. What follows is,
in part, an effort to modify the notions that Clemenceau's chief
contribution to the evolution of the Third Republic was the
negative one of being a harsh and destructive "Wrecker of
Ministries" and that France might have achieved stability had
it not been for his intransigence. It is argued that much of his
activity was based on the hope of implementing constructive
solutions to the problems of the Republic. His most important
goal was a social transformation that would guarantee both
political freedom and economic justice to the weak. For Clemenceau the Revolution of 1789 had initiated the process of
moral and political emancipation. But new conditions in the

1880s necessitated a second revolution, which would free the individual in the social and economic domain. It was to be nonviolent, implemented within the framework of the Republic; and such reforms as freedom of speech, press, assembly, and association were to be essential in order to facilitate the desired economic transformation.

Viewed in this light, Clemenceau's early life takes on new significance. Throughout the 1880s he and those on the far Left who called themselves Radical Socialists attacked the dominant laissez-faire prejudices of the age. They struggled for the rights of strikers and trade unions, for state protection of workers against the big companies, and for judicial and penal reform. They aimed, in short, to regulate capitalism and to break the power of what they called the "financial feudality."

The failure to discern how central these social and economic goals were to Clemenceau's political program constitutes the chief weakness in previous biographical treatments. This failure has resulted from two related factors: lack of sustained emphasis on the economic depression of the 1880s and neglect of the fact that, for Clemenceau, such issues as revision of the constitution and anticolonialism were an integral part of the Radical approach to the social question. His hatred for the Senate, for example, was rooted less in sterile political theory than in the fact that the Senate always vetoed social legislation. The modernity of his social ideals has been recognized by only a few historians, most notably by the American Leo A. Loubère in a series of articles on radicalism in France, published in the 1960s, and in a more recent study on radicalism in the Mediterranean departments.[2] This touches on a larger historiographical problem for the biographer of Clemenceau: that is, the absence of detailed studies on early Radical socialism, of which his first career was a part. In addition to Loubère's contributions, the only major works to date are those by Jacques Kayser and Jean-Thomas Nordmann.[3]

Although the creative aspects of Clemenceau's social goals for the Republic have been ignored, there remains one problem that has long baffled his biographers. This relates to his personality and to those "pernicious" tactics that often characterized his behavior. While I have tried to show that his reputation

as a wrecker of ministries is not entirely deserved, he was, nevertheless, incapable of compromise and often exhibited personality
traits that undermined his leadership potential and hence the
ideals he claimed to defend. Herein lies the contradiction of
his early life: how could he have hoped to achieve the reforms
he desired while alienating those whose help was essential and
while refusing to work for political office? It is true that the
ruling moderates found him unacceptable; but it is also true
that Clemenceau contributed to their mistrust and did little to
make himself acceptable. Contemptuous toward ministerial
positions and toward those who sought them, he often appeared,
even to his fellow Radicals, to prefer failure over success.

I do not believe that political analysis alone is enough to
explain this contradiction, for Clemenceau's early life was
marked by an essential dualism of character in which both
creative and destructive drives interacted in his private and
public behavior. In this book I argue that this polarity reflected
a more fundamental reality operating at the level of the unconscious: namely, a loss of self and an identity confusion,
both of which have roots in childhood and adolescence. I am
aware of the skepticism, often justified, with which many historians view psychoanalytic interpretations. For this reason,
some initial explanation concerning my approach is in order.

Twenty years have passed since William L. Langer, in an
address to the American Historical Association, urged his colleagues to begin applying the principles of modern psychology
to historical problems.[4] Several notable efforts in this direction,
however, have tended to discredit the approach—the study of
Woodrow Wilson by Sigmund Freud and William C. Bullitt,
which was published in 1967, being a prime example. Yet,
psychoanalytic methods have much to offer historians, particularly biographers, since they provide a systematic means for
viewing human personality in place of the unsystematic character studies on which many of us have relied in our teaching
and writing. Historians have a contribution of their own to
make in this regard. Knowledge of social and cultural forces
that have conditioned attitudes in the past is essential in order
to guard against a bias that is culturally bound or against the
tendency to view as abnormal what was characteristic of an age.

I have tried to keep this danger in mind in viewing Clemenceau. Many features of his early family life, especially the presence of a domineering father, were not unusual in the nineteenth century, as Jean-Louis Flandrin's recent study of the French family shows.[5] The same is true for other features of his life— from his decision to study medicine, which was in line with family tradition, to his fighting of duels. What must concern us is the degree to which familial and social forces influenced both his outlook and his success in adjusting to these forces. One should bear in mind Franz Alexander's warning that neurotic processes are only "quantitatively different" from normal ones.[6]

In the course of my research I found some of the principles of modern ego psychology to be helpful in understanding what I believe were very real inner tensions in Clemenceau's life. Freud's initial theories on the unconscious, which emphasized the link between motivation and repressed sexual strivings, have undergone many modifications over the past few decades. During the last thirty years or so, there has been increased stress on the concept of ego, or self, which is associated with the writings of such people as Anna Freud, Heinz Hartmann, Erik H. Erikson, Edith Jacobson, and many others. Of particular importance is the concept of ego identity, which is associated primarily, though not exclusively, with the theories of Erikson.[7] As David Rapaport has noted, these are extensions of Freudian ideas which complement those of Hartmann on autonomous ego development.[8] Erikson regards himself as a post-Freudian and sees his work as an attempt to extend Freud's study of the unconscious upward to "the enigma of consciousness." In particular, Eriksonian theory emphasizes the ego (as opposed to the id, or instinctual self), the ego's synthesizing functions, and its conditioning within a specific cultural and historical setting.[9]

If Erikson's formulations are used selectively and with an eye to their limitations, they can be useful to the biographer, since, by postulating a sequence of phases in the psychosocial development of the individual, they provide a framework for analyzing the whole life cycle—the first formulation in the history of psychoanalytic theory to do so.[10] These phases are characterized by developmental crises, each of which the individual must resolve before successfully confronting the next. Starting in infancy, these are *trust versus mistrust*, which corresponds to Freud's oral stage; *autonomy versus shame and doubt*, which corresponds to Freud's anal stage; *initiative versus guilt*, which encompasses Freud's ideas on the Oedipus conflict; *industry versus inferiority*, which corresponds to Freud's phallic stage. Next comes the crisis of *identity versus identity diffusion* in adolescence. From this point, Erikson sketches three psychosocial crises of adulthood, which are *intimacy versus isolation*, *generativity versus self-absorption*, and *ego integrity versus disgust and despair*.[11]

Erikson has developed his theories in biographical studies of Martin Luther and Mohandas Gandhi.[12] At the core of his ideas lies the concept of identity, which, he argues, has become as important for the study of personality in our time as sexuality was in Freud's. Erikson believes that identification with both real and fictitious people begins early in childhood. It is always a difficult process, especially during the period that we today call adolescence. At this point, ego synthesis, or the integration of all previous identifications, occurs. The final identity, while based on the perception of selfsameness, represents a selective assimilation and repudiation of childhood identifications and is not merely the sum of them.[13] The danger at this point is that there may be a confusion of roles; if there is, the identity crisis may be prolonged into adulthood and may become associated with a broad range of behavior.

Eriksonian theories are useful in examining Georges Clemenceau's early development, for I believe that the patterns of his first political career suggest a profound identity problem, which was rooted in the conflict between his own inner feelings and the role that had been imposed upon him by his rebel father, Benjamin. It will be helpful at this point to provide a brief overview of the theory presented in this book.

Biographers have long recognized the emotional bond that existed between Clemenceau and his father. In stressing this factor, they have usually pointed out the similarities in their ideologies and temperaments. Like the father, the son became essentially Jacobin in political outlook, a hater of injustice, often abrasive and authoritarian in his dealings with others. But there was another dimension in this pattern of father identification. An understanding of this dimension begins with an awareness that despite the image of Clemenceau as the "Tiger"—with all the attributes of power and mystery that this persona implied—there was a side of him that was seldom perceived by others. This side was marked by weakness, emotional vulnerability, and the need for approval and affection.

Clemenceau was always an emotional man, and those traits that could cause the Tiger of France to weep on several occasions in his public life can be discerned in his childhood. In chapter 1 we shall see that his emotional sensitivity owed much to his mother's influence during the first years of his life. His problems of adjustment, I believe, developed out of his effort to identify with his father in late childhood and adolescence. Clemenceau loved his father, but no matter how idyllic his reflections on his childhood may have been in the later years of his life, there can be little doubt that the tension created in the Clemenceau household by Benjamin's rigid standards and nervous behavior was trying for young Georges.

In 1946 a Freudian psychoanalyst named Pierre Lacombe, noting this neglected feature of Clemenceau's development, argued that there were in him actually two men, "one a destroyer, the other a creator." Lacombe conjectured that this duality was rooted in two sources. The first was Benjamin's perpetual anger, which "must have been meager nourishment for the sensitive heart of young Georges." The second was the Oedipus complex, or the child's unconscious rivalry with his father for the affection of the mother. According to Lacombe, these factors produced an unconscious hostility toward his father, who, in Georges's mind, came to represent all authority. Thus, the son's overthrowing of ministries in the 1880s was in reality an attack against the authority that symbolized Benjamin.[14]

Lacombe's analysis would make better sense had not the relations between father and son continued to be close throughout their lives. Yet, the notion of a polarity of drives within Clemenceau has much to recommend it, though, in my opinion, the source of this polarity was the difficulty that a sensitive boy experienced in the conflict between his father identification and his own quest for autonomous self-development. Indeed, Clemenceau's biographers have often indicated the problem of reconciling his post-1897 personality with his pre-1897 personality. But 1897 was the year of Benjamin's death, and as Lacombe has noted, that year marked the beginning of a change in Clemenceau. This study will show that Clemenceau's essentially uncompromising identification with his father's ideals necessarily created an obstacle to Clemenceau's independent personal and psychological self-development. Thus, it is possible to suggest that his fundamental psychological problem was the opposition between his striving for self-development and his father identification.

Two points must be kept in mind. First, the French Revolution, as idealized by Benjamin, made a deep impression on young Georges. There could be no betrayal of its ideals, for the role marked out for him early in life was that of defender of them. To interpret this aspect of his life as role-playing is by no means to imply that it was artificial or insincere. Such a role was an integral part of his father identification. "This admirable Revolution by which we exist," he told the Chamber of Deputies in 1891, "is not over . . . we are the actors in it, the same men are fighting the same enemies. What our grandfathers wanted, we want still."[15] Benjamin's standards were exacting and required, on the son's part, constant vigilance and strength of character in meeting the expectations of this role. As late as 1903 Clemenceau's friend the Danish literary critic Georg Brandes said of him, "Even now the son feels as if his father's eye were upon him. Occasionally the expression escapes him: 'If I were to do such-and-such a thing, my father would not call me his son.' "[16]

Second, Clemenceau's role as champion of his father's ideals, which began to assume form at the time of Benjamin's suffering at the hands of the Second Empire in the 1850s, coincided with Georges's own attempted ego synthesis of childhood identifications. His placing of self-development in opposition to father identification was bound to result in shame reactions—or the feeling that the inner self was unworthy of and unequal to the role model—and in an alternating perception of guilt. Since any attempt at asserting his own self-development demanded that he be emancipated from father identification, Clemenceau's continuing quest for his own true ego identity elicited guilt toward his father. This guilt demanded a submissive return to the childhood stance of father identification, which, in turn, produced guilt toward himself for his failure to become independent from any and all father identification. But guilt toward self once again demanded emancipation from father identification, thus starting a new cycle of Clemenceau's psychological conflict. As a result of this situation, he could not escape alternating feelings of guilt (toward his father and toward himself), and therefore, under the circumstances, the only available notion of self-identity was that of being a sufferer for his father's ideals.

Erikson has observed that shame and guilt incurred during the first struggles for ego autonomy form "one of the eternal sources of human anxiety and strife." He argues that in many cases the effects of these emotions are not apparent until later in life, when "conflicts over initiative may find expression in a self-restriction which keeps an individual from living up to his inner capacities."[17] While shame denotes a perception of inner weakness and unworthiness, guilt implies transgression of a moral boundary, especially in relation to an ego-ideal. Psychological guilt thus springs from self-awareness and the capacity for self-reflection and choice.[18]

The issue of psychological guilt as a dominant though often hidden factor in motivation is a difficult one. Helen B. Lewis, among other writers, recognizes the limitations in our ability to analyze both shame and guilt, but she believes that by focusing on them, we may better understand that "primary process" by which the self, as judge and regulator of self-directed hostility, allows "strangulated" feelings to find "compromise expression in neurotic symptoms."[19] Indeed, the human psyche has a variety of techniques for coping with the problem of guilt, which are often manifested in the form of psychological compromises. Such techniques range from confession and reparation to self-abasement and martyrdom; they may include what one writer terms an "intolerance of success" and a tendency "to sabotage oneself" in one's work and career.[20]

In Clemenceau's case, I believe that the evidence shows that the behavioral patterns and emotional cycles of his early life (which began to manifest themselves most clearly during his student years in Paris in the 1860s) are symptomatic of guilt-engendered drives that stem from his childhood relationship with his father. They are also suggestive of several related behavioral features during the height of his early political career, between 1880 and 1893. These include the syndrome of suffering and self-punishment, which is familiar to students of human behavior and which represents one of the primary techniques of the human psyche for resolving inner guilt.

It is to Clemenceau's self-identity as a sufferer for a cause, for example, that we can attribute his preoccupation with the role of martyrs in history and his solidarity with all sufferers among mankind, be they martyrs for a cause or victims of slavery, capitalist exploitation, or imperialist greed. These features of his character will be clearly seen in the chapters that follow. Many of them were, in fact, admirable traits that provided Clemenceau with the requisite empathy and understanding toward human problems that enabled him to formulate creative policies and goals for the young Republic. At times they imparted to him a vision of justice that transcended the selfish insularity of the bourgeois politicians of the Third Republic. But the so-called martyr complex that one discerns in the pre-1897 Clemenceau also required of him the sacrifice of his reputation and even his life on the altar of his father's ideals, and he did not hesitate to risk either, in Parliament or on the field of honor. Thus, his creative side had its counterpart in certain destructive and self-defeating drives.

More precisely, Clemenceau's pangs of guilt could be alleviated only by the process of externalization of guilt and by external punishment. Externalization of guilt toward his father found its expression in his intransigent defense of his father's ideals, and the boldness of this defense proved that he was indeed strong enough to measure up to his father's expectations. On the other hand, Clemenceau provided the external punishment that relieved the intensity of his guilt toward himself by engineering the defeat of those ideals. The engineering of his own political defeats—whether by alienating the majority in Parliament or by refusing any compromise of his principles—thus constituted a refusal to succeed as the champion of his father's ideals. It can hence be viewed as a form of self-punishment that was intended to alleviate the guilt he felt toward himself.

These complex delineations of character must not ignore the fact that there were powerful political and social forces that militated against the success of Clemenceau's Radical program. Yet, though they were aware of these forces, Watson and other biographers have also stressed that Clemenceau's own personality played an important role in causing his failures. The above observations, which will be developed in the pages that follow, help to explain why such an intelligent, capable, and even brilliant man as Clemenceau, despite the most noble motives and the most worthy vision for his country's future, achieved so little during the twenty-three years of his first political career.

Several institutions and individuals have aided me in the preparation of this study. A University of Delaware Summer Faculty Research Grant enabled me to begin collecting microfilm materials relating to the life of Georges Clemenceau, and a grant from the American Philosophical Society made it possible for me to visit France during the initial stages of research. Special appreciation is due to Madame Boilot and her staff at the Musée Clemenceau in Paris; to Albert Krebs of the Bibliothèque Nationale, whose articles on Clemenceau's youth are well known to scholars in this field and who gave me valuable assistance and advice; and to Georges Clemenceau, grandson of the French statesman, who introduced me to several of his grandfather's former associates and graciously invited me to spend a few days at the ancestral chatêau of L'Aubraie in the Vendée. I also wish to thank Katharine M. Wood, Jennie A. Spurgeon, and Joyce A. Storm of the Reference Department of the University of Delaware Library for their help during research for the book. One of my colleagues in the Department of History at the University of Delaware, Professor Stephen Lukashevich, read the completed manuscript and offered many useful criticisms and suggestions. Finally, I wish to thank my wife, Diane Marie Ellis, for her encouragement and help during the long period of research and writing.

Naturally, any errors of either fact or interpretation are entirely my own.

The Early Life of
Georges Clemenceau

Which I meantersay, if the ghost of a man's own father
cannot be allowed to claim his attention, what can, Sir?

Joe Gargery to Pip in
Dickens's *Great Expectations*

ONE

Identity Quest &
Identity Diffusion, 1841-1870

The transmission of ideals from one generation to the next is never as simple as it appears to be. Relationships within the family and the interaction between the family and the social milieu affect both the formation of ideals and the manner in which the child integrates them as he moves from one developmental stage to another.[1] As the spokesman for radicalism during the first decades of the Third Republic, Georges Clemenceau prided himself on being a man of principles; these were less the product of a formal system of thought than of ego standards that he had acquired within the family circle. This chapter will trace the evolution of his ideals in an effort to show that the role they dictated for him conflicted with his own sense of inner self. This conflict lay at the heart of his early identity problems and is one of the most important keys in understanding his subsequent career.

Clemenceau was a Vendean, a fact he never let others forget. He was born on September 28, 1841, in the village of Mouilleron-en-Pareds, which is about fifty miles southeast of Nantes. It was a typical hamlet of the *Bocage*, lost amid hollows and coppice, the surrounding fields fenced off with mud walls and hedges.[2] The house in which he was born belonged to his mother's parents, François and Emma Gautreau. His mother, the twenty-four-year-old Sophie Emma, had insisted on undergoing her confinement there, as she had done when her first child, Emma, had been born the year before, rather than at L'Aubraie, the ancestral château of her husband, Benjamin, which was located near the village of Féaule in the commune of

3

Sainte-Hermine and in which she had lived since her marriage in 1839. L'Aubraie was a depressing place for such an event. Besides, she did not like her father-in-law, Paul-Jean, who had not wanted his son to marry her. The reason was that the Gautreaus, who belonged to the petit bourgeoisie in Mouilleron and owned only a few modest properties, had little to offer besides Sophie Emma. Old Paul-Jean knew the value of good marriages, for that was how L'Aubraie had been brought into the family shortly after the Revolution.

A modern visitor to Mouilleron senses the isolation and timelessness of the place. A visitor in the 1840s would have been even more struck by its severity. To the west the shores along the Bay of Biscay, stretching south from Nantes to the old Protestant stronghold of La Rochelle, are lined with dunes and marshes that cut off seaborne trade. A great plain runs inland toward the *Bocage,* a wooded country of poor people and rocky soil, its farms and hamlets joined by dirt roads that wind through groves and thickets. Adversity had always been their lot, but the Vendeans were rich in passion for king and Mother Church. Here the last bloody struggles between Catholics and Huguenots took place in the late sixteenth century. More recently, in 1793, the Vendeans had risen in revolt against the revolutionary regime in Paris. The ensuing civil war between royalist *blancs* and republican *bleus,* along with the ferocity of the Republic's suppression of the revolt, had left a legacy of hate.

The Clemenceaus were not nobles, but in the fifty years or so before Georges's birth their manner of living at L'Aubraie had exhibited aristocratic pretensions. Georges's direct male ancestral line can be traced back to the early sixteenth century. By the early seventeenth century, Protestantism had become a distinguishing trait of this line, the apothecary Paul having been a member of the Church of Mareuil. In 1623 he had married another Protestant named Charlotte Charretier. Their children had been baptized as Protestants, but with the revocation of the Edict of Nantes in 1685, the family had been forced to convert to Catholicism. Religion does not appear to have had a significant influence on Georges's immediate paternal ancestors. His grandfather was a nominal Catholic, but his father, Benjamin, who was born at L'Aubraie in 1810, was an atheist, whose heroes could be seen in the portraits of Robespierre and Saint-Just that hung in the château. The Gautreaus, on the other hand, were devout Protestants; and Georges's mother was a firm believer and a member of the church of Mouilleron-Sainte-Hermine.[3]

Georges's great-grandfather, grandfather, and father were all doctors. The study of medicine not only set them apart as men of learning, in contrast to the ignorance and credulity around them, but was also a method for scientific training that could be applied to the management of their agricultural interests. One family home was at Colombier, near Georges's birthplace. The other, L'Aubraie, was a brooding, rundown château with interior oak beams that still showed the marks of burns from the religious wars. Here the Clemenceaus planted, tended their livestock, hunted, and sometimes prescribed remedies for the peasants. During the Revolution the family's social status had been enhanced by Georges's great-grandfather, Pierre-Paul, who served as a medical officer for the republican armies of the *bleus* during the civil war and later sat in the Council of Five Hundred under the Directory and in the Corps Législatif under Napoleon.[4]

The traditions of Protestantism and republicanism in Georges's background signified minority status for his family in this milieu. But he had a deep love for the Vendeans, whose differences from his own family and whose history of passion and violence could not help but stir his imagination. Whether digging for bullets in the trees around Mouilleron or listening to his grandmother Joubert tell about the rebel siege of Montaigu, he was intrigued by the peculiarities of this Catholic and royalist region. His later literary works dwell on the people he had known in childhood. There are stories of quail-hunting around Sainte-Hermine, many portraits of local characters, and descriptions of visits to such coastal towns as La Tranche-sur-mer, where bronzed lean fishermen appeared to him as "a vestige of primitive races." He saw in his fellow countrymen a reflection of his own intense commitment to ideals. "I love the Vendeans," he once said, "they have an ideal, and to defend that ideal they have something stubborn, narrow, savage, which I like."[5]

In 1843 Georges's parents moved to Nantes.[6] It was here,

along the rue Crébillion, that he grew up, although he spent
vacations with the Clemenceaus at L'Aubraie and often visited
his mother's parents in nearby Mouilleron. His father, Benjamin, inherited L'Aubraie in 1860, and the family moved back
at that time. Benjamin's initial move to Nantes was a significant
step for him, and the anger and frustration that appear to have
prompted it are relevant to our understanding of Georges's later
identity problems.

Parenthood evokes memories of one's own childhood and
the difficulties experienced in identifying with one's parents.[7]
What is known about Benjamin suggests that by the time his
first two children were born, he was attempting to resolve an
inner crisis that prompted him to affirm a separate identity from
his father, Paul-Jean, whom he perceived as being weak in
character and lacking in ideals. Benjamin's mother, Gabrielle
Joubert, was, by contrast, a strong and energetic woman. One
surviving letter, which she wrote to him while he was in Paris
in 1830, shows both her intelligence and her affection for her
son.[8] Georges remembered that when he was a boy, his grandmother was the "linchpin" that held the household together at
L'Aubraie and that she was far superior to her husband, whose
chief interests were his farms and who inspected his livestock
in a white tie and high hat.[9] Paul-Jean did become mayor of
La Réorthe, which included the area around L'Aubraie, but
that was the extent of his political activity. There was one other
member of the family, Benjamin's younger brother, Paul; he was
a reactionary who in any case showed only sporadic interest in
anything other than his guns and dogs. Paul-Jean is supposed
to have dubbed his younger son the marquis, his older son the
sans-culotte.

One of Benjamin's earliest memories was of standing at the
bridge at L'Aubraie and hearing the news about Napoleon's
defeat at Waterloo.[10] Sometime during his youth he developed
a fascination for the heroes of the Revolution—especially Robespierre and Saint-Just—and a conviction that the Revolution had
been the most noble experiment in history. By the age of twenty
he had already known the first of many personal disappointments
when the Revolution of 1830 failed to establish the Republic.
After the installation of Louis Philippe, Benjamin arrived in

Paris to begin his medical studies. Here he became part of the romantic rebellion of the Left Bank, an admirer of Jules Michelet and Louis Blanc, and a champion of the new doctrine of positivism, with its belief in the superiority of science over religion and metaphysics. He idolized Victor Hugo, whose play *Hernani* was shocking Parisian literary circles because of its mocking of kings and aristocrats. Benjamin got his medical degree in 1835; then he traveled briefly in Switzerland before returning to L'Aubraie. His subsequent courtship of Sophie Emma and his father's opposition to his marriage into a family that was inferior in wealth and status further embittered what was no doubt an already precarious father-son relationship.

Benjamin had neither the ambition nor the talent to become a successful country doctor.[11] Increasingly he perceived his identity in terms of an almost legendary past, of the revolutionary Republic that had toppled kings and priests and that, in promoting the idea of the career open to talents, had given meaning to the lives of men such as himself. But the Rights of Man had been betrayed; in looking around him it was not hard to find the culprit. His private notebooks bristled with denunciations of the Church. Religion had always produced "inertia and stupid resignation." A new society must eradicate it, for "it is hard to believe that a doctrine that has produced only misery and tyranny for two thousand years can suddenly give birth to happiness and liberty." The day of reckoning was inevitable: "That great current of ideas that has flowed across France since the Constituent Assembly, sometimes large and powerful, sometimes dammed up in its banks or hidden under the earth, is not destroyed; rather, it has temporarily disappeared."[12]

The move to Nantes gave Benjamin a chance to assert his own identity as a worker for the Republic, and it was not long after 1843 that he joined a small group of business and professional men who called themselves the Republican Commission of Nantes. It met almost every day in a reading room at the corner of rue Jean-Jacques Rousseau and the place Graslin, where its members talked and plotted, always on guard against police spies. Between these activities and the solitary hours that he spent in his library at home, Benjamin indulged his tastes as a dilettante—painting, making lithographs, playing the violin. Already he resembled the description left in later years by Georges's friend, the writer Gustave Geffroy: "Neither sturdy hates nor mocking and revengeful irony were lacking in him. . . . There was in him a great capacity for enthusiasm and indignation, and his contempt for social evil alternated with his admiration for the beauty of literature and art . . . . his hands folded behind him, in a gray coat, straw hat and coarse boots, clean-shaven, his piercing eyes sheltered by glasses, a faint smile playing over his lips, full of wit between his silences."[13]

Benjamin's share of the family estate enabled him to bring up his children in relative comfort. Four more were born after Emma and Georges: Adrienne in 1850, Sophie in 1854, Paul in 1857, and Albert in 1861.[14] Benjamin deeply loved his children, but his own nervous distractions and authoritarianism, combined with traditional notions of child rearing, created an unsettled atmosphere in which Georges passed his first years. The father's hatred for social evil and his sensitivity to the issues of human freedom and justice did not entail private tenderness and affection in his dealings with young children.

In Georges's earliest memories of him, his father appears as a man who was "always angry." Benjamin was "unpleasant to approach, always boiling over," and if the boy wandered into his father's library, he was told, "Georges, get out of here; you are not in your place." During the first years at Nantes, Georges saw very little of his father during the daytime. Mealtimes, which were such an important part of the ritual of bourgeois families of that era, were in his family no occasion for idle chatter. Benjamin monopolized the time, discussing his reading, blurting out his philosophy "in fits and starts," and ensuring that the gods of the Revolution were ever present: "He spoke of Danton, of Robespierre. He was for Robespierre, against Danton."[15]

The Revolution of 1848 rekindled and magnified Benjamin's staunch republicanism. Georges long remembered standing at the window of the house in Nantes and seeing his father arrive in a highly emotional state. Georges's older sister, Emma, explained to her brother that "the King is dead."[16] Benjamin's reading club in Nantes sent a resolution congratulating the new Provisional Government and extolling the events in Paris as "a revolution without equal in history," a document that Benjamin signed personally.[17] At Colombier he planted a "liberty tree," and he kept to his death a copy of the original proclamation of the Provisional Government, which he had received from his old Parisian friend Étienne Arago, who was a minister in the Provisional Government.[18] When further violence broke out in June as the Parisian workers, angry over abolition of the National Workshops, went to the barricades for a second time, the new and conservative National Assembly appealed to the provinces for aid against the rebels. At L'Aubraie, where the family was just starting its summer vacation, Georges recalled witnessing this scene: "All the bourgeois Vendeans had armed and equipped themselves, and one day, I recall, I walked into the kitchen and saw my uncle melting up bullets. My uncle Paul was getting ready to go. My father learned of it and stormed in like the wind and said to my uncle, 'Paul, if you go to defend those swine I'll go myself. I'll go and fight on the side of the Parisians.' "[19]

Neither brother went, however. After three days of bloody fighting, the rebels were beaten. After a few months, Louis Napoleon became president of the dying Republic, which was soon to be followed by the Second Empire. Benjamin's hopes were again crushed, but there was always the hope of achieving his goals through his children. The collapse of the Republic in the three years following the Revolution of 1848 marked a change in his relations with Georges. This change, as will be shown below, entailed a significant psychological readjustment for his eldest son, at the heart of which was a shift from the maternal constellation to a paternal one.

Erikson has stressed the crucial importance during infancy and early childhood of achieving a sense of trust, autonomy, and initiative, while overcoming corresponding feelings of shame, doubt, and guilt. The mother is the central figure in the child's achievement of these goals, for it is she who enables him to move from psychobiological dependency to a greater sense of self. The term "self" has many definitions, but it is used here to denote one's inner feelings and perceptions and one's knowledge of these.[20] "Ego identity," on the other hand, is the integration of this experienced self with what Robert W. White has termed "the requirements of social living."[21] In young Clemenceau's case there were significant differences between the image of self that he acquired during his first years and the one that he formed in early adolescence, which he strove to project to others.

During his first ten years, Georges's most tender emotional investments were directed toward Sophie Emma, who has been described as a woman of both firmness of spirit and gentle sweetness.[22] There can be little doubt that his attachment for her was a deep and lasting one and that under her care he achieved a sense of trust. She was always, for him, "une femme admirable" who counseled him with "words from the heart," and he was her "beloved" son. At some point in his youth she gave him a little box, and every year, on his birthday, she placed in it small souvenirs—money or a book such as an early edition of the play *The Marriage of Figaro*. He carried this box to his grave.[23]

It is important to remember that Georges was probably the center of attention during these first years, since the third child, Adrienne, was not born until nine years later, in 1850. His older sister, Emma, seems to have been especially fond of him. A photograph of the two children taken around 1848 shows her in a very protective stance toward her little brother—her hand grasps his, and her arm is around his shoulder. It will be recalled that it was she who tried to explain to him what was happening when the agitated father arrived home with news of the Revolution of 1848. She and Albert, the youngest child, had especially close relationships with Georges throughout their lives.[24] The comfort and security that young Georges felt within this circle must have been especially strong, for even in his old age he remembered that the birth of Adrienne had been a "disagreeable date" in his life, since the attention demanded by the new infant meant that he had had to go to a private school rather than continuing to be tutored by his mother, who had taught herself Latin so that she could instruct her children.[25]

In later life, Clemenceau recalled the home of his mother's parents in Mouilleron as being a happy place where he had "danced very often." He long retained memories of his Grandmother Gautreau, a strong-willed Huguenot woman, as she sat reading her Bible. His Grandfather Gautreau, "rustic and a bit unpolished," used to bounce him on his knee and say, "Ah, little Georges, when I get to heaven it will give me great pleasure to learn that you've made a fine speech like Jules Favre." Conversely, the boy did not like visits to L'Aubraie, where he obviously felt the tension between his father and grandfather: "When I was able to mount my horse and gallop in the fields, life was beautiful. Until then it was deadly. I can understand why my mother wanted to undergo her confinement elsewhere."[26]

Such a reaction is not surprising for one whose early character formation showed traits of deep emotional sensitivity. All his life he remembered being moved by accounts in the works of Charles Dickens of American newspaper notices describing runaway slaves who were identifiable because of some physical mutilation. He wept as a boy while watching a performance of *Uncle Tom's Cabin* in a theater in Nantes, and his well-marked copy of the novel can still be seen today.[27] Abraham Lincoln was one of his earliest heroes; even at the end of his life he called him "one of the greatest men who ever lived" and said that he had always wanted to be like him.[28]

The Protestant tradition, as embodied in his mother, is equally relevant to the development of his early character traits. David Robin Watson has noted that as a boy, Georges learned the Bible well.[29] But there was conflict between the parents over this issue. At some point a worried Benjamin extracted from Sophie Emma a vow that even if he should die, she would not allow any of the children to be baptized or to receive religious instruction. "You know the promise you have made to me and sworn upon your honor," he wrote her in 1858, "I remind you of it, and if you should fail to do so, I would feel constrained to hate you."[30]

Nevertheless, despite Georges's lifelong atheism, there were always traces of the religious aspect of the maternal influence.[31] The genuine moral sensitivity and compassion toward the weak and oppressed that one sees in his early political career surely owed something to his mother's Protestant heritage. In his first writings at the age of twenty, for example, he denounced the "corrupt and debased clergy" who had influenced Louis XIV to revoke the Edict of Nantes. He sympathized with the sufferings of the Huguenots, and he argued that their martyrdom had helped to prepare the way for "the great day of reparation" in 1789.[32]

After the birth of Adrienne, Georges attended a private school; then, in 1853, he entered the fifth form of the lycée at Nantes. It is curious to note that one of his first teachers, the father of the writer Jules Vallès, impressed him as being "a violent man" who seemed to want "to swallow everything up."[33] For it was during this same period that Georges was beginning to be engulfed by new demands and pressures from his father, whose previous attitude of neglect was changing to one of great attentiveness. In the light of Benjamin's own frustrations it is easy to see how he perceived his son to be an extension of himself, even if the father's narcissistic requirements entailed the sacrifice of young Georges's emotional needs.

More and more Benjamin doted on the boy—selecting his readings, painting his portrait, seeking out the best instructors to teach him the use of swords and pistols so that he would be able to defend his honor and principles. Now Georges accompanied his father to the reading club in Nantes, where he was thrust among "strange people who had seen the Revolution and Napoleon." Sometimes Benjamin would take the floor and pace back and forth, denouncing the priests and aristocrats. "You see that man in the corner there?" he would ask Georges. "He was an old friend of Marat's." The son did not know who Marat was, except that the name conjured up images of blood and a woman named Charlotte Corday. Georges and his father went hunting and horseback riding together, and they had long talks about literature and philosophy. The substance of these talks is not hard to guess, judging from the son's comments in later life: "I think that the only influence that had any impact on me was that of my father. Where did he get his ideas? Certainly not from his family, almost all of whom were hostile to him. I think he got them from Michelet, of whom he always spoke with the greatest respect. My father was basically a romantic who had translated into politics and sociology the literary ideas of people such as Victor Hugo."[34] Proof of the enduring impact of these discussions can be seen in Georges's first writings: he praised Hugo as his model for courage and integrity and declared his allegiance to Michelet's philosophy of history, with its fixed idea of the Republic's triumphing over religious and political injustice.[35]

Benjamin took a special interest in what Georges was learning at the lycée, whose curriculum was heavy with rhetoric, elocution, and translation of the classics. The boy's overall record was not distinguished, but he excelled in science, composition, philosophy, and English, which he practiced by reading such novels as *Robinson Crusoe* and *Uncle Tom's Cabin*. Benjamin worried over what his son was learning about religion, and family mealtimes now became the occasion for grillings:

> He would say to me at dinner, "What have you learned today?" I would tell him. I would go over the clerical theories that had been served up to me during the day on the soul, life, death, and so forth, and he would discuss them. I was caught between two fires. The next day in class—I was very outspoken—I would turn to my philosophy teacher and say, "But sir! There is a counterargument to what you are saying. How can you reconcile this thing and that? . . . Once, pointing my finger at my teacher, I said, "But you are losing the thread of the argument." His response was, "Leave the room!"[36]

As Georges entered the period of what today is called adolescence, it was normal for him to strive to identify with his father, to emulate his physical and mental attributes, to incorporate his powers and virtues. Benjamin, moreover, exercised an additional appeal in his fanatical adherence to an idealized past, or to what Erikson has termed an "*ethos of action* in the form of ideal types and techniques fascinating enough to replace the heroes of picture book and fairy tale."[37] Georges could not help but have been overwhelmed by the almost fairytale world of the Great Revolution: "At L'Aubraie there were portraits of Saint-Just, Robespierre, and others in every corner. My father used to tell me they were gods and that there was none besides them."[38] But to say that Georges Clemenceau loved his father and sought to incorporate within himself his father's vision of the past tells only half the story. Identification with a stern father entailed emotional readjustments for a boy who had hitherto enjoyed the unconditional love of an affectionate mother. These readjustments became especially painful as the father began to assume the image of a noble sufferer for his ideals.

Benjamin was arrested briefly in Nantes following Louis Napoleon's coup d'état of December 2, 1851. He was arrested again in March of 1858 during the crackdown against liberals that followed Orsini's attempt to assassinate Napoleon III in Paris. He was sentenced to be transported to a penal colony in Algeria. His family were beside themselves: Georges's older sister, Emma, suffered a nervous collapse, lingering for weeks near death. Because of this, there was great sympathy in Nantes for the family, but Benjamin asked for neither help nor pity. He rebuffed a friend who visited him in the Nantes jail, and he tore up the letter of introduction from the bishop of Nantes to the bishop of Algiers, which the friend had brought. On the day that Benjamin was to be sent away, Georges accompanied his mother to the jail. In the presence of the guards he vowed to his father, "I will avenge you!" Benjamin replied, "If you want to avenge me, work!"[39]

But Benjamin got only as far as Marseilles. The public outcry in Nantes against the arrest of Dr. Clemenceau, in addition to the condition of his daughter, put pressure on the authorities, who finally ordered his release. Benjamin told the prefect of police in Marseilles: "You'll see, I don't have to bind my son to Hannibal's vow. You're going to have your hands full with this boy yet!"[40]

These events, which occurred at a significant stage in Georges's development, exacerbated the problems of adjustment that were mentioned earlier. Erikson has noted that identity formation begins where the usefulness of identification ends. For Georges to have resolved his adolescent identity crisis successfully would have necessitated a healthy and stable integration of all earlier identifications as well as a perception, on his part, of continuity and selfsameness. It also would have required some degree of role experimentation in order to prevent a premature definition of self which in his case helped to produce an identity diffusion and a permanent fixation at an adolescent level of conflict.[41]

But Benjamin's suffering and the damage that it inflicted on the family increased Georges's difficulties in freeing himself from father identification. It is possible that these difficulties preceded the arrest in 1858 and entailed more than the so-called oedipal situation, in which the boy imitates the father who possesses the desired object of love and affection—namely, the mother. During the early years at Nantes, Benjamin's behavior and perpetual anger may well have produced anxiety in the sensitive boy, who was attached to his mother. Identification with the source of anxiety is one of the defense mechanisms of the ego, a phenomenon that is understandable in a household such as Georges's.[42] "Defensive identification" with a stern and powerful father was capable of producing in Georges shame reactions toward the sensitive and vulnerable aspects of his character and toward their association with an earlier stage of dependency.[43] Shame produces feelings of inferiority and fear of being unequal to rigorous expectations; it can be, and often is, incorporated into guilt or self-reproach for one's failure to achieve an identity that is consistent with the experienced self. As noted earlier, such guilt requires both self-awareness and the capacity to reflect on oneself and the psychological choices that lie ahead. In the case of sixteen-year-old Georges, the probable source of the inner guilt that was to become an important regulator of his adult drives lay in the psychological pressures that were created in the transition from maternal to paternal spheres. On the one hand lay Georges's knowledge of the true self experienced during the earlier stages of maternal dependency; on the other lay his uncompromising duty toward the role fashioned by his father, a role whose accompanying emotional pressures were intensified by the father's suffering to such an extent that the young boy felt compelled to make a public avowal of his determination to avenge the injury done to his father and the family.

Finally, since Georges's *earliest* identification with his father was based on the latter's power and anger, without corresponding traits of affection and tenderness, his adolescent attempt to integrate all earlier identifications was weakened. Edith Jacob-

son has shown that lack of "wholeness," as well as constancy
and consistency, in the parental model may weaken the child's
awareness of a coherent self. He is thus incapable of integrating
into his own ego identity selective features of the role model.
Such a situation produces a "fusion" with the model in which
"likeness and difference are equally frightening, because likeness
threatens to destroy the self and difference the object."[44]

As Georges approached the end of adolescence, his identity
was being increasingly defined as that of being a defender of
and sufferer for his father's ideals. This role and the familial and
social forces that helped to shape it were to give him a rather
remarkable store of energy; but the expenditure of that energy
and the loss of self that this entailed were to be costly for his
own development.

THE CHALLENGE OF OCCUPATION AND INTIMACY

Georges passed his *baccalauréat* examination in the summer
of 1858, and in November he enrolled in the Preparatory School
of Medicine and Pharmacy of Nantes. His decision to study
medicine was made "without hesitation" because that was the
family tradition.[45] There was still the question, however, of
what kind of doctor he was to become; and this was related
directly to the problem of identity. Another challenge was the
need to establish intimacy with others, which included, though
was not limited to, a finding of oneself through achieving solidarity and a sense of shared identity with a member of the
opposite sex. A stable solution to the latter problem required
Georges to meet his prior need for ego autonomy, but this would
have entailed a decreasing of identification with his father.
In this section I will trace Georges's reaction to these challenges
during the years 1858 to 1865; I will also show how the patterns
of his emotional conflicts tended to crystallize and to produce
identity diffusion, defined here in Erikson's terms as "a split in
self-images" and a loss of centrality.[46]

Georges took his first examination in the summer of 1859,
rating a "very satisfactory" in anatomy, chemistry, natural history, and external pathology. In the *concours*, or competitive

examination, which was given that November, he earned the title of *externe des hospices*, achieving the higher level of intern the next year. He pursued practical training at the Hôtel Dieu and the Hôpital Général in Nantes throughout this period.[47] After his preparatory training he had to complete his medical education at a regular medical faculty, for which he chose the Faculty of Medicine at the University of Paris. In November, 1861, he arrived in the capital and found a room on the Left Bank along the rue de l'Estrapade. His father went with him.

The Paris of the Second Empire was a city of almost two million people, its medieval façade vanishing under the hand of Baron Haussmann. Young Clemenceau fell in love with the city. Since his father was paying the bills, he could pursue his training without worrying about money, at the same time beginning the work that his father had in mind for him. On taking his first *concours* in December, he was placed as an extern at La Pitié after scoring tenth among 330 students. From the outset, Benjamin was busy introducing Georges into republican circles, most of whose members were still dazed by the failure of 1848 and by Napoleon's coup of December, 1851. Georges became a protégé of his father's friend Étienne Arago, who had just returned from exile in Holland. The journalist Henri Lefort, who was a friend of Victor Hugo's, was another of Benjamin's acquaintances. "It was to him that my father took me when we arrived in Paris," Georges recalled later, "it was more important to my father to see me frequent Lefort's place than the Faculty of Medicine, for through Lefort, who had known Hugo . . . all doors were opened."[48]

In the Latin Quarter, the same milieu in which Benjamin had worked three decades earlier, Georges began to carry out his role as defender of his father's ideals. The Left Bank was alive with activity among the youth of the schools who hated the Empire and its censorship. The heroes of the hour were Victor Hugo, who was now in exile; Michelet, in a self-imposed exile to the provinces; Edgar Quinet, in exile since 1851 for his attacks on Catholicism; and such exiled political figures as Louis Blanc and Alexandre Ledru-Rollin. Some people of Georges's generation regarded the latter two figures as heroes of the past, the "graybeards of '48," whom history had passed by; but such was not the case with young Clemenceau or those with whom he now associated in the Latin Quarter. His new friends were law and medical students, poets and journalists, disciples of Proudhon and the almost legendary Auguste Blanqui. The group included the law students Gustave Tridon, André Rousselle, and Eugène Protot; medical students Aristide Rey, Jean-Paul Dubois, and Gustave Dourlen; a former theology student named Germain Casse; and a young journalist from Lyons, Pierre Denis.

One month after Georges arrived in Paris, he and his friends had founded a newspaper called *Le Travail, journal littéraire et scientifique*. Like dozens of other student newspapers, it was short lived, for the police closed it down after only nine issues had appeared. Casse was the editor, with Clemenceau, Denis, and Rousselle forming the regular staff. Other contributors included Ferdinand Taule, who became a good friend of Georges's, and an obscure young writer named Émile Zola.

Georges's first writings exhibited the moralism and combativeness that one might have expected from his desire to prove worthy of parental ideals. "We are strong because we fight for an idea," he wrote, "we can be forced to conceal our thought, but not to compromise it."[49] To one young writer who had argued that God inspires certain men to be examples for humanity, Georges responded that he would select his own models without the aid of Providence. These models were those of his father, such as Michelet, for whose philosophy that freedom and justice marched through history Georges proclaimed his highest regard.[50] Idealism formed the main theme of his reviews of plays that he had seen at the Odéon: "The only goal of art is to moralize the masses. It should create better people in order to guide them along the path to a better future." He hated all writers who were favorable to the Empire, especially Edmond About, whose serialized romances were favorites of the empress. Georges denounced About's writings as "turgid and pretentious," and when one of About's plays, *Gaëtana*, opened at the Odéon on January 3, 1862, young Clemenceau was among those whose catcalls disrupted the performance. To About's protests against "the rascals of Paris," Clemenceau responded in *Le Travail:* "We return to the author all the contempt he inspires in us, a contempt certainly shared by the youth of the schools."[51]

The image of a tough and vigorous fighter, which Georges tried to project, could not mask the emotionalism and often the sentimentality that were a part of his inner self. After complaining that Alphonse Daudet's play *La Dernière Idole* demoralized the viewer because of its lack of optimism and idealism, he wrote: "Leave us our tender illusions of twenty years. We still want to believe in friendship and especially in love. Do not tear down our last idol. We still need to grasp the hand of a friend and to count upon the affection of a mother."[52]

But the essay that most fully reflected Clemenceau's early character formation was one entitled "The Martyrs of History." In it one sees both an intense emotionalism and a deep fascination with those who suffer for ideals. "It is beautiful," he wrote, "to suffer and die for a principle, for an idea, as did Socrates or Jesus Christ." Those who were "guilty of genius" had usually fallen victim to the mob, but fear had not prevented these "holy martyrs of society" from defending their ideals, even if it meant, as in the case of Spartacus or Brutus, the sacrifice of one's reputation in history as well as one's life. History had vindicated them, Clemenceau argued, and now it was the turn of the generation of 1793 to be vindicated. It was true, he said, that the men of the French Revolution had used violence to achieve their goals, but that was only because of the tenacity of the opposition. For the *conventionnels,* "no price was too high to pay for the triumph of their principles. Without them, I ask you, where would we be today?"[53]

Clemenceau's fascination with the notion that suffering was the price of progress lasted all his life.[54] Its relevance to his own perceived role as a sufferer for his father's ideals is evident; for on February 24, 1862, just two days after this essay appeared, Georges did something that he knew would get him into trouble. He and some of the staff on *Le Travail* staged a rally at the place de la Bastille to celebrate the overthrow of Louis Philippe fourteen years earlier. They handed out placards in the working-class district of Saint-Antoine, announcing the rally; but few workers showed up, and the protesters did little more than shout cheers to the Republic and sing a few stanzas from a current student favorite called "Le Lion du Quartier Latin." The police moved in with nightsticks and broke up the rally. The effectiveness of the police apparently convinced Georges that suffering was best contemplated from a distance, for he fled the scene. The police found him two days later in his apartment and hauled him away in a crowded Black Maria (where he had to sit on the lap of a butcher who had just murdered someone); at the Mazas jail they forced him to bathe in a communal tub of water "the color of café au lait."[55]

Georges had now experienced his father's humiliation of 1858. Benjamin came to Paris, but was unable to get Georges out of jail. Writing to Sophie Emma, Benjamin said that the demonstrators had been bludgeoned and that he wept while hearing these accounts. "I wish only to be certain of living long enough," he told his wife, "to see the day of vengeance repay these crimes." Nevertheless, Benjamin showed satisfaction with what Georges had done, for he also told his wife: "It has been said that the vanity of fathers in regard to their children is almost as great as their affection. So, if it is any consolation to you, just know that your son was making for himself a position proportionate to his age and the milieu in which he lived. He counted for something in the gallery of the Odéon and was a lion in the Latin Quarter."[56]

Young Clemenceau was formally charged in April under an 1848 law banning riotous assemblies. He was fined and sentenced to one month in jail, which, combined with the time he had already spent there, added up to seventy-seven days at Mazas. Le Travail also folded, as the police cracked down on the editors, meting out fines and sentences to Casse, Rousselle, and Taule for "outrage against morality and the Catholic religion."[57]

After his release in May, Georges helped to found a new journal, Le Matin. He contributed only one article, a review of Étienne Arago's historical novel on the Vendean revolt, and the paper ceased publication after a few issues.[58] In the meantime, Georges was finding new opportunities for intrigue. La Pitié, where he had resumed his medical duties, was located near Sainte-Pélagie prison, where his friends Ferdinand Taule and Eugène Carré of Le Travail were still serving out their sentences. While visiting them, Clemenceau got to know Auguste Scheurer-Kestner, a chemist from Alsace whose father was one of Benjamin's friends. Auguste, who had been imprisoned for encouraging student resistance to the Empire, managed the chemical works of his father-in-law, Charles Kestner, in the little town of Thann in Alsace.[59] Georges was also able to meet Blanqui himself; he long remembered during their first encounter the "shock of burning black rays that shot forth from his white, emaciated face."[60] He immediately fell under the spell of this self-annointed heir of Babeuf and the preacher of permanent revolution against injustice. Blanqui symbolized for Clemenceau the lonely martyr suffering for his principles, or, as Clemenceau later described him, "a living reproach to lesser men," whose solitary life taught "the lofty and severe lesson of an unchangeable soul."[61]

Clemenceau continued his visits to Blanqui for several months during 1862 and early 1863. It was not long before "L'Enfermé," as Blanqui's youthful disciples called him, involved Georges in his intrigues outside prison. On one occasion he sent him to Brussels to pick up a printing press from an emigré doctor. Clemenceau and his roommate, J. A. Lafont, kept the press in their apartment, despite the dangers from the police, who were keeping watch over the former editors of Le Travail. But this collaboration halted one day when another of Blanqui's disciples showed up, demanding the press. The reason for Blanqui's anger was that someone had told him that Clemenceau was associating with one of Blanqui's rivals, the journalist Charles Delescluze.[62]

Relations between the two cooled for a time after this episode, but Clemenceau always had a deep admiration for the old man and, in his later political career, spent a good deal of time defending him in Parliament. But Clemenceau's admiration is best understood in light of an earlier psychological disposition; that is, it sprang less from Blanqui's vague ideas on revolution and a classless society than from his courage and his willingness to suffer as a martyr for his beliefs. Blanqui hence fortified Clemenceau's father identification; in fact, Benjamin, who spent some of his time in Paris in 1862 and 1863, possibly encouraged this process. He, too, admired Blanqui and is said to have accompanied his son on several visits to Blanqui in the prison of Sainte-Pélagie.

In light of the time that Clemenceau had devoted to republican conspiracies against the Empire, it is not surprising that his medical studies suffered. In October of 1862, when he took the *concours* for the post of intern, his performance was so dismal that he was assigned to the Bicêtre Hospital, which was the home of four thousand aged and infirm men. Many of the patients suffered from mental disorders. Clemenceau hated it there, writing to Scheurer-Kestner in February of 1863 that he had been "installed for a year in the midst of fools, idiots, and cretins" and that his new milieu had forced him "to moderate some of the theories I have on the influence of environment."[63] In July he was suspended for two months for being absent without leave and was moved back to La Pitié.[64] In the fall he again took the *concours;* and once more, having failed to earn the rank of intern, he resumed his work as provisional intern at La Pitié.

Around early 1863 the number of Clemenceau's political intrigues decreased, and it was during this period that for the first time he began to try to cope with the demands of intimacy in his life. This was no easy task; it involved considerable emotional pressures, which stemmed from his perception of what his father required of him. One problem was how to communicate his feelings to a father who, despite his deep love for his son, lacked those character traits that would have made him sensitive and understanding with regard to matters of the heart. Georges found in Auguste Scheurer-Kestner and Étienne Arago individuals in whom he could confide, but to no one could he reveal his innermost feelings more than to a man named Gustave Jourdan.

Jourdan was a moderate republican and a bit of a dilettant who, after his marriage to a wealthy Parisian widow, passed much of his time talking philosophy with students in Latin Quarter cafés. Clemenceau met him one day in a café on the boulevard Saint-Michel. He was twenty years older than Georges, and in matters of the heart, he became a kind of surrogate father who in turn viewed his new friend as "a younger brother whom I love" and "a substitute for the brother and son I've never had."[65] Both Jourdan and Arago had their hands full in comforting their protégé during the bitter disappointment of his first romance. The episode clearly illustrates the sensitivity and vulnerability of the real Clemenceau; and his first failure to achieve any lasting sense of psychological intimacy with a woman—which, as noted earlier, would have included a feeling of solidarity and shared identity—was to have lasting repercussions in his life.

The young woman was Hortense Kestner, his friend Auguste's sister-in-law. Georges had met her on a visit to Auguste in Thann during the summer of 1863. She was beautiful, loved poetry and music, and had already received several proposals of marriage from prominent young men. Clemenceau fell madly in love with her, but Hortense was not responsive. Nor were her parents: the difference in age between the two concerned them (Hortense was one year older than he), but Clemenceau's own behavior was probably more upsetting to them. In the words of Auguste, who in an unpublished journal later recorded both his impressions of the affair and of the letters that he received from Georges, "They also found him abrupt, which he was, and odd, which he was not."[66]

Clemenceau could not understand the real difficulty, however, and perceived his main problem to be the overcoming of the parents' hostility so that he could communicate his feelings directly to Hortense. In early January of 1864 he wrote to Arago: "If, as I do not doubt, you have been so good as to believe me when I told you I love this young girl whom you know, you will well understand why it's hard for me to follow your last advice in this regard." Clemenceau stressed that he was not afraid of learning the truth: "So be it! If necessary, I will submit to this failure. It seems to me that I am within my rights in asking to be refused only by Mademoiselle Kestner or at least by her father and mother. I'm not in any way bashful in this matter, and then, but only then, will it be possible for me to forget."[67]

He resolved to go to Thann and lay out his feelings to Hortense's parents. Arago called him in and tried to dissuade him, but Clemenceau was adamant. Arago then wrote to Scheurer-Kestner that "this brave Clemenceau" wanted only "a *yes* or *no* from the father, mother, or daughter. You love and appreciate Clemenceau as I do, which is why I address myself directly to you in these circumstances."[68] A few days later Arago tried again to persuade Clemenceau to renounce his hopes, but he found that he had "an insistence bordering on folly."[69]

Clemenceau went to Thann in February. Precisely what happened is unclear, but apparently Hortense's parents discouraged his designs on the basis of the age difference between the couple. He persisted anyway, asking Auguste to seek the advice of his brother-in-law Victor Chauffour on how to handle the situation. Back in Paris, on February 9, Clemenceau wrote a long letter to Auguste, which shows his despair:

> And now, tell me, dear friend, have you spoken with your brother-in-law? What did he say? What do you both think? These are the questions that I ask myself every day and that are still unanswered for me. Don't be afraid to write me and tell me the whole truth, whatever it is. I prefer it to uncertainty. Here I pass my time weighing each of your words, interpreting each one according to my mood. Invariably, the conclusion is that I'm very much afraid. Then I tell myself it is mad to hope—the dread of learning what I fear overcomes my wish to know the truth. I float back and forth between these two feelings. Certainly, I would like to hear from you, but I would probably leave your letter on the table for an hour, turning it over and over without daring to open it. Ah, why can't I think of the words to make you understand what I feel? I told you the other day of all the great speeches I make when you are not here. It's different now. Every day I plan great feats of eloquence, then when I try to write it all down, everything freezes up. If I haven't been table to make you feel what is in my heart, it is the fault of words, my poor friend, and not of feelings.

He did, however, have a ready answer to the argument about the difference in age: "Well! My God! Age is a guarantee. I don't pretend to deny it. But tell me, do not ideas, sentiment, and character provide a host of moral guarantees of considerable weight and of perhaps a more elevated order?" Clemenceau revealed that he sensed a great change in his life as a result of the affair, that he was on the eve of "a great joy or a great sorrow." In a very significant passage he noted that he had just written to his father about the whole situation, but that since his father was ill, his mother had responded with some words of the heart. One sees the turmoil within young Clemenceau and the ambivalence that he felt when exposing his inner self to his father: "My father is and has always been, above everything else, my friend. Since I reached the age of reason, I have never heard an order come out of his mouth, and I have never had happiness or pain that we have not shared. . . . It is not when I experience an honest and sincere emotion that I should start hiding from him."[70]

Throughout the spring and summer of 1864 Clemenceau persisted in this one-way courtship, arranging clandestine meetings with Auguste in the taverns of Mulhouse in Alsace, falling into such morbid states that he suffered "a fear of being buried alive."[71] Finally, in September, he sent Hortense a written proposal, which she refused. It was a crushing blow to his ego; months later Jourdan, who was still trying to comfort Clemenceau, admitted to him that he had derived some satisfaction from the whole affair, "for your sake, because I love to see you that way, knowing that your pride will return, and for mine, because having never actually experienced these tender emotions, it gives me great pleasure to think about them."[72]

Several times in his journal Scheurer-Kestner, writing in 1893, suggests that the Hortense episode had a "deadly influence" on the subsequent life of his friend, that the rancor and storminess of his life might have been tempered by a woman like Hortense. Scheurer-Kestner was also able to perceive that there was a different person behind the mask of iron will and determination: "I will not attempt a psychological analysis of his character, so strong and yet so tender. The contrast between Clemenceau's head and heart shows up in every line. As a man, he remained what he had been as a student. I have always found him to have the same heart he had then. But experience did not ripen him, and after hurting himself because of his lack of common sense, he ended up hurting all others around him without realizing it."[73]

Hortense eventually married Charles Floquet, the man

with whom Clemenceau, showing no apparent ill feelings, would work in politics in later years. But his love for her had been no passing infatuation, and he appears not to have given up hope entirely until she became engaged in 1869. At that time he himself married the American woman Mary Plummer, a decision that was in part a compensation for his loss of Hortense, which helps to explain his failure to build a lasting marital relationship. But, as will be seen, Clemenceau's failure in the latter regard also suggests that his inability to achieve any enduring sense of psychological intimacy with women may have been rooted in identity conflicts so profound that even a favorable response by Hortense might not have brought him the happiness he was seeking.

The impression one has of Clemenceau after 1864 is that he was a suffering youth in need of healing his wounds. Healing required solitude and withdrawal, but any withdrawal seemed to betray his duty to his father's ideals to keep up the fight against the Second Empire. For the moment, Clemenceau was tired of the struggle. In April of 1864 he had written to Scheurer-Kestner that the police were keeping an eye on everything that he and his friends were doing, which included the planning of a new journal to be called *Les Écoles de France:* "It isn't a bad journal, the best you can say about it is that the editor is inevitably destined to end up in Sainte-Pélagie."[74] These plans never materialized; nor did those he made with Ferdinand Taule, Aristide Rey, Jean-Paul Dubois, and Gustave Dourlen to create a fraternal association of medical students in Paris, whose goal was to be improvement of the curriculum and reform of the rules governing student life. Clemenceau was selected president of a committee that was formed to draw up bylaws, but the dean of the Faculty of Medicine and the prefect of police banned a general assembly of students that was to debate the proposals.[75]

For the moment, Clemenceau was resolved to finish his studies. He could take the *concours* again, which was the avenue for gaining distinction in medicine; or he could elect to write an intern thesis and thus get his degree. He chose the latter—that rather belatedly in early 1865—and asked Charles Robin, professor of histology, to direct his thesis. It was an

appropriate choice for someone who wanted to write a work
of philosophy rather than medicine. Robin was a doctor and
a philosopher, a friend of republicans such as Jules Michelet
and Léon Gambetta, and one of the chief spokesmen for the
doctrine of scientific positivism.[76]

Clemenceau finished the thesis in the spring of 1865, en-
titling it *De la génération des éléments anatomiques*. It was
little more than a rehash of one of Robin's pet notions: the
doctrine of spontaneous generation, an old idea revived of late
because improved microscopes showed new microorganisms in
putrefactive matter. Proponents of the theory argued that these
and all living cells were spontaneously generated from inorganic
forms. Debate waxed hot after Pasteur, a Catholic, began to
discredit the notion; for belief in spontaneous generation eliminated the necessity for an initial divine creation, something
that even Darwinian theory could not dispel.[77]

Clemenceau's preface set the tone of dogmatic materialism
in the thesis: "To observe phenomena precisely is the point of
departure for all science; to group and interpret it is the goal.
I do not furnish new observations. I assemble facts." He added
that "I alone am responsible for the opinions I express. I do
not hold them because I have written this work; I have written
this work because I hold them."[78] Then followed over two
hundred pages in which he attacked all supernatural explanations for the origins of life. Man was nothing more than the
synthesis of atomic elements or cells that had spontaneously
generated to produce an embryo in the fertilized egg. Man had
no soul, for life processes were so mathematical that "there is
not a moment for the introduction of the soul into the embryo."[79]
All this was characteristic of much nineteenth-century French
thought, but it is a mistake to view Clemenceau's political values
as the offspring of a well-defined philosophical system. He did
not need Comte or Robin to lead him to materialist ideas, and
in fact, there was much in the thesis, as he himself recognized,
that was inconsistent with the positivist belief in empirical veri-
fication, especially his attitude toward the origins of life, which
lay outside the realm of observable phenomena.[80]

Clemenceau defended the thesis in May of 1865. Although
he was almost tripped up by one member of the jury, who kept

quizzing him on scarlet fever, Robin came to his rescue; and the committee passed him, awarding him a diploma.[81] He was also honored when the thesis was published by J. B. Baillière et Fils; a second edition, containing a preface by Robin, appeared two years later.

Nevertheless, in 1865 Clemenceau was still a very depressed young man, and for several months he had been thinking of leaving for America. In later life he claimed that his motive had been to study democracy in action.[82] In fact, deeper psychological forces were at work. Georges's longing for solitude sprang from his inability thus far to attain a firm sense of self which would have enabled him to cope with sexual failure as well as with other demands of adult life. Depression and the urge to withdraw were normal reactions,[83] but he had also resolved to extend for himself what Erikson has termed the adolescent psychosocial moratorium—that period between youth and adulthood during which the individual experiments with roles and tries to achieve continuity between what he was as a child and what he is to become as an adult.[84] A successful outcome to this indefinite moratorium meant that he had to remove himself from the one object that seemed to pose the greatest threat to his own ego autonomy. That object was his own father.

The decision to delay the critical decisions of life was in some respects a psychological triumph for Georges, but it produced painful and ambivalent emotional reactions. In January of 1865 he happened to go to Basel to attend the funeral of a friend named Colonel Charras. Charras, the husband of one of Hortense's sisters, had been forced into exile in 1851. At Basel, Clemenceau told Scheurer-Kastner that he was definitely leaving for America, and from Paris, on February 10, 1865, Clemenceau wrote him a letter that revealed a much different man from the cocky young medical student of 1861. The letter showed his seeming desire to abandon his life to circumstances: "You know why I'm going, why ask me more? What will I do? I simply don't know. I'm going, that's all. Fate will take care of the rest—surgery in the federal army, perhaps something more, perhaps nothing." Georges was also determined to work out his problems without help from anyone: "I don't want anyone to feel sorry for me. If I'm cowardly or brave in the face of this unhappiness, where I go, what I think, what I try, what I do, all this is only an affair between me and me." There was the sense of guilt toward his father:

> I leave behind me only one regret—my father. I told you one evening that he would forgive me, and you answered that I would not forgive myself. If you are my friend, then hope that this day never arrives. Finally, when this last heart-breaking experience is over, I will be free of all attachments (who can say whether this is good or bad), and I'll go where the wind blows. I hope you don't mind, my dear friend, if I don't pursue any further this psychological study you asked from me. Besides being useless, close analysis becomes painful.

Finally, there was his longing for withdrawal: "I find a great attraction (I don't know with what mixture of pride and bitterness) in withdrawing into myself and not opening up for anyone. That is my last consolation."[85]

But Benjamin was still reluctant to cut the symbiotic ties with his son, though he agreed to support him financially.[86] On July 26 he accompanied him to London, where both of them met John Stuart Mill. Mill asked young Clemenceau to translate into French his *Auguste Comte and Positivism,* and it was in return for this translation that J. B. Baillière et Fils agreed to publish a second edition of Clemenceau's thesis. In early September, Georges left his father and headed for Liverpool, where he boarded the steamer *Etna* for the two-week voyage to New York. Though he was to make several return visits to France, America was his home for the next four years.

MORATORIUM IN AMERICA

In his old age, Clemenceau burned the bulk of his private papers relating to this episode in his life. Enough is known, however, to enable us to formulate several conclusions regarding the significance of this stage in his development. First, he did attempt a moderate degree of role experimentation. One product of this attempt was his letters to *Le Temps* on American reconstruction and the plight of the former slaves. These letters were based on observations and experiences that both enhanced his compassion for oppressed peoples and strengthened his early belief in the principle of avenging justice in history. Second, his effort to attain ego autonomy was only a partial and temporary success, and his failure to come to terms with his own sense of self and his father identification began to feed an inner reservoir of rage and self-reproach, which ensured that he would remain fixated on this level of identity conflicts well into adulthood. Finally, his first and last attempt to achieve intimacy through marriage was in fact a pseudo intimacy whose weakness from the outset reflected and interacted with his own identity conflicts.

One of Georges's letters to Scheurer-Kestner in December of 1867 reflects the alternating moods of pride, cynicism, and humor in the young doctor's role experimentation:

> I'm teaching myself to become wise, honest, and moderate, *respectable* as they say here. . . . Every day I get twenty-four hours older: every evening when I go to bed, I look at myself in the mirror, and I find a more pensive expression than the day before. I'm becoming serious and grave enough to make a monument jealous. I talk about the balance of power in Europe, and I put on my gloves. In a few months I'll be buttoning up my frockcoat right to the chin and buying a cane, perhaps even some rubbers. I'm watching myself live, and when that no longer interests me, I watch others live. When I run into imbeciles, I speak of *my experience,* and at other times I permit myself a "when I was young."[87]

In New York he had found an apartment at 215 West 12th Street in Greenwich Village. The stream of Irish immigrants had swollen the population of the city to nearly one million, and the city of gaslights and brownstones was already becoming an urban monster. Greenwich Village was not yet a famous bohemian quarter, but writers and artists were already living in the "French colony" around Washington Square. Some of the Americans whom Clemenceau had met earlier in Paris took the young doctor under their wing. One was Edward Howard House, drama critic for the New York *Tribune.* Others included a lawyer named Eugene Bush and a young man named John

Durand, son of the famous engraver Asher Brown Durand. Clemenceau also got to know Horace Greeley at the *Tribune,* who was one of the Americans he most admired, and Charles Anderson Dana of the *Sun.*

He was soon at home in the city, maintaining a credit account at Pfaff's restaurant on Broadway, frequenting the reading rooms of Cooper Union, and becoming a regular visitor to Astor Library on Lafayette Street. He at first cultivated the image, and in a rather extravagant way, of the intriguing foreigner and exile from the French Empire. He had brought several trunks of clothes—striped trousers and fleece-lined overcoats—and even his own private library, the freight charges on which at Le Havre he had sent to his friend Gustave Jourdan. Benjamin's regular allowance was not enough, for Georges borrowed from friends such as John Durand, to whom he had to write embarrassing notes on the matter of his debts.[88] At one point he tried to sell subscriptions for the newspaper of Charles Delescluze; his lack of success, he wrote to Scheurer-Kestner, was "the beginning and end of my commercial career. After this I have rested like God on the seventh day, and, like Him, I have never rested again."[89] The letters that he received from Jourdan (which are among the only ones from this period that Clemenceau could not bring himself to burn in his old age) were sometimes scolding where money matters were concerned: "This miserable question of money makes me worry about you," he told him. "You have too much—for your father has been good to you—to make it necessary to renounce any grand projects, and you don't have enough to make it unnecessary to earn more."[90]

For a time, Clemenceau busied himself with the task of translating Mill's book on Comte. But he was bored by it, confessing to Scheurer-Kestner that the style was "heavy and stuffy" and that he had "had the good sense" to destroy the introduction he had written.[91] What he found much more interesting was his new job as foreign correspondent for the liberal French daily *Le Temps.* Jourdan helped him get the position shortly after his arrival in New York, and the monthly salary of thirty dollars was a handy supplement to the allowance from his father. The editors assigned him the task of reporting generally on developments in America. Since his earlier political activities had given him a bad name in the eyes of the French censors, the editors entitled his column "Letters from the United States" and signed it with a pseudonym.[92]

Clemenceau's letters to Le Temps—ninety-four in all—are significant not only because of their reflection of his own attitudes but also because of their value as a contemporary analysis of Reconstruction politics. Fortunately, Jourdan seems to have dissuaded him from an early plan "to study America in the light of Positivist method."[93] As a result the letters have a freshness and spontaneity that make them interesting reading today. Clemenceau traveled to many regions, including the war-torn South, and he was a frequent visitor to Philadelphia, Baltimore, and Washington. With a note from Dana, he landed an interview with William Henry Seward, the secretary of state, and at some point he also met Ulysses S. Grant.[94] In general, he admired the equality of American life and, as he told Jourdan, the way in which custom was more important than law. His first letter to Le Temps, in the fall of 1865, stressed the American capacity for change: "The people of the United States have a peculiar faculty for adjusting themselves to circumstances and learning by experience, suddenly changing their course and thus nearly always disappointing prophets of disaster. The Americans will make mistakes . . . , but in the end, when truth and justice have taken some kind of shape . . . , the people will seize upon them."[95]

There was much that he found unattractive, however. Rallies of armed Fenians in New York upset him, and he seems to have had little understanding of the problems of the Irish in America.[96] Politics struck him as a "carnival," with freedom to "insult and deride and bear false witness," and he thought that the Americans had "an unbalanced streak in their nature," much like the people of southern France.[97] Fundamentalist preachers intrigued him, and in a letter to his father he suggested that the practices of the Shakers had a pathological source.[98] Puritan staidness, on the other hand, irritated him, especially as exemplified in laws on drinking. In November of 1867 he described for Le Temps a meeting at Cooper Institute, where Horace Greeley spoke to an audience of "parsons, religious old women, and fanatical puritans." It was decided, he said, "that morality, the Bible, Providence, as well as order and propriety, demand that every Sunday New York take on the aspect of a cemetery."[99] In a more serious vein, Clemenceau attacked those wealthy industrialists and manufacturers who promoted high tariffs, arguing that tariffs were incompatible with a new and free country like America.[100]

The political struggle in postwar America attracted his greatest interest, and running through his letters is a deep concern over the misery of the former slaves and over the future that they faced. He saw hate and prejudice against them everywhere, and in one trip to the South, he witnessed the lynching of a Negro.[101] To Le Temps he wrote that the blacks had become "a nomad population, congregated in the towns and suffering wretchedly there, destined to be driven back eventually by poverty into the country, where they will be forced to submit to the harshest terms imposed by their former masters."[102] Bigotry was not confined to the South. After attending a meeting of New York Democrats, he wrote: "Any Democrat who did not manage to hint in his speech that the negro is a degenerate gorilla, would be considered lacking in enthusiasm." He noted that after shedding their blood for the Union, many blacks were now "being forced to bargain for, perhaps in the end to lose entirely, the rights which they have already purchased so dearly." Their real misfortune was in not owning any land: "There cannot be real emancipation for men who do not possess at least a small portion of the soil. We have had an example in Russia. In spite of the war, and the confiscation bills, which remain dead letters, every inch of land in the Southern states belongs to the former rebels."[103]

Clemenceau was at first sympathetic with President Andrew Johnson, who sought lenient treatment for the former Confederate States. But the young Frenchman soon sided with such radicals as Charles Sumner and Thaddeus Stevens, who insisted that the South was still not entitled to representation since it persisted in denying rights to blacks. Clemenceau believed that "any question which has not been settled justly remains unsettled forever," and he saw the opportunity to destroy once and for all the "temper of oligarchial pride" in the southern aristocracy. In addition, he pointed out that although the Fourteenth Amendment had granted citizenship but not suffrage to the Negro, it was a positive step, since the Supreme Court was bound to side with Johnson: "As we all know, there is never a lack of legal texts any more than of religious texts, when men seek to stifle their consciences and proclaim the necessity and need of injustice."[104]

Clemenceau argued that the process of radical reconstruction constituted a "second American Revolution" and that if this revolution failed, "the final and complete emancipation of the colored people will be deferred indefinitely." His heroes were Wendell Phillips, Charles Sumner, William Henry Seward, and Secretary of War Edwin M. Stanton, whom he called "the Carnot of the American war." His greatest idol was Thaddeus Stevens, the "Old Commoner" from Pennsylvania. Like Blanqui, Stevens represented to him one of those solitary individualists who "leaps over the barrier himself, and lets anyone follow him who can." He once witnessed the sick and aging radical leader being carried into the House of Representatives on a stretcher: "Mr. Stevens is carried in, his illness progressing rapidly, but his energies mounting still faster. Once in a while a sardonic smile, like a grimace, flickers over his livid face. If it were not for the fire smoldering in the depths of his piercing eyes, one might imagine life had already fled from that inert body, but it still nurses all the wrath of a Robespierre."[105]

For three months in 1868 Clemenceau reported the events of Johnson's impeachment trial in the Senate, not a little mystified by the arrangement of the executive and the legislative in American democracy. He was disappointed by the Senate's failure to convict the man who was retarding "the march of progress upon this continent."[106] Afterwards he covered the presidential election of 1868, but he could not take the challenge of the Democrats seriously: "The Democrats simply will not understand that the revolution which has been carried out in spite of them is not of the kind that can be undone. . . . The demand for the abolition of slavery was made not so much by the Republican party as by the conscience of the whole nation. There can and must be a reaction against the work of a single party, but there can be none against the decrees of the human conscience, prompted by justice."[107]

Clemenceau's role as a commentator on American affairs presents an important side of his character. That was his compassion for the weak, in this case the victims of slavery. This trait enabled him to see the link between moral and political issues, and his conviction that postponement of full equality for black people would compound and perpetuate racial strife proved to be well founded. Many of the most recent American scholars of the Reconstruction era support the substance of those arguments that he set forth in his letters to *Le Temps*.[108] The plight of the former slaves also enhanced his sensitivity to the issue of racial oppression in debates over colonialism during his later career and placed him in opposition to the notions of inferior and superior races, which were characteristic of much nineteenth-century thought.[109] It is true that one of his last letters uses the language of social Darwinism: "Can the African, with his natural indolence, compete successfully with white labor? . . . In this ruthless struggle for existence carried on by human society, those who are weaker physically, intellectually or morally must in the end yield to the stronger."[110] While the idea of the survival of the fittest was becoming fashionable at this time among men with "scientific" views of society, one must, in Clemenceau's case, distinguish the rhetoric from the deed. Much of his early career was spent in defense of the weak and belies the notion of Clemenceau as a social Darwinist.

The letters also show the power that the paternal legacy continued to hold over him. Whether in comparisons of various American radicals such as Stevens with the heroes of the French Revolution or in the repeated use of such words as "principle," "right," and "justice," Benjamin's ideals are everywhere apparent. Both the language and the symbolism that the son invoked are similar to those in his later parliamentary speeches. Especially important was the concept of justice. Young Clemenceau wrote in one letter to *Le Temps*: "There is only one method of ending all difficulties, and that is justice, not force. . . . The power which crushed the one [slavery] is the same power that nourishes and eventually will assure the triumph of the others— avenging justice."[111]

The paternal influence weighed heavily on young Clemenceau in other ways during his years abroad. In the first year, especially, he was often depressed and lonely, feelings that may have been occasioned as much by guilt over his self-imposed moratorium as by his continued brooding over Hortense. In February of 1866 he received terrible news from Paris: his friend Jourdan had died of cholera. In his old age, Clemenceau recalled his sense of isolation afterwards: "I really had the feeling that I had lost all support to which I could cling—I was alone."[112] A few months later he decided to go home. He stopped in Paris to visit his old friends. In what may have been an attempt to reaffirm his identification with his father, he joined a society called Act According to Your Beliefs, whose pledge bound its members "never to receive any sacraments for birth, marriage, or death."[113] He went to L'Aubraie, but he soon returned to New York, apparently against Benjamin's wishes. For during the summer of 1867, Benjamin turned down his son's request for money to invest in western lands and ordered him to come home for good. When Georges refused, Benjamin cut off his allowance altogether.[114]

There was now an open break with his father. What transpired between father and son over the latter's determination to stay in America is not known. But it is certain that there was tension and that in refusing to go back to L'Aubraie, even if it meant supporting himself financially, Clemenceau was making another determined effort to assert his own identity. But as in 1865, it was painful for Georges to do so, and on occasions one sees him forcefully reminding others (and himself) that he was still the upholder of his father's ideals, even if the emotional burden that this entailed was heavy. In a letter of September, 1867, to an unidentified woman who had expressed sympathy to him for the doomed Maximilian and his wife, Carlotta, in Mexico, he said:

> My God! Yes, I know, these people are always charming. We know that beforehand: they've been that way for five or six thousand years. They have the recipe for all the virtues and the secret of all the graces. They smile? How delicious. They weep? How touching! They let you live? What exquisite benevolence! They crush the life out of

you? That's the misfortune of their situation. Well! Let me tell you something: all these emperors, kings, archdukes, and princes are great, sublime, generous, and superb; their princesses are everything pleasing to you. But I hate them, with a merciless hatred, as they used to hate in the old days of '93, when that imbecile of a king Louis XVI was called the execrable tyrant. Between us and them there is a war to the death. . . . You think I'm savage; what's worse is that I'm intractable, and on this matter, I will never change. . . . I really doubt there is another atheist who regrets as much as I do the absence of Providence. I would abandon everything to His supreme justice, and that would relieve me of hate. But it is sad to think that all evil men slumber under the same sun as the good.

He revealed that he had written home, posing "modest conditions" to his father concerning a return to France. "I hope my father will accept them," he said. In a passing allusion to the Hortense affair, he revealed his own ambivalent feelings toward his inner self and, as in one of his letters to Scheurer-Kestner in 1864, used the imagery of being buried alive in order to express his feelings: "After a long struggle I have finally renounced the last of my illusions. I expect nothing, I hope nothing more and desire nothing more. I am searching for a cemetery where I can bury myself alive."[115]

With only his salary from *Le Temps*, Clemenceau had to find a job. His friend Eugene Bush introduced him to Catherine Aiken, who ran a finishing school in Stamford, Connecticut, called Miss Aiken's Seminary for Young Ladies. She needed a part-time teacher of French and equitation, and Clemenceau accepted the job. He was a popular teacher with his students, though he was somewhat brusque and eccentric in the classroom.[116] Among his students was the eighteen-year-old Mary Plummer, who had been born in 1849 in Springfield, Massachusetts, where her father practiced dentistry. He later moved his family to a farm in Wisconsin, where he died in 1860. Mary had a wealthy uncle in New York, named Horace Taylor, who brought her east and began financing her education at Stamford. To her friends she was known as the "beautiful" Mary Plummer, and her new French teacher took a keen interest in her.

By the spring of 1868 Clemenceau had become engaged to her, but his eagerness to live up to his principles (and his Latin Quarter pledge of 1866) almost wrecked the possibility of marriage; for Horace Taylor, Mary's uncle, insisted on a church wedding. Clemenceau was just as adamant, and on June 27 he boarded the *Ville de Paris* and returned to France without her. He showed little apparent regret, writing to Scheurer-Kestner, a few days before leaving New York, that he intended to spend three or four months in France and that if Auguste would visit him, he would find "the most friendly man in the world."[117] At L'Aubraie he was reconciled with his father, though in the fall he began laying new plans for a visit to Germany.[118] His stand on principle with Horace Taylor seems to have pleased him, for some time during this period he sketched the outline of a play in which the hero was a young man who suffers for refusing to be married in church. It was to be entitled *Le Puritain*.[119]

Then, in November, he received word that Mary's uncle had capitulated on the matter of a civil ceremony. Clemenceau returned to New York, only to come home again in late January of 1869. Why he did so is not clear, though it is significant that while he was in America, he had heard the news of Hortense's formal engagement to Charles Floquet. From Paris, on February 3, he wrote a somewhat penitent letter to Scheurer-Kestner: "You'll be happy to learn that my spirits are in all respects everything you could desire. After a long time I've recognized my foolishness and have admired with good faith your wisdom, as well as the friendly patience with which you've listened to my silliness and supported by ridiculous blusterings. My only excuse, you know it, is that I was young. Today, I'm a little older and am, if not more modest, at least more moderate."[120]

He told Scheurer-Kestner that he was himself engaged to a young American "miss," and a few days later he described her to him: "Brunette, 29 teeth (3 still on their way): size—medium, etc., etc. Character—I dare not talk about it after knowing her for only two years. Ideas—still being formed. Religion—it doesn't go very deep. The parents raised a fuss about having a minister. I raised a fuss about not having one . . . they had to give in to me."[121]

If, in fact, Clemenceau had held out any last hopes for Hortense, they were dashed by her marriage to Floquet on April 6. The next month, Georges returned to New York. His wedding, which was performed by Oakey Hall, the mayor of New York, took place on June 23 at the home of Mary's uncle on Fifth Avenue. That same month, Clemenceau brought his new bride to L'Aubraie. He was at pains to demonstrate to his friends that he was now a happy man. To Scheurer-Kestner he wrote: "What have I done, said, or insinuated that has led you to believe, suppose, or imagine that I, G. Clemenceau, Vendean by birth and American by profession, was ever the unhappiest man in the world? Did I have gloomy airs and melancholy looks? Have I accused nature and execrated society? Have I pointed a gun at my young breast?"[122]

For one year after returning to L'Aubraie, Clemenceau occupied himself with practicing medicine in the vicinity. He undoubtedly had affection for his new wife, but his marriage to her—which was the culmination of his lengthy moratorium and of his effort to achieve identity and intimacy in his life—offered little possibility of satisfying these longings. For Mary, the starkness of L'Aubraie, coupled with her poor French, made adjustment difficult in a new country, and she never understood the stormier side of her husband's character. In addition, Benjamin was aloof in his dealings with her, although Georges's mother and sisters were friendly and kind and helped out with the new baby, Madeleine, who was born on June 2, 1870.

As he settled into L'Aubraie, it looked as if Georges's life would be like that of his father. The Second Empire, which was no longer the repressive regime of post-1851 days, seemed more solidly established than ever. Then, in July of 1870, came word that Napoleon III had declared war on Prussia. Clemenceau reacted with mixed feelings: invasion and defeat at the hands of Von Moltke's armies would be a disaster, but so would victory on the part of the imperial regime that he had hated since childhood. For weeks he waited as the accounts reaching L'Aubraie told of French defeats. He decided to leave his wife and baby and to head for Paris to see what was happening. He arrived on September 1 and moved in with his friend from student days, J. A. Lafont, at 19, rue Capron in Montmarte. The decision to go to Paris was to have a decisive impact on his life. Our study will now focus on Clemenceau's entry into public life during the Franco-Prussian War and the Paris Commune of 1870–71. In the ensuing chapters we will examine the degree to which his continuing identity conflicts influenced both his public and his private life. What the present chapter has tried to show, in brief, is how these conflicts began: the sensitive and emotionally vulnerable boy, who had been pulled from a maternal constellation by a strong father whose mystical visions and own suffering enhanced his appeal as a role model, found in early youth that his role in life was defined as the defender of and sufferer for his father's ideals. The weakening of the son's autonomous development and his inability to achieve a sense of continuity that would link the inner self of childhood with the "tough" character traits demanded by his role led to identity diffusion, to weakness in coping with the demands of intimacy, and to an extended psychosocial moratorium, which ultimately failed.

TWO

The Radical of Montmartre
1870-1880

THE WAR AND THE COMMUNE

Clemenceau began his political career in 1870 with the help of his father's old friend Étienne Arago. His activities during the following decade may be seen as an effort to adapt his father identification to the issues and needs of his own generation and to do so in terms that were psychologically acceptable to himself. His experiences during the civil war of 1871 were significant as the first act in a postmoratorium effort to conduct his life with the force and dignity that he perceived as being characteristic of his father's ideals.

Politically, these experiences determined a future course for him of seeking nonviolent reform within the framework of the Republic. But they also confirmed him in the role of being a sufferer for his father's ideals; such was the result of the unjust accusations that he was responsible for the murders of Generals Claude Lecomte and Clément Thomas on March 18, 1871, and the subsequent opprobrium that he earned by trying to steer a middle course between the supporters and the opponents of the Paris Commune. One corollary of this role was inner tension, which influenced his own continuing quest for ego autonomy and which contributed to a temporary psychological withdrawal around 1877.

Upon arriving in Paris in 1870, Clemenceau renewed his ties with many of the republicans he had known in the early 1860s. Since July, many of them had been making plans in case the Empire went down in defeat. They did not have to wait long. On September 2 the army of Marshal MacMahon, who

41

was trying to relieve Metz, was smashed at Sedan, and Napoleon himself was captured. The road to Paris lay open.

The shock reached the capital the next day. On the afternoon of September 4 a crowd invaded the halls of the Corps Législatif and demanded the creation of a republic. The Left opposition, partly in an effort to stave off the more radical Jacobin and Blanquist elements within the city, had helped to prepare this demonstration.[1] Clemenceau and one of his old friends from Latin Quarter days, Arthur Ranc, were in the crowd. Sporting the kepis of the Parisian National Guard, they followed as Gambetta led the march to the Hôtel de Ville to proclaim the Republic. The new Government of National Defense made Arago the mayor of Paris and gave him the task of choosing temporary mayors for the twenty arrondissements of the city. Arago selected Clemenceau as provisional mayor of the eighteenth arrondissement, which encompassed Montmartre, and ordered him, along with the other mayors, to "supervise with vigilance the arming of citizens and to be ready night and day to uphold national defense."[2]

This was undoubtedly a great moment for Clemenceau. After the years of depression and uncertainty abroad, he was suddenly thrust into the center of a historic event in which he had a chance to emulate the triumphs of his father's heroes. He believed that, as in 1792, the Republic could proclaim the *levée en masse* and drive out the invader. The new government, whose members ranged from Léon Gambetta to more conservative republicans such as Jules Simon and Ernest Picard, recognized the realities of the situation: the regime born on September 4 was the child of radical Paris, not of conservative France, and its survival depended on its ability to defeat the Prussians. The Blanquists and other extremist elements were already demanding the creation of a commune patterned after that of the Great Revolution. Within the various quarters of the city they were organizing "vigilance committees," and they were beginning to exert power through the National Guard. With the provinces disorganized and Bazaine trapped at Metz, the burden of defense rested on this citizen militia. But it had little coordination and even worse discipline. As thousands of respectable bourgeois fled the city, the working-class regiments, which were easily swayed by the vigilance committees, were gaining the upper hand. Their distrust of the bourgeois officials at the Hôtel de Ville was evident in their demand that military officers be elected.[3]

Montmartre, one of the largest and poorest sections of Paris, was dominated by the butte where Sacred Heart Basilica would later be built. Its shops and taverns were hotbeds of political extremism and working-class discontent. But since fear of the Prussians dominated all other concerns, Clemenceau's vigorous activities on behalf of the war effort soon won for him the support of most of the inhabitants. "You would say he is one of those wild doctors invented by Eugène Sue in his novels," the writer Edmond de Goncourt noted in his diary.[4] Clemenceau lived up to the image, forming committees to enforce conscription laws and placarding the walls with warnings that shirkers would be prosecuted to the limit of the law. He supervised the distribution of rifles and bullets, and in a meeting on September 14, he tried to gain the confidence of local working-class leaders by urging the election of his old idol Blanqui as commander of the 169th Battalion. As the Prussians were surrounding the city on September 23, he appealed to the past in an effort to shore up the courage of the people:

> Shall France be swallowed up and disappear, or shall she resume her former rank in the vanguard of the peoples?
> That is the question facing us today and it is up to us to answer it.
> The enemy is at the gates of the city. The day is not far off, perhaps, when our breasts will be the last rampart of *la patrie*.
> Each of us knows his duty.
> We are the children of the Revolution. Let us be inspired by the example of our fathers in 1792, and like them, we shall conquer.
> *Vive la France!*
> *Vive la Republique!*[5]

The Parisians held out with a stubbornness that baffled even Bismarck, whose generals soon determined to starve the city out rather than make a direct assault. In Montmartre, Clemenceau urged aggressive action against the enemy. As rifles ran short, he approved the plans of a group of workers to make petrol bombs; but the government, which was at times more afraid of the Parisians than of the Prussians, ordered him to surrender them. He could not understand such apathy. Convinced that the National Guard, whose four hundred thousand members outnumbered the Prussians, could break out and win a decisive victory, he was outraged at any hint of indifference or lack of discipline, especially in his arrondissement.[6] Then, on October 31, he learned that Bazaine had surrendered at Metz and that Adolphe Thiers, bearing a safe-conduct from Bismarck, was urging that an armistice be accepted. Clemenceau placarded the walls of Montmartre with an announcement that "the citizens of the 18th arrondissement protest with indignation against an armistice that the government can accept only by committing treason."[7]

For the next few hours all authority within the city seemed to collapse. At the Hôtel de Ville a crowd led by revolutionaries from the Belleville National Guard held several ministers captive in their own conference rooms. Auguste Blanqui and Félix Pyat were there, denouncing the government for refusing to proclaim the *levée en masse* and for wasting the National Guard in ill-planned sorties. Rescue finally came at the hands of loyal Breton *mobiles*, but peace was restored only when the ministers promised both to conduct a plebescite on the Government of National Defense and to hold new mayoral elections in the twenty arrondissements.[8]

In the confusion of the situation, many mayors, including Clemenceau, thought that the promise for new elections would mean the creation of a Commune of Paris. When this proved not to be the case, he sent a note of resignation to Arago.[9] Although Clemenceau had not participated in the violence of October 31, he had sympathized with those who were demanding more efficient use of the National Guard and the proclamation of a national *levée en masse*. On November 3 the frightened and sobered city gave the Government of National Defense an overwhelming vote of confidence. In the mayoral elections in Montmartre, Clemenceau, with over nine thousand votes, beat the government's candidate. Clemenceau's friend J. A. Lafont was elected deputy mayor; but two other figures, both of whom were members of the Montmartre vigilance committee, were also elected deputy mayors. One was Victor Jaclard, a local union organizer, an amiable fellow with whom the newly elected mayor could work. But the other was Simon Dereure, a former delegate to the International, who had built his reputation as a revolutionary while organizing shoemakers in Montmartre. He had also helped to organize representatives of local vigilance committees into a central committee, which met at the headquarters of the International. Clemenceau may have sensed that he could not trust him, but he also knew that Dereure was a powerful voice in these illegal committees.

As the siege wore on through November and December, Clemenceau devoted most of his efforts to alleviating the plight of the inhabitants of his district. He created committees on health and hygiene, and he established distribution centers for clothes and shoes. With the help of Louise Michel, the "red virgin," who was one of the most prominent workers in the women's military auxiliary group known as the Amazons of the Seine, he organized ambulance brigades and relief supplies of medicine, milk, vegetables, and horse meat for the children of Montmartre. Michel also helped him to organize free schools in the arrondissement. When he discovered that some of the teachers were sending their pupils to mass during class hours, he dispatched a circular to all school directors: "You are to receive the children for teaching and watching over them, not for sending them to church during class hours."[10]

Despite the circumstances of the siege, his spirits were high. On December 20 he wrote to Mary, in English:

My dear little wife Mary,
    Another balloon is going to leave tonight. I wish I could go with it and take a little trip to Féaule. . . . I am well in every way, my most ardent wish is that little wife Mary and little baby Maddie may be as well and buoyant as I am. Yes dear, buoyant I am. Buoyant we all are: for here everything is motion and activity. We have the best reasons in the world to be full of hope, and we all feel now that all our efforts will be rewarded with success. In fact it is hardly possible otherwise, for, since the beginning of the siege we have all been at work with great activity.

Everything that could be done, has been done. We have
made cannons, guns, cartridges; powder, etc., etc. We have
armed and equipped the *Garde Nationale,* organized a new
army. We have fortified Paris in such a manner that the
Prussians did not dare attack our walls. Now the time has
come when we may go and attack them. . . .

. . . I *guess* the Prussians will soon find they have a
hard nut to crack, as a yankee would say. The spirit of the
people has never been so good as it is now. They are very
patient, since they know that the government means to
fight to the very end, and will *never* treat with the enemy,
whatever may happen. There is not the slightest disturb-
ance in the city, and there will be none. It is remarkable
how the people, to whatever party they may happen [to
belong], are united and mean to remain united against
our common enemy. In reading today the relation of what
the Prussians are doing in the unhappy part of France
which they are burning and plundering I cannot but feel
very thankful that you are in such a remote part of the
country.

He advised Mary, for the sake of her health, to stop breast-
feeding Little Maddie, and he concluded with "warmest kisses
to the little baby and little mother, my *warmest* love to them,
may they be as *brave* and *patient* as I wish them to be."[11]

Clemenceau's optimistic tone (which was perhaps meant
to convey the determination of Paris in case the letter fell into
Prussian hands) did not reflect the reality of the situation. The
attacks by the National Guard against Prussian lines always
ended in bloody futility; and with each failure, the frustration
and rage among Parisians grew more intense. On January 18,
1871, the German Empire was proclaimed at Versailles. In
Paris the government ordered one last attempt to break the
encirclement, but a final sortie, which took place in the direction
of Buzenval, ended in disaster. In a stormy meeting of the
mayors, Clemenceau urged that resistance be continued; but
since the bakeries and butcher shops were empty and since
any hopes of rescue by the forces of Gambetta (who had escaped the city in early October to organize the provinces) were
fading, the situation was hopeless. On January 26 Jules Favre
was seeking out Bismarck so that they could discuss an armistice.

Bismarck agreed to a truce of three weeks in order to allow France to elect a National Assembly, which would then decide whether to accept the terms. Elections were scheduled for February 8. Throughout the country, hundreds of local committees sprang up with lists of candidates. Most of these candidates, unlike those in Paris, were committed to peace. At Bordeaux, Gambetta, who had not been consulted about the armistice, resigned in disgust. Shortly before doing so, he had written to Clemenceau, asking him to take the post of mayor of Lyons.[12] Gambetta's resignation ended this possibility, but now Clemenceau saw his name on several Parisian electoral lists for the new Assembly, which was scheduled to meet in Bordeaux on February 12. Five groups included him on their lists, alongside such figures as Louis Blanc, Victor Hugo, and Edgar Quinet. When the ballots were counted, Clemenceau had been elected in twenty-seventh place among the forty-three new Paris representatives, most of whom held radical republican or moderate socialist ideas. Rural and conservative France, however, had rebuked its upstart capital and had elected twice as many monarchists as republicans. The majority of the monarchists favored peace.[13]

Clemenceau took his seat in the new Assembly at Bordeaux on February 16. He soon discovered the reactionary mood of the majority, many of whom had wanted the monarchy to be restored. For the moment they were content to make Thiers the provisional executive. On February 19 Clemenceau tried, without success, to remove restrictions on public viewing of the debates, which he called "a heritage of imperial traditions." On another occasion he took aim at the Bonapartists and provoked a lengthy debate by presenting a petition from the so-called Positivist Club of Paris, demanding that Corsica be expelled from the French Republic.[14]

Bismarck's demands included an indemnity of five billion gold francs, military occupation of eastern France until this was paid, and the annexation of Alsace and part of Lorraine to the new German Reich. As the vote on these terms drew near, the deputies from Alsace and Lorraine, including Scheurer-Kestner, protested that France could not surrender these areas without destroying its integrity. Clemenceau agreed, persisting in his belief that if France only had leaders such as those of 1792, defeat could still be turned into victory. On March 1 he voted against acceptance of the terms. The vote was 546 for and 107 against; after it was taken, the deputies from Alsace and Lorraine and some of those from Paris walked out of the Assembly.[15] Clemenceau did not resign, since he believed that he could still be useful in the trials that lay ahead. Indeed, one of the peace provisions allowed the Prussians to make a victory march through Paris and to occupy it for two days. On March 1 Clemenceau ordered that a placard be posted in Montmartre (it was probably prepared during a brief trip to Paris on February 20), urging his fellow citizens not to resist the Prussians and reminding them that "only the Republic can avenge and repair our disasters."[16]

The Prussians had their victory parade, but a sullen National Guard still had its rifles and nearly two hundred cannons purchased by public subscription during the siege. Moreover, a central committee of the National Guard, formed by representatives of working-class battalions, was being organized. With the old vigilance committees, it filled the temporary power vacuum in the city, and on March 1 it had moved most of the cannons to an artillery park on the summit of Montmartre in order to keep them out of Prussian hands.

Clemenceau left Bordeaux for Paris on March 5. Shortly after he arrived he was called to a meeting of the mayors at the Hôtel de Ville. There, a nervous Picard, now minister of the interior, told them that despite apparent calm in the city, the situation could become critical. He tried to cut short Clemenceau's protests by telling him that "we can't allow these cannons to go wandering about like this on the streets any longer." But Clemenceau answered that he had just visited Montmartre and had found that the battalions that were guarding the guns were willing to surrender them. As a measure of good faith, he suggested the creation of a central artillery park, which would be commanded by the Parisian deputy Victor Schoelcher, where battalions from different quarters of the city could alternately guard the cannons. Vautrain, who was mayor of the fourth arrondissement, argued that it was time to "take the bull by the horns" and arrest the Central Committee. Cooler heads prevailed for the moment, and the mayors charged Clemenceau with the responsibility of negotiating for the return of the guns.[17]

On March 10 Clemenceau wrote a letter to Gen. Aurelle de Paladines, the former Bonapartist whom the government had just designated as commander of the National Guard. Recognizing how little authority the general had, Clemenceau promised him that the guns would be turned over the next day. Aurelle was convinced of Clemenceau's sincerity, as he testified later, but when his forces arrived at the designated spot on place Royale, they were told that the agreement had been repudiated. Apparently only one battalion, the bourgeois Sixty-first, had agreed to cooperate with Clemenceau.[18] The Montmartre vigilance committee, including Clemenceau's deputy mayors Jaclard and Dereure, had vetoed the agreement. The Central Committee had also had a hand in the matter, having concluded that Clemenceau did not really speak for the government.

In fact, the actions of the government were undermining Clemenceau's efforts to resolve the matter of the guns peacefully. The Assembly of Bordeaux, which was anxious for a resumption of normal business activity, had decreed an end to the wartime moratorium on rents and commercial debts. In addition, on March 11, news reached Paris that the new session of the Assembly, which was scheduled for the twentieth, would meet at Versailles instead of Paris. On the same day the tough old army commander Joseph Vinoy suppressed five of the most radical Parisian newspapers. The latter measure especially alarmed Clemenceau. He went to see Thiers, who had just arrived from Bordeaux, and told him that he would already have received the cannons if the Assembly had not decided to move to Versailles and if the newspapers had not been suppressed. Clemenceau promised to continue working for return of the cannons, and Thiers, in turn, promised to do nothing to aggravate the situation.[19]

As the new session of the Assembly approached, however, businessmen were warning Thiers that the financial operations of the country could not be restored so long as the situation in Paris was in doubt. With the provinces demobilized and the loyalty of the Paris National Guard in question, he knew that he had to risk a surprise move. On the evening of March 17 he ordered Vinoy to retrieve the cannons by force while the city slept. It fell to Gen. Claude Lecomte's brigade to seize the guns of Montmartre. By four o'clock on the morning of March 18 he had done so; only one young sentry named Turpin was wounded in the brief skirmish. But one detail prevented the operation from being carried out smoothly: someone had forgotten to bring along horses to pull the artillery pieces away.

What happened at this point was to have a profound influence on Clemenceau's political and psychological development. The events of March 18, 1871, which culminated in the outbreak of civil war, were the first in a series of events that caused him to become one of the most controversial figures of the Third Republic. His efforts to achieve a compromise between two extremes ended by his earning the enmity of both sides. It was a "good initiation into the stupidity of public life," he said in later years, "I found myself between two groups that both wished me dead."[20] On this day he found that the historic moment of 1870, which had allowed him to play the role that his father had marked out for him and that had thus far invigorated him with such "buoyant" emotions, also contained a violent challenge; the trauma was to strain his inner resources and, at one point, to reduce the brusque and fearless mayor of Montmartre to tears. The political and psychological consequences of this experience are further examined below. First, it is necessary to determine exactly what happened.

In 1872, Clemenceau tried to reconstruct the events of March 18 of the previous year, calling upon witnesses to confirm his account.[21] His own version, which must be weighed against other sources, shows the picture of a compassionate man who was committed to justice for the weak but who, in his devotion to legality and nonviolence, was thwarted by circumstances over which he had little control. In his account he remembers that Simon Dereure awakened him around six o'clock with the news of Thiers's coup. Dereure suspected that the mayor was working with the Versailles government, but Clemenceau denounced Thiers's treachery and left to see General Lecomte at the summit of Montmartre. There Clemenceau expressed his surprise to the general over Thiers's action. Lecomte said that he would not discuss the matter and that he was only following orders. Clemenceau answered that Lecomte had better move the guns as soon as possible, since news of the coup was starting to spread.

Clemenceau then walked over to the guardhouse at 6, rue des Rossiers, where about a hundred prisoners who had been taken in the dawn skirmish were being detained in the courtyard. Inside he found the wounded Turpin, who was being attended by Louise Michel. Clemenceau returned to his office to get a stretcher for Turpin, but when he came back, Lecomte, fearing that the mayor might be trying to "parade the corpse" in order to stir up the growing crowd, refused to give him permission to move the wounded man. Clemenceau assured Lecomte that he would answer for order in his arrondissement, but the general refused to yield. Heading back down the slope, the mayor noticed a national guardsman berating one of the soldiers of the line who had taken part in the operation. As Clemenceau neared his office on the rue de Vieux Chemin, another guardsman began denouncing him for what had happened. At the square in front of his office, about twenty people, Dereure among them, were complaining bitterly about treason and betrayal.

Lecomte, meanwhile, was losing control over the situation. His refusal to allow Turpin to be removed had angered several people; at the same time, Louise Michel had left the scene, spreading word of the incident.[22] With every minute the size and confidence of the crowd grew, and it began to press in on Lecomte's lines. He gave the order to fire, but it was ignored. Suddenly his own men, joined by elements of the National Guard, lifted their rifles and began shouting cheers to the Republic. Lecomte was beaten and then was taken to an old dance hall on rue Cligancourt, which was called the Château-Rouge, along with the officers and military constabulary who had accompanied him. Some of the latter were also hustled off to a guardhouse near Clemenceau's office.[23]

Alone in his office, Clemenceau heard the ring of the tocsin. The square began to fill up with guardsmen and, to his surprise, soldiers of the line. A little after eight o'clock the detachment of military constabulary arrived under guard. Clemenceau apologized to its captain, but forbade the prisoners to leave the nearby guardhouse for fear the sight of them would stir up the crowds. Guardsmen crowded into his office, and among them Clemenceau spotted one of his former assistants for food supply, who was now a member of the Central Committee. The man turned on him, saying: "Yes! You negotiated with us merely to lull us to sleep, and you can never hope to make me believe that you were not conniving with the government all along!"

Stung by these words, Clemenceau was speechless. According to his own account, a "tear of rage" appeared on his cheek, causing his accuser to apologize for his remarks. But the mayor knew that others were thinking the same thing; now he grew alarmed lest they take their vengeance out on the prisoners. To his relief, Capt. Simon Mayer, the commander of the 169th Battalion, a man whom Clemenceau had known and liked during the siege, came in around ten o'clock with news that he and his men were guarding Lecomte and his officers at the Château-Rouge. Mayer promised that he would safeguard the prisoners and that he would be answerable to the mayor on their account. At about the same time, Clemenceau's deputy Jaclard arrived, and the mayor told him that if the government were overthrown, the Prussians would occupy Paris. Jaclard agreed, but told Clemenceau that he, Jaclard, could not with honor abandon the revolution now. He promised, however, that he would go to the Château-Rouge and that he would report any new developments. It was a promise that he apparently failed to keep.

Around eleven o'clock, Clemenceau sent out a friend to find other mayors or deputies who could come to Montmartre and lend him the weight of their authority. Around one o'clock the deputies Édouard Lockroy and Col. A. J. Langlois, who had been summoned by the deputy Henri-Louis Tolain, appeared at Clemenceau's office. He told them what was happening, and then he sent them out for more help. Langlois managed to see Thiers, who ordered him to go back to Clemenceau with instructions "to do everything possible to see that Lecomte is saved."[24] But Thiers seems to have already abandoned the general and his men to their fate. His own minister of war was warning him that only about six thousand of the four hundred thousand guardsmen could be relied on. The insurrection was spreading to Belleville, and by three o'clock, Thiers had decided to abandon Paris. He ordered the government to follow him to Versailles.

At the same time, Clemenceau faced an open violation of his authority in his own office. The local vigilance committee began holding a meeting in an adjoining room, and he was barely able to convince its members to go elsewhere. What they were discussing is not known. It is possible that they had heard about Clemenceau's appeals for help and that they were debating whether the prisoners should be removed. In any case, shortly after three o'clock the local National Guard committee ordered Simon Mayer to move Lecomte and his men back to 6, rue des Rossiers. Mayer was barely able to protect them from a mob of drunks, prostitutes, guardsmen, and soldiers of the line who had left their units. When he arrived on the summit of Montmartre, new trouble erupted. Around four o'clock, Gen. Clément Thomas, a former commander of the National Guard, was arrested by a guardsman and taken to the rue des Rossiers. The crowd that had gathered there began to demand that both generals be executed.

Captain Mayer ran to get Clemenceau. Louis Valigranne, commander of the 129th Battalion, tried to calm the crowd, but he barely managed to escape so that he could warn the mayor.[25] For, up to this point, Clemenceau had not had any word that there was trouble or that Lecomte and his men had been moved from the Château-Rouge. Mayer reached the mayor's office at half past four, and the two men headed back up the slope, Clemenceau fastening on his sash of office as he ran. But at this moment the crowd was bursting into the house at 6, rue des Rossiers and was dragging the men out. First Thomas, next Lecomte, was placed against a stone wall in an adjoining garden, then shot, and the crowd began to defile the bodies of the two slain soldiers.

Clemenceau arrived moments later. The crowd spotted his sash of office and began to hurl insults, accusing him of working with Thiers. Entering the rue des Rossiers, he met a detachment of guardsmen who were taking away the other prisoners, who, by some miracle, had been spared by the crowd. He stopped one of the officers, a Captain Buegot, and asked where he was taking them. Buegot, who later testified that Clemen-

ceau was "scared and very pale," answered that he was moving
them to the headquarters of the local vigilance committee for
safety.[26] Clemenceau then walked toward the house at 6, rue
des Rossiers, recalling in his account an eerie sensation of empti-
ness in the street as the last prisoners passed by. His account
describes what happened next:

> Suddenly a terriffic noise broke out, and the mob that
> filled the courtyard of the house at No. 6 poured into the
> street in the grip of some sort of frenzy.
> There were chasseurs, soldiers of the line, national
> guardsmen, women, and children. All were raving like
> savage beasts without realizing what they were doing. I
> observed then the pathological phenomenon that one might
> call blood lust. A breath of madness seemed to have passed
> over this mob: children perched upon a wall were waving
> indescribable trophies; women, dishevelled and wasted,
> flung their bare arms about while uttering raucous cries,
> having taken leave of their senses. I saw some of them
> weeping while they cried out louder than others. Men were
> dancing about and jostling each other in a sort of frenzied
> agitation. It was one of those nervous outbursts, so frequent
> in the Middle Ages, which still occur among masses of
> human beings under the stress of some powerful emotion.

Clemenceau did not go into the house where the mutilated
bodies now lay, feeling, as he wrote in his account, that he
"would not come out alive." He began to descend the hill,
ignoring the taunts and cries that others deserved to be killed.
Some guardsmen pointed their rifles at him; he retraced his
steps, faced his accusers, and denounced the killings as a dis-
grace to the Republic. He then managed to make his way to
the headquarters of the vigilance committee on the rue Chaus-
sée-Clignancourt to find out what had happened to the prisoners.
Langlois and Lockroy soon joined him, and both the Central
Committee and the vigilance committee, disclaiming responsibility for the deaths, agreed to free after dark both the officers
whom they held and the constabulary in the guardhouse near
Clemenceau's office. "They certainly owe him their lives," Langlois later testified with regard to Clemenceau's efforts. Two days
after the event, Langlois also told the Assembly at Versailles

that Clemenceau had "exposed his life. If you had seen how he treated the assassins . . . you would find it hard to understand how he was not shot."[27]

As both a mayor and a deputy, Clemenceau emerged as one of the chief spokesmen for reconciliation between Paris and Versailles. He believed that civil war could be averted, that the bulk of the city's population belonged to the party of order, and that compromise on the part of Thiers could prevent further violence. In a meeting on the afternoon of March 19 Clemenceau and the other mayors decided that they would try to persuade the National Assembly to agree to hold municipal elections, which would grant Paris greater autonomy, on condition that the insurgents surrender the Hôtel de Ville and postpone their announced plans for election of a commune, or a new city government. The Central Committee balked on the matter of giving up the Hôtel de Ville, but it agreed to wait on the matter of new elections pending action from Versailles.

In the Opera Hall at Versailles on March 20, Clemenceau proposed the election of a Paris municipal council, which would choose its own president. He warned the deputies about the threatening danger: "In the city of Paris there is no longer a constituted authority, except for some tottering municipalities that before long will be powerless to contain the wave that threatens to flood them. If you want to get out of this terrible situation . . . we must create an authority in the city of Paris . . . . around which all men who wish to see order reestablished can group themselves." But the Assembly, which was outraged over the murders of Lecomte and Thomas, was in no mood for conciliation. When Clemenceau charged that in deserting Paris the government had abandoned its post, several ministers and deputies interrupted to deny this. When he hinted that the abortive coup of Thiers was responsible for the situation, the minister of public instruction accused him of speaking the language of insurrection. From the tribune the next day, Clemenceau blamed the government as "the first cause of present events," and the response was so violent that he apologized for inflaming the debate. Jules Favre delivered such a vigorous harangue against the "blood stained minority" in Paris that Clemenceau temporarily withdrew his proposal.[28]

The Assembly's attitude reduced the credibility of the mayors in Paris. That night, Clemenceau, Lockroy, and Schoelcher went to the Central Committee to ask it to postpone its plans to elect a commune. Their request was denied. The next day the mayors issued a placard condemning the elections as illegal. As a result, revolutionaries took over their offices in all twenty arrondissements.[29] Back at Versailles on March 24, Clemenceau tried to speak again, but he was told to wait until the next day. As the session closed, he warned his colleagues, "You take the responsiblity, gentlemen, for what is about to happen."[30]

The Central Committee proceeded with plans for an election. It urged the mayors to back the plans, promising that their offices would be returned. On the twenty-fifth, Clemenceau returned from Versailles with news that the Assembly was contemplating the restoration of the monarchy. This proved to be false, but it caused one faction of the mayors, including Clemenceau, to sign the Central Committee's election decree. At Versailles the Assembly rejected Louis Blanc's proposal to approve the action of the mayors. Then, in a confused election on March 26, which saw less than half of the qualified voters go to the polls, the Parisians returned a municipal council on which revolutionaries of all shades outnumbered the moderates four to one.[31]

On the next day, Clemenceau resigned his post as deputy, but he continued to work for reconciliation, even after fighting had broken out between Versailles and Paris on April 2. For five weeks he remained in Paris, working with Lockroy, Schoelcher, Floquet, and several former mayors in a new group called the Republican Union for the Rights of Paris. Its goal was to persuade both the Commune and the National Assembly to accept a three-point program: recognition of the Republic; recognition of Paris's right to govern itself; and recognition of the National Guard and its right to bear arms.[32] But the Paris revolutionaries had determined their course, and Thiers, who was determined to crush the rebellion, was merely playing for time. The union planned a meeting at Bordeaux with representatives of other cities. In order to attend it, Clemenceau slipped out of Paris on May 10, using the papers of an American friend. When he was halted at Saint-Denis, he got by the Versailles soldiers by pretending that he spoke only English. Then he learned that the government had banned the meeting and had already arrested three of the Parisian delegates, although Floquet had escaped. As Clemenceau later wrote to a friend, Thiers had "judged it advisable to cut off the last branch of salvation to which the country could cling."[33]

Finding himself stranded in the countryside, Clemenceau tried to reenter Paris, but found that the city gates were blocked by troops. He made his way to Nantes, where the father of the future politician René Waldeck-Rousseau forged a passport for him. From there he went to L'Aubraie and rejoined his family. Meanwhile, the Commune was approaching a bloody denouement. After the cruelest excesses on both sides, the Versailles troops crushed the insurrection. In what came to be known as Bloody Week in May of 1871, at least seventeen thousand people were killed and another thirty-six thousand imprisoned.

Clemenceau's experiences during the war and the Commune strengthened certain features of his political outlook. For six months, under extraordinary conditions, he had labored on behalf of the two ideals that he had first associated with his father in 1848: the Republic and the Parisians. In so doing, he had identified for years to come those forces that were opposed to his ideals: the Prussians, the monarchists, the generals who had lost the war but now gloated over how they had broken the spirit of Paris, and the self-righteous bourgeois types like Thiers who could "shed blood without flinching." His hatred of violence extended to the revolutionary fanatics who were willing to spill blood in the interest of some vague utopia.[34] Distaste for even the doctrinal implication of violence was a major reason for his hostility to collectivist ideas in the 1880s.

By the same token, his involvement in the events that led to the murders of Lecomte and Thomas earned him a reciprocal hatred from the Right, many of whose members believed that he had been, at best, derelict in his duty, or, at worst, a coward. Even among some conservative republicans he was tainted by this episode. "When one brags about doing his duty," Jules Simon told him in the National Assembly two days after the killings, "he should look twice before telling others that they have not done theirs."[35] David Robin Watson has claimed both that Clemenceau's association with the Commune was responsible in later years for "a sort of tacit veto" among conservatives and moderates, which kept him out of office, and that his failure to join the Commune, on the other hand, weakened his future efforts to build a Radical party.[36] It is true that Clemenceau's role in the events of 1871 damaged his potential ability to achieve his ideals. This damage, however, was rooted less in how others perceived him after his ordeal than in how he perceived himself.

For the psychological consequences were as profound as the hardening of political attitudes mentioned above. To be placed between two groups, both of which, in his own words, "wished me dead," added confirmation to an earlier perception that his identity in life was to be that of a sufferer for his father's ideals. Both the physical danger and the abuse that he subsequently endured must be linked psychologically to the attitude that he first expressed in his tribute to the "Martyrs of History" of 1862, in which he eulogized those who were willing to sacrifice life and reputation for an ideal. Furthermore, his self-image as a martyr for the Republic was enhanced by the fact that his suffering in 1871 had resulted from external circumstances, not from the kind of consciously invited punishment that had landed him in Mazas in 1862.

Clemenceau's self-image as a sufferer had some beneficial results; in the next section, one sees how, as a member of the Municipal Council of Paris, he readily associated himself with the victims of the war and the Commune. But the kind of psychological predisposition that one sees in Clemenceau may produce a variety of other emotional reactions. One, as indicated in the previous chapter, is shame, or the feeling that the true self is inadequate to bridge the gap between one's ego and one's ego ideal. Gerhart Piers and Milton B. Singer stress that intense feelings of shame produce an unconscious threat to the ego that denotes a primitive fear of abandonment and of the withdrawal of parental love and approval.[37] Clemenceau was able to externalize part of this reaction by proving to the world that he possessed the courage and the manliness to suffer and to risk his life and career. During the parliamentary investigation of 1871 into the causes of the insurrection, a very emotional Clemenceau energetically defended his actions before a panel which, despite its hostility toward him, could find no evidence of wrongdoing on his part. A commander, Nöel Poussargues, who was with Lecomte on the morning of March 18, charged that Clemenceau was responsible for what happened in that his facile assurances to Lecomte that he could keep order in his arrondissement had put the general off guard. Clemenceau challenged him to a duel with pistols, and in the Bois de Verrières, Clemenceau won the fight by wounding Poussargues in the leg.[38] But Clemenceau's enemies refused to forget. In later years, one of the most extreme of them, the rightest editor Ernest Judet, repeated Poussargues's charges, hinting darkly that Clemenceau had been in league with the Central Committee.[39] Not a scrap of evidence was produced in support of these charges. Nevertheless, the fact that such things concerning him could be believed by others, including the widow of General Thomas, who regarded Clemenceau as her husband's murderer,[40] strengthened Clemenceau's self-image as a sufferer and added fuel to his compensatory efforts to prove that he was worthy of his father's ideals.

MUNICIPAL COUNCIL TO CHAMBER OF DEPUTIES

It has been stressed that Clemenceau's self-identity as a sufferer helped to create his feeling of solidarity with all sufferers of mankind. Aside from the psychological conflicts that were inherent in this role, such an identity also provided him with certain strengths. It sharpened his sensitivity to issues involving human justice, and it often enabled him to transcend the limitations and prejudices of class origins that characterized the outlook of many of his colleagues. It provided him with a remarkable store of energy. Equally important, it gave him the physical and moral courage to stand in opposition to the pressures of majority opinion. These positive features of his identity role were apparent during the years 1871 to 1876 as he tried to defend the interests of the Parisians against the government and Assembly at Versailles. Although biographers have given little attention to this phase of his career, it was important in the

development of his awareness of social and economic problems
and thus has a bearing on the policies that he would propose a
few years later.

He returned to Paris in July of 1871, leaving his wife and
daughter at L'Aubraie and taking up residence in a small apartment on rue Miromesnil in the eighth arrondissement. The city
was still numbed by the tragedy. Many homes and shops had
gone up in flames, and the disruption of everyday life—not to
mention the arrests and sentencings that were still being carried out—made it hard for the thousands of innocent victims.
In Montmartre, at 20, rue des Trois-Frères, Clemenceau opened
a clinic, where for two days of each week he treated the poor
free of charge. His office was usually packed on consulting days,
and here he witnessed the real problems of working-class families: the drudgery in sweatshops, the cramped living quarters,
the ignorance with regard to hygiene and diet.

But politics, not medicine, was still his chief concern, and
whether the Republic might yet survive. The royalists in the
National Assembly had initially hoped to restore the monarchy.
For the moment, the determination of the Bourbon pretender,
the comte de Chambord, to replace the tricolor with the white
flag of the Bourbons prevented this solution.[41] With Bona-
partism discredited, the Republic was the only alternative. It
was not, however, the kind of republic that Clemenceau envisioned. Thiers, who now took the title of president, declared
that the Republic must either be a conservative one or not exist
at all. To this end, radical Paris must be kept in line. At Versailles the Assembly had finally voted through a new form of
government for the city, in which the Municipal Council would
be only an advisory body directly under the control of the
prefect of the Seine. The body would be composed of four representatives from each of the twenty arrondissements.[42] Clemenceau decided to stand as a candidate from the Clignancourt
Quarter of the eighteenth arrondissement. On July 23, in an
election in which few people voted, he won a seat with just over
sixteen hundred votes.

The council began meeting in August at the Luxembourg
Palace under the presidency of a former mayor named Joseph
Vautrain. The council had a small right wing that was composed

of representatives from wealthy sections of the city, but the majority tended to be moderate or radical republicans who were united in their resentment over subjugation of the city. Two of Clemenceau's friends from student days, J. A. Lafont and Jean-Paul Dubois, were members, as was Charles Floquet. Clemenceau soon began to play a prominent role in the work of the council, serving on committees that dealt with public assistance and instruction, health and hygiene, finance, architectural landmarks, and aid to neglected and abandoned children.[43]

He was a frequent participant in debates of the council, and often he was a very excitable polemicist when the topic involved public aid to religion. During debate on the budget of 1872, he attacked the laws on communal aid to religion as being a violation of both liberty of conscience and the independence of the Commune. The same year he almost disrupted the sittings by violently denouncing religious subsidies as being a tax on everyone that benefited the moral needs of only a few. He frequently challenged the competence of the teaching congregations and urged the council to enforce standards. His emotionalism on these occasions was matched only by that which he displayed when his record as mayor of Montmartre was questioned or when he felt that the government was undermining the autonomy of the Municipal Council. Once he stormed in and interrupted the discussion with news that one of the mayors, who had been selected by Versailles, had barred a municipal councillor from jury duty on grounds of his "intellectual incapacity." He demanded that the prefect take action, since the councillor had been elected by universal suffrage. The people of Paris had thus been the real object of the insult.[44]

His more substantive labor, however, was devoted to the poor people of Paris. He fumed at the bureaucrats who frustrated the efforts of citizens to collect indemnities for war damage, noting that the latter were usually poor and illiterate or were from families of individuals who had been condemned for taking part in the insurrection. Lack of teachers and classrooms, especially in the poorer sections of Paris, concerned him. He urged that money be spent on schools and foster homes rather than on rebuilding damaged churches. Clemenceau brought his medical knowledge to bear on the one area that interested him

most: public health. Lack of space in Parisian hospitals, lack
of isolated wards for women recuperating from childbirth, and
the need for new laboratories were problems he often brought
to the attention of his colleagues. In August, 1874, he denounced
those "harmless" neighborhood cemeteries, citing the latest scientific findings to prove that there were dangers of infection
and urging that all cemeteries be moved outside the city.[45]

One aspect of his work that won him recognition was that
of aid to neglected and abandoned children. In March of 1872
he charged that state protection of illegitimate children was
ineffective, and he criticized the endless bureaucratic obstacles
that unwed mothers had to face. Later, as a member of the
Committee on Public Assistance, he wrote a detailed report
outlining reforms that were needed in aid programs to found-
lings. Noting that there had been much progress in hygiene
in Parisian hospitals, he nevertheless emphasized the continuing
increases in infant mortality and proposed that sick children be
placed in the countryside rather than in hospitals, where danger
from infection was much greater. He contended that indigent
or unwed mothers should give up their babies only in cases
of extreme hardship. Instead of giving subsidies to wet nurses,
who often bottle-fed the children, payments should be made
to the mothers, who could then nurse their own babies. This
would help to prevent abandonment and would halt the climb
in infant mortality.[46]

For nearly five years Clemenceau devoted his time to work
of this sort, first as secretary, then as vice-president, and finally,
on November 29, 1875, as president of the Municipal Council.
In his opening speech he lauded the council for its work in
"paying off the criminal follies of the Empire." That Parisian
credit was now on a par with that of the state was a tribute
to the courage and sacrifice of the city's people. He argued
that Paris was "an immense laboratory" for French ideas and
genius:

> The dominant characteristic of our municipality . . .
> is that of being profoundly imbued with the laic spirit.
> That is, in accordance with the traditions of the French
> Revolution, we wish to separate the domain of law, which
> everyone should obey, from the domain of religious belief,

which is accepted only by a fraction of the citizens. Upon this terrain is engaged the great struggle that we are the anxious witnesses of and that characterizes the end of the century. . . . Animated by the true traditions of the French spirit, of high heart and determined spirit, we await the clash.[47]

But the Municipal Council was a limited forum for carrying out his role as a leader in this struggle. Even as president of this body he could do little to help those who had been condemned for participating in the Commune. Thousands were still in prison or in hiding, exiled in New Caledonia, separated from friends and family. He worried over the families of those who were in jail, over friends such as Louise Michel, to whom he sometimes sent money in New Caledonia, and over Auguste Blanqui, who was jailed at Clairvaux after having been condemned by a council of war in 1872.[48] To the exiled Arthur Ranc he wrote: "My heart is with you. Call on me for anything and know that I am your devoted friend."[49] But the power to begin healing the wounds of civil war by proclaiming amnesty for the communards did not lay at Paris.

It lay at Versailles, where Thiers directed the destinies of France. Even Thiers was in trouble with the Assembly, which was frustrated over the failure to restore the monarchy and was restive over Thiers's support of a republic, even a conservative one. In May of 1873 the duc de Broglie rallied the majority against Thiers, whose replacement was the more malleable Marshal MacMahon. Though the legitimist comte de Chambord had not changed his mind over the issue of the flag, the Assembly could no longer delay giving the nation a constitution. In order to postpone the decision about restoration of the monarchy to a more favorable time, the royalists passed the Septennate, which gave MacMahon a seven-year term. The "organic laws" of 1875 provided for a Chamber of Deputies, with representatives from single-member constituencies to be elected by universal manhood suffrage. A Senate, which would represent rural and conservative France, would serve as a check on the lower house. Some senators were to be chosen for life by the outgoing National Assembly, whereas others were to be selected by departmental electoral colleges composed of deputies, municipal councillors, and other local officials. The president of the Republic would be elected by both houses sitting together as a National Assembly. Thus was made the Constitution of 1875, which was republican in name but royalist in spirit.[50]

In Montmartre an "advanced republican committee" asked Clemenceau to run in the elections for the Chamber of Deputies, which were scheduled for February 20, 1876. Clemenceau accepted, announcing his program at the old meeting hall known as the cirque Fernando. This program, which was similar to the one that Gambetta had laid out at Belleville in 1869, called for "the completion of the great renovation of 1789 that has been abandoned by the French bourgeoisie." Its main points included amnesty for the communards; abolition of the death penalty; freedom of speech, press, and assembly; administrative decentralization; restoration of Paris as the capital; the separation of Church and state, accompanied by free and obligatory primary education; expulsion of the Jesuits; the election of judges; equal military service, with militias replacing professional armies; imposition of income and inheritance taxes; and adoption of the electoral reform known as the *scrutin de liste*. This last reform would replace single-member constituencies with slates of candidates, and this, it was hoped, would encourage the growth of disciplined parties.

These points were becoming familiar ones in the ideology of Radical republicanism; they were almost identical to the platforms of many other candidates throughout Paris. It should also be stressed that while amnesty for the communards ranked high among the goals of the Radicals, the first priority for republican candidates during the elections of 1876 was the consolidation of the republican form of government.[51]

Clemenceau won an easy victory in Montmartre, capturing over fifteen thousand votes against an opponent named Arrault. The final tally, after the second ballot, gave encouragement to those who believed that despite the monarchist victory of 1871, republicanism was on the rise. Although the Right dominated the Senate, republicans captured 367 of the 532 seats in the Chamber of Deputies. But the various republican factions, which tended to group around individuals, only faintly resembled real parties. In the Left Center were 75 deputies who preferred the conservative republic of Thiers. The Republican Left, which was dominated by Jules Ferry, numbered 185, while Gambetta's Republican Union had 86. The Extreme Left, which was dominated by men such as Louis Blanc, numbered 34, although only about 27, Clemenceau among them, could be classified in Loubère's terms as "hard core" Radicals. Jacques Kayser has noted that about 60 deputies, or 11 percent of the Chamber as a whole, could be loosely termed "radical" in that they favored such measures as amnesty for the communards and separation of Church and state. Over half of them had dual membership in the Extreme Left and Gambetta's Republican Union, since dual membership was commonplace until 1881.[52]

In tracing Clemenceau's efforts to formulate an ideological role that would express his striving for an identity, it is essential to understand the nature of the minority movement that he associated himself with on the Extreme Left. Among its 34 members the liberal professions were dominant, including 10 lawyers and 10 medical men. One would expect that many of these were also property owners.[53] The proportion of lawyers on the Extreme Left was similar to that in other republican groups, but the proportion of those with medical training— about 29 percent—was much higher than among the moderate republican factions. If one takes only the 27 hard-core Radicals, the proportion of doctors was even higher, about 40 percent. At thirty-five years of age, Clemenceau was the youngest among the latter group, whose average age was just over fifty-seven.[54]

Among radicals as a whole, the areas most heavily represented were the departments of the lower south (35 percent) and the Seine (just over 24 percent). Leadership of the movement by those who had been born or educated in Paris was a feature that would last for more than a decade.[55] Among hard-core Radicals, one sees two generations represented. The first was that of 1848 and included—besides Louis Blanc—François-Vincent Raspail, who had spent the bulk of his eighty-two years fighting for the Republic and for social medicine;[56] Madier de Montjau, who had sat in the Legislative Assembly in 1850 and had been elected representative for the Drôme to the

National Assembly in 1874; and many lesser known figures, all doctors, who had been active in 1848 and had been arrested after Napoleon's coup of 1851. They included Jean Moreau, the *"médecin des pauvres"* from Creuse; Émile Vernhes from Hérault; Paul Massot from the Pyrénées-Orientales; Alfred Leconte, a pharmacist and journalist from Indre; and Jean Turigny, who had long been one of the leaders of the republican movement in Nièvre and was now a popular doctor in the Gros-Callou Quarter of Paris.

The new generation of Radicals was typified by people like Clemenceau. Its political initiation was the Second Empire rather than the Second Republic, since most of its members, except for a few like Floquet, had been born in the 1830s and 1840s.[57] Clemenceau had known many of them as a student or during the war and the Commune: Germain Casse, Georges Perin, Édouard Lockroy, Victor Schoelcher, and Léon Laurent-Pichat. Others included Benjamin Raspail, son of the elder Raspail; Désiré Barodet, a schoolteacher who had once been mayor of Lyons; Martin Nadaud, a former worker who had a deep interest in labor questions; and Joseph Alfred Naquet, a brilliant chemist who had been a representative from the Vaucluse to the National Assembly and who was one of the most fascinating of the early Radical leaders.[58] As was true for Radicals as a whole, the hard-core Radicals came primarily from Paris and the lower South and included such individuals as Jean-Louis Greppo, Émile Brelay, Alfred Talandier, Gaston de Douville-Maillefeu, Alphonse Gent, Jacques Marcou, Pierre Ducamp, Augustin Daumas, Édouard Millaud, and Victor Bousquet.

The new Chamber convened at Versailles in March, and Clemenceau emerged as a major spokesman for his group. Showing the same nervous intensity that he had exhibited on the Municipal Council, he let no challenge from the Right go unanswered, and before long he had tried to pick fights with Bonapartists such as Paul de Cassagnac and Robert Mitchell.[59] He was convinced that the nation had declared itself in favor of the Republic, and he had little patience with those who wished to delay the implementing of reforms, starting with a program of amnesty. Gambetta, realizing that republican unity did not exist, was much more cautious and did not want to alienate conservative opinion. He also realized that President MacMahon, who felt himself to be the equal of the Chamber, would not hesitate to dissolve it should it press too hard. He had already selected a ministry headed by J. A. Dufaure, who had once served the July Monarchy.

Clemenceau refused to adjust his goals to these political realities. On the very first day that the Chamber met, he and Lockroy engaged in heated exchanges with Gambetta over the matter of amnesty.[60] Their remonstrances did little good, however, and on March 12 the Extreme Left held its own caucus at the home of Victor Hugo and decided to press immediately for a bill that would give full amnesty for those "condemned for acts relative to the events of April and May, 1871."[61] On the twenty-first the elder Raspail presented the bill to the Chamber, while Hugo presented it to the Senate. It failed in committee. On May 16 Clemenceau followed Lockroy and the elder Raspail to the tribune to urge that the bill be accepted by the Chamber as a whole.

"I am at this tribune," he said, "in order to fulfill a duty, a difficult duty." He argued that the Dufaure ministry was opposing amnesty because it believed that it would dishonor the country by conceding that the condemned of the Commune were simply victims of civil disaccord. Such, however, was the case, Clemenceau said. It was not that a "gang of bandits" had descended upon the city, but that the city had been the victim of "a series of fatalities" from which it could not escape: "From the Empire to invasion, defeat, disorganization, and after blow upon blow, to the convulsions of the most hideous civil war."

He described in detail the background of March 18, from the famine and cold and psychological conditions—which had been bred by war and siege—to the entry of the Prussian soldiers. "If you examine the history of insurrections," he told the Chamber, "you will not find one where premeditation has been less." He urged an end to repression, claiming that at least seventeen thousand people had already been shot without trial, that fifty thousand had been arrested, and that one hundred thousand had been driven into exile. Rehabilitation was better than vengeance; had not the Convention sought to rehabilitate

the Vendeans, and Louis XVIII the regicides? Turning to Dufaure and his ministers, Clemenceau appealed to them to have
confidence in their own ability to achieve a reconciliation of
classes that would produce "the social appeasement that we all
desire."[62]

On May 18 the proposal got only fifty votes in the Chamber;
it got only nine in the Senate a few days later. Bitter over
Gambetta's failure to support the bill, Clemenceau was among
fourteen Radicals who gathered at Louis Blanc's home a few
days later and called for a total break from the Republican
Union.[63] It was not until May of the following year, when the
seize mai crisis seemed to threaten the Republic, that he again
gave full support to his former hero. In December of 1876
Dufaure had resigned his ministry, having been plagued with
controversy over the issue of further prosecution of the communards. Against his will, MacMahon called on the moderate
republican senator Jules Simon. On May 15, 1877, after Simon
had been defeated in the Chamber over the press law, Mac-
Mahon replaced him with the duc de Broglie, whose views were
more in harmony with his own. The new cabinet included the
reactionary Bardy de Fortou at the Ministry of the Interior,
as well as two Bonapartists. MacMahon adjourned the Chamber; then, in a violent session on June 16, he dissolved it with
a call for new elections the following October.

Clemenceau called MacMahon's actions "an insurrection of
the ruling classes against the national will" and accused "the
black armies of clericalism" of having supported the president.[64]
He also worked with Gambetta in organizing committees and
propaganda and in establishing liaison with republican groups
in the provinces. In Montmartre he had no opposition in October, and he garnered nearly nineteen thousand votes. The
elections as a whole confirmed the nation's conversion to republicanism: 340 of the original 363 republican deputies were returned, which was still a majority and represented a moral victory in light of all the efforts made by the government.[65]

There was still the possibility that MacMahon would at-
tempt a coup d'état. On November 6, the day before the new
Chamber was to meet, the Left formed the Committee of
Eighteen to serve as a permanent council, as had the great

Committee of Public Safety. Clemenceau, Blanc, Lockroy, and de Montjau represented the Extreme Left, which met daily in Paris to plan strategy. Though Broglie and his cabinet were overthrown, MacMahon refused to buckle under. Gambetta, who was afraid that there might be a coup similar to that of 1851, worked with several members of the Committee of Eighteen to make plans for meeting force with force. Clemenceau appears, from the limited evidence regarding this "revolutionary resistance," to have served as Gambetta's right-hand man, claiming in later years that Gambetta had confided his plans only to "a very small number of friends" and that most of the members on the Committee of Eighteen did not know what was going on.[66] Gambetta evidently intended, in case there were a coup, to seek assistance from certain republican generals, to enlist support from the provinces, and if necessary, to withdraw to fortified cities in the north such as Lille. The majority on the Committee of Eighteen, doubting that there was any danger, rejected these plans when Gambetta finally revealed them.[67]

Clemenceau, who always believed that a coup had been prepared, was furious at their timidity, and in later years he condemned some of his colleagues on the committee for "hiding behind us" when the Republic was in danger.[68] In any case, MacMahon saved them the need for making further decisions on the matter. He gave up the fight and called on Dufaure to form a Left Center ministry, which included Charles de Freycinet of the Republican Left. The *seize mai* crisis had greatly undermined the political strength of monarchism, and by early 1879 the dominance of the republicans was confirmed by their control of both the Senate and the presidency.

For just under two years following the *seize mai* crisis, there was a slackening in Clemenceau's pace. He made no speeches in or out of Parliament for the remainder of 1877; nor did he make any for the whole of 1878.[69] Not until his speech of February 21, 1879, attacking limited amnesty did he begin to emerge once more as a leading spokesman for radicalism. Wormser attributes his reticence during this period to his discouragement over lack of republican support for revision of the monarchist constitution of 1875.[70] But the evidence suggests that more was involved, that, in fact, he was experiencing a

new stage of psychological development that necessitated a retreat from the battles in which he had been engaged for the
past seven years. In the following section I will examine this
phenomenon and the psychological compromise that Clemenceau
tried to make between the demands of his role and the demands
of his inner self.

RETREAT, REJUVENATION, AND THE FOUNDING OF *La Justice*

Erikson has argued that one cannot separate identity conflicts in an individual from contemporary crises in historical
development, since both interact with and help to define each
other.[71] For Clemenceau, the resolution of the *seize mai* crisis
seemed to hold out great promise for the eventual triumph of
the Republic of his ideals, but a promise whose attainment
required further labor, discipline, and sacrifice. In mid 1877
the deputy from Montmartre suddenly faded from the scene; in
trying to understand why he did so, one should begin by recalling his words to Scheurer-Kestner in 1865, that he found
"a great attraction" in withdrawing into himself. At that time
his depression had been caused by the inability to cope with
sexual failure and the problems of intimacy, which were related
to his identity conflicts. In 1877 his mood was likewise linked
with continuing identity problems and the inner tension that
he had experienced for seven years as the defender of his father's
ideals.

Contrary to the image of Clemenceau that has often been
projected by his biographers, the discipline and self-abnegation
that are essential to a sufferer for a noble cause did not come
easily to him. From the sensitive young boy, dependent on the
affection of his mother, to the young student, shattered by his
first courtship, one sees an ego of pronounced fragility and in-
security. It is easy, therefore, to understand both the difficulties
that he encountered in trying to live up to his role and the
nervous tension—which was apparent throughout his entire life
—that resulted from his feelings of inadequacy as well as guilt
should be ever stumble or prove unworthy of expectations.

Indeed, the Clemenceau of the 1870s and 1880s was often

like a tightly coiled spring. Those around him could not help
but notice the tension, which always seemed to be on the verge
of erupting. His friend Camille Pelletan wrote of his "nervous
abruptness" and his "sang-froid always on guard." Gustave
Geffroy spoke of his "rapid gestures" and "quick speech" and
compared him to "a doctor, giving orders as sharp and precise
as a medical prescription." Louis Andrieux was struck by his
"vehemence against oppression"; the writer Léon Daudet, by
his "impulsiveness, sudden temper, changing moods." Describing one of his speeches in the Chamber, the newspaper *Le
Temps* noted his "abrupt movements" and "concentrated energy"
and said that his sentences were "short, vigorous, and go rapidly
to the point."[72]

Such *nervosité* in physical traits and speech patterns was
more than a simple quirk of personality. It was a feature of the
intense emotionalism that accompanied his determination to
defend his ideals. This determination prompted him, for example, to respond to those on the Right who interrupted his
speech on amnesty in May of 1876 with a challenge: "I will
speak on whatever I wish to speak, and if you have any observations to make to me, I am ready to receive them here or elsewhere."[73] The brusque and combative façade signified stress
and tension beneath the surface, and it was only on rare occasions that he permitted people to get a glimpse of the other
feelings that existed there. In 1883, on the death of his friend
from Latin Quarter days Jean-Paul Dubois, for example, he
stood at the graveside almost weeping over the loss of a com-
panion "so good, so loyal, so generous" who had shared the pain
of this "abominable struggle."[74]

There are indications that by the late 1870s this stress was
affecting Clemenceau's private life as well. During much of
the time that he had served on the Paris Municipal Council,
he had been separated from his wife, Mary, who remained at
L'Aubraie. In 1872 she had given birth to a second daughter,
Thérèse, and, in 1873, to a son, Michel. By 1876, when Clemenceau entered the Chamber of Deputies, the family was finally
united and living in Paris, first in a flat on rue Montaigne and
later in an apartment on rue Clément-Marot. Judging from the
sentiments in his letter to Mary during the siege, Clemenceau

was capable of being a tender, caring husband. She seems to have been extremely attached to him. According to an interview given by "an intimate friend" of Mary's to the New York *World* in 1892, the couple enjoyed a harmonious union until about 1878. "He was everything to her," Mary's friend said, "she knew every little foible, every little characteristic." But in 1878, when Michel was five years old, a change came over Clemenceau. He began to grow irritable and depressed; he was unable to sleep, and his insomnia seems to have lasted for several years. "If he has insomnia one night," the friend quoted Mary as saying, "I know he will make a speech next day; if the insomnia lasts two nights I am sure there is going to be a great scene in the Chamber, and if it continues a third night then a ministry is likely to be overthrown."[75]

It was at about the same time that his depression became noticeable to his wife that he began to have a series of affairs with other women, though his relationships with them could only be described as efforts toward pseudo intimacy. If his grandson Georges Gatineau-Clemenceau is to be believed, he even appeared with his mistresses in public, as if to show off his latest conquest. There was Rose Caron, the *cantatrice* of the Opéra; Léonie Leblanc, an actress who is reputed also to have been the mistress of the duc d'Aumale; and Suzanne Reichenberg, a young actress at the Comédie-Française, who was the wife of the baron de Bourgoing.[76]

A souring toward domesticity in a man who is entering his late thirties is by no means abnormal; nor should one be surprised to find a politician of that era keeping a mistress. In fact, Clemenceau continued to live with his wife until 1892, content with the double standard that gave men, though not women, sexual license outside the home. But there was a price to be paid for such behavior on the part of a man who preached the highest principles in politics. Mary's friend mentioned how Paris laughed at the rumors of Clemenceau's affairs, thinking it "droll" that the man "who had led so straight-laced a life and who had always talked about principle in the home life, should do as other men do."[77] For several years, Mary endured her husband's infidelities; however, the relationship was anything but stable. In 1884, for example, when Clemenceau departed on a tour of the cholera-stricken areas around Marseilles, he left a note entrusting the upbringing of his children, should he not return, to his friend Cornélius Herz.[78]

The details concerning the causes for Clemenceau's estrangement from his wife and for his continuing marital problems may never be known. What little evidence is available, however, indicates behavioral patterns that were not entirely consistent with what is otherwise known about Clemenceau's feelings. His letters during the Hortense affair, for example, show a sensitive man who was desperately searching for adult love and intimacy, not a man who would be content with repeated attempts and failures with young actresses. Furthermore, Clemenceau did not strike others as being a promiscuous man; in fact, for some he had "the character of a Puritan" in him.[79] One of his friends, Georg Brandes, once noted that even in intimate conversation Clemenceau never let his attitude toward women be known; he once remarked of the risqué novels of a writer named Pierre Louys that "they ought not even to be touched."[80] In this light, and in light of what is evident concerning his earlier identity problems, it is possible to suggest that in the late 1870s Clemenceau was still functioning at an essentially adolescent level of identity conflict, still desperately striving to find his own identity role even if this process distracted him from his role as defender of his father's ideals.

One should compare, for example, Ernest Judet's description of the young deputy in 1877 with Clemenceau's own self-description to Scheurer-Kestner when he was in New York ten years earlier, which included the references to examining himself in the mirror, buttoning up his collar to the chin, and buying himself a cane: "His blunt demeanor, his mocking smile, his impudent, cunning eyes, his magnificent cane under a waving arm, his hat planted on the side of his head with an affectation of provocative poses, of the radical dandyism that would later form part of his so-called *bien parisienne* originality—all his person radiated self-satisfaction."[81] Judet, of course, hated Clemenceau, but there was truth in his description. At about the time that his marriage began to fall apart, Clemenceau gravitated toward the world of high society. He was in demand for dinner parties and gala affairs, sought after by the leading salons of such women as Madame Ménard-Dorian. He took his morning horseback rides in the Bois de Boulogne, wore the finest clothes, smoked expensive cigars, visited the best cafés and restaurants, and was a frequent visitor at the Opéra and the Comédie-Française. His reputation as a man who was deadly with swords and pistols was no doubt an appealing aspect of his role, although the only man he ever seriously injured was Commander Poussargues in 1871.[82]

Erikson has stressed that the counterpart to intimacy is isolation, the eschewing of all relationships that might lead to intimacy.[83] It would be incorrect to portray the early Clemenceau as being totally isolated in his personal relationships. He enjoyed the friendship, not of politicians, but of writers and artists such as Alphonse Daudet and especially the painter Édouard Manet, whom he met in late 1879.[84] As Wormser has pointed out, however, Clemenceau was genuinely close to few people throughout his life.[85] His tendency to draw into himself was an obstacle on the political front as well, especially in his efforts to organize a Radical party in the 1880s. At the time of his withdrawal from politics in the late 1870s, this tendency did not escape the notice of others. On March 18, 1879, for example, Blanqui wrote him a letter from his cell at Clairvaux, congratulating him on his amnesty speech the previous month. Clemenceau never did receive this letter, but Blanqui's attempt to encourage him in his renewed activism gives an indication of some contemporary perceptions of Clemenceau's attitudes at this point. "Don't sulk in your tent," Blanqui warned him. "Don't let yourself be disarmed by any man or woman. Above all, don't disarm yourself in search of tranquility."[86]

Clemenceau's speech of February, 1879—his first major address in almost three years—had come after Louis Blanc and the Radicals had proposed a new amnesty bill. The ministry of W. H. Waddington, who had replaced Dufaure, had countered with a measure for partial amnesty. Under the Waddington proposal, amnesty would result from executive pardon and would be available to all who were not charged with certain atrocious crimes and who were not "enemies of society." Clemenceau denounced the bill as "an expedient for safeguarding the benefits of repression while repudiating the appearances."

He argued that the Republic was strong enough to implement full amnesty and that halfway measures were certain to create further agitation. Blanc's bill got only 99 votes, while the government's measure passed by 343 to 94, with the Radicals casting their votes in the end for the government's bill.[87]

Despite this setback, Clemenceau proved during the next month that he was still a man who could not be taken lightly. Émile de Marcère, the minister of the interior, had prosecuted the editors of *La Lanterne* for a series of articles on abuses in the Paris Prefecture of Police. As the episode unfolded, there were charges that de Marcère was protecting certain officials who had been ready to carry out a coup d'état in 1877.[88] In the Chamber on March 3 Clemenceau charged de Marcère with trying to hide the truth. He contended that it was the police, not the Parisians, who were responsible for agitation because of their secret agents, their beatings of prisoners, and their dossiers on private citizens. Rather than investigating the charges, Clemenceau said, de Marcère had sided with the prefecture, most of whose posts were still held by personnel from the Empire. The attack demoralized the already vulnerable minister, and he resigned, the first minister to be toppled by Clemenceau.[89]

By early 1879, therefore, Clemenceau was ending the withdrawal that had characterized his behavior since the *seize mai* crisis. Several political factors help to account for his new surge of energy, all of which reminded him of his ongoing duty to be true to his role as the defender of his father's ideals, whatever personal problems he faced. One factor was the changing attitude of Gambetta, whom Clemenceau had admired since his Latin Quarter days. By the late 1870s Gambetta was beginning to embrace the doctrine known as Opportunism. The term was first used as an epithet for those who refused to enact reforms— particularly amnesty—until the time was right. The social and economic features of Opportunism, which reflected the outlook of those libertarian moderates who now dominated the country's political institutions, will be examined in the next chapter. For the moment it need only be noted that, for Clemenceau, Gambetta's unwillingness to move quickly on the matter of amnesty symbolized a betrayal of the ideals that had been laid down at Belleville in 1869.[90]

A second factor may well have been the fate of Blanqui, who had been jailed at Clairvaux since 1872. By the spring of 1879 the amnesty controversy centered briefly around him, especially after his victory in April against one of Gambetta's friends in a by-election at Bordeaux. Because of Blanqui's condemnation in 1872, a parliamentary committee voided his election. No doubt, the affair gave to the Radicals a dynamic emotional issue in their attack on moderate republicans. But it is a mistake to assume that, for Clemenceau, political calculation was the only or even the primary motivation. Since the 1860s Blanqui had been a powerful image in the "ethos of action" that Clemenceau had inherited from his father, and in 1879 Clemenceau was outraged at the treatment of Blanqui. In his report to his electors of Montmartre at the cirque Fernando on May 11, Clemenceau defended Blanqui's election and ridiculed the government's fear of him. As a symbolic gesture, the old revolutionary was named honorary president of the session.[91] During the same month, in the Chamber, Clemenceau attacked the committee that had voided the election of Blanqui, but his demand that the latter be temporarily released so that he could come and defend himself was voted down.[92] On June 9 the government pardoned Blanqui rather than granting him amnesty, and in an additional show of self-confidence the majority voted two weeks later to return the capital to Paris.

A third factor was the refusal of the Opportunist majority to commit itself to separation of Church and state. Clemenceau wished neither the crushing of Catholicism nor the denial of religious freedom, but he did believe that no reform was possible until the secular power of the Church, which he saw as synonymous with the Right, was broken. His goal was the nullification of the Concordat of 1801, which he viewed as having given the Church certain funds and privileges within society that always enabled it to resist the rights and demands of the state.[93] The Opportunists wished to maintain the concordat as a means of controlling the clergy, who were paid servants of the state. Thus, in March of 1879, Jules Ferry, who was then minister of public instruction, presented to the Chamber a bill to restore state control over education. Any teaching congregation that was not authorized by the Concordat of 1801 was forbidden to direct public or private educational institutions. At the cirque Fernando on May 11 Clemenceau denounced Ferry's proposals as "useless, ineffectual, and dangerous." They were useless, he said, because laws against unauthorized congregations were already on the books. They were ineffectual because they ignored authorized congregations, where the instruction was identical. They were dangerous because they indicated to the country that these proposals were the maximum it could expect.[94] Ferry's proposals nevertheless passed in the Chamber and were sent on to the Senate for debate.

Finally, the factor that may have been most important in inducing Clemenceau to take up the banner of his father's ideals once more was the encouragement that came from Benjamin himself. In order that his son, like Gambetta and many others, could have his own newspaper to promote his views, Benjamin sold one of his farms in the Vendée and contributed a total of 300,000 francs.[95] The result was *La Justice,* whose first issue appeared on January 16, 1880. That issue set the future political tone of the journal: "The great formula of the Revolution— Liberty, Equality, and Fraternity—which contains in these words all the rights of man, all social reforms, all precepts of morality, is summed up in an even briefer formula: Justice!"

Clemenceau took the title of political director, recruiting Camille Pelletan as editor in chief. Camille was the son of Eugène Pelletan, who had served on the Government of National Defense in 1870. Other writers included Charles Longuet, Karl Marx's son-in-law; Stéphen Pichon, a young law student who had left his studies to work for Clemenceau; and a host of young Radicals such as Édouard Durranc, Léon Millot, Julien and Mario Sermet, Constans Laurent, Louis Mullem, and Sutter Laumann. Pelletan did the bulk of the political writing since Clemenceau felt that his main task was to be at the tribune of the Chamber. The paper printed his speeches in full, however, and issued reprints of them to earn extra money. There were also sections on current art and literature, often written by Gustave Geffroy. Like the half dozen other Radical newspapers in Paris, *La Justice* had a limited circulation (never above

fifteen thousand), and more than once it appeared to be ready
to collapse for lack of funds. Nevertheless, it was to become the
most important mouthpiece for French radicalism.

Clemenceau was not overly fond of his editor, Pelletan,
whose bohemian appearance and absinthe drinking differed
from his own correct bearing. But he found friendship among
the young "Clemencistes," who were, in the words of Geffroy,
"a family, all adopted by Clemenceau." Pichon, plus two others
who joined the staff later—Alexandre Millerand and a young
lawyer named Georges Laguerre—Clemenceau referred to as
"my three colts." He maintained an office at the journal, which
was located in Montmartre at 10, rue du Faubourg, and he usually dropped by every evening to read proofs for the next day's
edition. Afterwards, he stayed on past midnight, drinking coffee
or adjourning to a nearby restaurant. Geffroy remembered him
as being a warm and relaxed man on these occasions.[96]

During the first months of publication, the subject that most
occupied *La Justice* was still that of amnesty. The previous
December, Clemenceau had spoken in the Chamber during an
interpellation by Lockroy on the government's application of
the partial amnesty measure. He had attacked the minister of
justice, Le Royer, for the arbitrary manner in which the government was handling the cases of unpardoned communards.
Lockroy's motion of no confidence failed by a vote of 246 to
108; but 50 members of Gambetta's Republican Union had
supported the Radical position, and an additional 53 republicans, 38 from among Gambetta's followers, had abstained. This
poor showing fatally weakened Waddington, who resigned on
December 21.[97] Clearly, many republicans were coming to share
Clemenceau's belief that only total amnesty could bring harmony
to the nation.

By early 1880 about eight hundred communards remained
unpardoned. In *La Justice* and in a major speech at the cirque
Fernando on April 12, Clemenceau kept the amnesty issue alive.
On May 23 a socialist demonstration to commemorate 1871 was
held at Père-Lachaise Cemetery; it gave further proof of the
need to settle the matter once and for all. The police brutally
dispersed the small crowd. The deputies for Paris met and
decided to send Clemenceau, Louis Blanc, and Benjamin Ras-

pail to demand an explanation from Ernest Constans, minister of the interior. Against the advice of some of his colleagues, Clemenceau, who was not satisfied with Constans's claim that the rally had posed a danger to order and that his men had used moderation, decided to challenge the ministry over the matter.[98] In the Chamber, on May 28, he ridiculed Constans's belief that the rally had been organized by foreigners and charged him with wishing only to appease conservative sentiment. But Clemenceau's motion of censure got only twenty-eight votes.[99]

Clemenceau's utter failure was a source of some amusement in the press, and his image was not helped by his decision immediately afterwards to go to Switzerland to serve as a second to Henri Rochefort, who had challenged a brother-in-law of the prefect of police to a duel over a matter arising from the May 23 rally.[100] But it was just such incidents that persuaded Gambetta that the time for complete amnesty had come. In June, one of his followers was defeated in a Paris by-election by a communard. Gambetta now urged the prime minister, Freycinet, to bring in a bill for complete amnesty. This was done on June 19, with Gambetta himself leaving his chair as president of the Chamber in order to defend the measure. It passed on June 21 by a vote of 312 to 136. In July the Senate, knowing that further opposition was useless, also passed it after attaching an amendment that excluded those who had been guilty of arson or murder.

While passage of the final amnesty measure depended largely on Gambetta's efforts, Clemenceau had played an important role in persuading him and other moderates to take this stand. Clemenceau's speech in the Chamber on December 16, 1879, for example, had helped to rally a substantial number of Gambetta's followers to the Radical point of view. The subsequent resignation of Waddington had proved that the agitation with regard to amnesty was a political liability for Opportunist cabinets. In addition, Clemenceau's defense of Blanqui, his speech of April 12, 1880, at the cirque Fernando, and his attack on Constans following the May 23 rally at Père-Lachaise had all helped to keep the amnesty question alive.

It is true that some Radicals promoted amnesty because they believed that the denial of it was encouraging the revolu-

tionary Left, especially after Jules Guesde had begun to organize the French Workers' Party at Marseilles in October of
1879. But it is an error to regard Clemenceau as just another
bourgeois politician motivated by a desire to win support in a
working-class constituency. His sympathy for the communards
was genuine; and his belief, first expressed in his speech of
May 16, 1876, that delay of full amnesty would be the first step
in alienating significant portions of the working classes from
the new Republic, would be borne out by events.[101]

Clemenceau long regarded the achievement of amnesty as
the first and one of the most important accomplishments of his
early political career.[102] By 1880 he was becoming the most
visible spokesman for radicalism in France. In the next chapter
I will examine in detail the nature of his political and economic
goals during the period 1880 to 1885. I will also attempt to
answer a fundamental question relating to the seeming contradictions of Clemenceau's post-1880 career: After he had failed
to weaken his father's power over him during both his moratorium of the late 1860s and his withdrawal of the late 1870s,
how did Clemenceau eventually manage to satisfy his own inner
need for ego autonomy and identity?

No doubt, he was able to sublimate certain drives that
remained unsatisfied in his private life. Erikson notes that the
life stage of generativity—or the urge to found and guide the
next generation through one's own offspring—may, for some
individuals, be applied on a broader level and may encompass
the more general drives of productivity and creativity.[103] It is
useful to recall Geffroy's words—that Clemenceau found a home
at La Justice and that the editors and critics there were a
"family," all "adopted" by him. But the pattern of Clemenceau's
behavior after 1880 suggests an even more complex psychological process at work, which produced what was mentioned at
the outset of this study as an alternating perception of guilt and
the need for self-punishment.

THREE

The Creator & the Destroyer
1880-1885

THE DUALISM OF CHARACTER

Throughout Clemenceau's post-1880 career one detects both creative and destructive drives in his personality. The contradictions inherent in his tendency to undermine his own ideals baffled his contemporaries as it has baffled modern historians. The latter have generally assessed his political activities during this period as being negative in character. They speak of his "sterility" and "wild destructiveness," or they dwell on his reputation as the *tombeur des ministères* who "could not replace those he destroyed." He is regarded as a "spiteful, insolent adversary," an "isolated gladiator," a "surly and implacable fighter," a man who existed "by and for his passions." His tactic of leading the Radicals to join the monarchist Right in order to topple republican cabinets is seen as a chief cause of parliamentary instability in the Third Republic.[1]

In analyzing Clemenceau's behavior, it is important to keep in mind the unitary nature of motivation and the fact that character traits spring from a series of related strivings.[2] In his comments on ambivalence, Franz Alexander has argued that the difference between love of self and love of others is the only genuine polarity of personality.[3] No matter how deep Clemenceau's love for his father, the persistent demands of self for emancipation from the paternal influence were bound to create conflict. It has been suggested that guilt toward his father and toward himself was a distinguishing feature of this conflict, a powerful regulatory emotion whose first symptomatic expression appeared during his student years and during his subsequent

psychosocial moratorium. One recalls, for example, his outlook
on the eve of his departure for America and the tension that was
engendered by the dual wish to withdraw into himself and to
please his father, who, as he wrote to Scheurer-Kestner, he
hoped would forgive him. Similarly, the visible patterns of his
psychological withdrawal between 1877 and 1880 suggest a conflict between the inner demands of self (which may have been
intensified by the birth of Michel and the possible revival of his
own early identification problems) and the ego-ideal represented by Benjamin.

Guilt may be an incentive to action and creativity.[4] We
have seen in Clemenceau's case that his self-perception as a
suffererer and his corresponding ability to empathize with the
weak had several positive qualities when applied to the social
and political problems of France in the 1870s. But guilt can
also have debilitating and self-defeating results. One sees in
the post-1880 Clemenceau a destructiveness that was less outer-
than inner-directed and that, I believe, can be assessed as an
unconscious desire to ensure the defeat of his ideals as a gesture
of expiation toward the denied or reduced self. Jacobson has
noted that many brilliant and gifted individuals with deep-
rooted identity problems may boast of their individualism, but
in reality they have no sense of belonging. Their ambitions are
often "obsessively driving" and exhibit moral perfectionism (as
was true in Clemenceau's political intransigence), but success
is often condemned by the conscience. Failure, and the psychological atonement that it provides, may be a psychic necessity.[5]

This chapter will explore these features of Clemenceau's
character and will try to indicate the ways in which they produced the idiosyncrasies of his political behavior. Specifically,
it will examine the nature of his political and economic goals,
his defense of industrial workers, his anticolonial campaign, and
finally, his abortive efforts to create a reformist movement. Before doing so, however, it is first essential to strip away some of
the myths surrounding his early career and the age of which
it was a part.

From the founding of *La Justice* to his defeat during the
Panama scandal of 1893, Clemenceau played a role in every
major event that affected the development of the Third Re-

public. This was a critical period in French history, during which the beliefs and attitudes of dominant political forces tended to crystalize on social questions.[6] When viewed as an integral part of the diverse reactions to the economic crisis of the 1880s, Clemenceau's activities assume greater importance than historians have ascribed to them. As a newspaper editor, as a popular deputy for a working-class district in Paris, and, after 1885, for a Radical stronghold in the Var, and as the most effective orator for the Extreme Left in Parliament, he was in a strong position to challenge the policies of the Opportunist majority.

His speeches themselves, which were always an event in the Chamber of Deputies, commanded the attention of the often unruly benches. Between 1880 and 1885—the most active period of his early career—he made a total of thirty-six speeches in the Chamber, twenty-three of which dealt with domestic issues and thirteen with foreign affairs. He also had great oratorical success in seven major addresses to his constituents at the cirque Fernando and in four additional speeches to rallies in Marseilles, Lille, Bordeaux, and Draguignan in the Var.

Clemenceau's activities have provided a ready explanation for those who seek reasons for the Republic's failure to achieve stability, but such a view ignores the complexities and contradictions within the early Republic itself. Would France have known stability had Clemenceau never entered Parliament? In order to answer that question, several considerations must be kept in mind.

First, the Third Republic was a parliamentary democracy in which the legislative branch of government ruled supreme. Here the tensions and divisions rooted in a turbulent past produced a multiplicity of groupings that made any coalition a tenuous affair. Those that were formed were marked by an extreme fluidity; in them a deputy's vote was determined less by ideology or by his place on the political spectrum than by his individual response to a myriad of specific day-to-day political problems.[7] In addition, the individuals in these shifting factions were often men of extreme localism who had little sense of party discipline or broad national interests, but were instead characterized by what one writer has termed an *optique ar-*

rondissementière.[8] In 1876, some 70 percent of the deputies had been born in or near the areas that they represented; almost 58 percent had already served as members of General Councils; and 33 percent had served as mayors or municipal councillors.[9] Other features of this parliamentary arrangement, such as the system of powerful committees and the device known as the interpellation, meant that instability was an inevitable feature of French democracy.

In fact, Clemenceau's power to wreck ministries during the period 1880 to 1885 has been exaggerated, endowing him with political strength that he did not have and obscuring the degree of conflict in the moderate majority. During this period the parliamentary extremes accounted for only 31 percent of the deputies, and while Clemenceau certainly led the attacks on such individuals as Gambetta, Freycinet, and Ferry, the moderates whose votes were essential in overturning these leaders were not motivated solely by Clemenceau's speeches. While he frequently ridiculed the process of "replastering" fallen cabinets,[10] he was defensive about the charge of being a systematic destroyer, and he tried to impress on others, and with reason, the extent of the moderates' responsibility.[11] It was after his early political career had ended that he appears to have begun to savor his reputation as a power broker. In a 1901 interview with Alexandre Zévaès, for example, he did not challenge the assertion that he had overthrown "ten or so ministries," and he used the famous aphorism "They were always the same ministry."[12]

It is difficult to determine exactly how many of the twenty-three cabinet turnovers between 1876 and 1893 were caused by Clemenceau. The events related to the *seize-mai* affair accounted for four of the twenty-three; one fell in the Senate; and in the cases of six cabinets, the prime minister resigned for reasons other than a defeat of a motion of confidence.[13] In the collapse of four other cabinets, Clemenceau's opposition was likewise of no consequence: that of René Goblet (1886–87), which fell as the result of an effort on the part of moderates, in concert with the Right, to get rid of Georges Boulanger as minister of war; that of Charles Floquet (1888–89), which was supported by Clemenceau and the Radicals on the vote of confidence that brought it down; and the two cabinets of Émile Loubet (1892) and Alexandre Ribot (1892–93), which fell because of events relating to Panama and which no one has ever accused Clemenceau of destroying.

Of the remaining eight, Clemenceau is often credited with wrecking the first Ferry cabinet (1880–81), the short-lived Gambetta cabinet (1881–82), the second Freycinet cabinet (January–August 1882), and the second Ferry cabinet (1883–85).[14] This chapter will show that while Clemenceau was among their most outspoken opponents, other factors proved ultimately to be more decisive in their downfall. It required more than the combined votes of the Extreme Left and the Extreme Right to topple Gambetta, for example, and the depth of hostility among many moderates toward him is often overlooked by historians. By the same token, both Gambetta and de Marcère helped to carry the day against Freycinet in July of 1882. In addition, the same session that witnessed Clemenceau's dramatic indictment of Ferry over the Tonkin imbroglio in March, 1885, also saw the less dramatic but possibly more decisive attack on Ferry's colonial policies by the moderate Ribot.

It was only after the elections of 1885, which gave the extremes a combined strength of 56 percent in the Chamber, that Clemenceau was truly in a position to engineer the defeat of moderate cabinets. One might hold him accountable for the fall of the third Freycinet ministry in 1886, less because of his active opposition than because he refused to do anything to save it. There is little question concerning the decisiveness of his intervention in the fall of Maurice Rouvier in 1887. He played an equally crucial part in the undoing of Pierre Tirard's ministry in 1888, and also in that of the fourth Freycinet ministry of 1892. In general, therefore, Clemenceau played a decisive role in the fall of three cabinets, a passive role in the fall of one, and an active, though not decisive, role in the fall of four others. One should also include the fall of de Marcère in 1879 (which did not entail the resignation of the entire ministry) as well as Clemenceau's contributory role in the weakening of Waddington the same year.

Clemenceau must thus bear some blame for ministerial instability, especially for the period after 1885; but in weighing his responsibility, one must remember that no deputy could overthrow a cabinet singlehandedly and that the fate of a ministry under the Third Republic, as an examination of voting patterns on motions of confidence will show, depended on a variety of complex factors.

A second consideration with regard to the instability of the Republic is that the failure of the Opportunists to enact social and economic reforms was far more important than the intransigence of the Radicals in producing unrest during the 1880s. In the eyes of many workers the social and democratic Republic had long held out the promise of economic emancipation, and after the consolidation of the Republic in 1877 they had believed that the conditions of their lives would be improved.[15] But the first years of the Third Republic were barren of social legislation. An example of the inertia of the ruling classes was the fact that almost every piece of economic legislation introduced in the Chamber of Deputies came from private members. Such proposals failed or were killed in the Senate. Where questions of social welfare arose, the Opportunist Republic, reflecting the interest of bourgeois and rural France, invoked the orthodoxy of economic liberalism. The gap between promise and performance was a central factor in the social tensions of the 1880s, and as one recent historian, Bernard H. Moss, has demonstrated, it was one of the primary reasons for the eventual creation of a separate workers' movement with a revolutionary program.[16]

The Opportunist philosophy that Clemenceau denounced for its timidity and negativism constituted the outlook of powerful forces in French society.[17] A recent study by Sanford Elwitt has greatly enhanced our understanding of that alliance between petty producers and an industrial bourgeoisie that dominated the political life of the Third Republic. Victorious over the old Orleanist financial bourgeoisie during the *seize-mai* affair, this new "republican bourgeoisie" nevertheless embraced similar values regarding property relationships and "kept its distance from sweeping programs of social reform."[18] What John B. Christopher has termed the "peculiar inflexibility" of this social class was especially apparent in its aversion to any tax reform that would have been essential in order to pay for social programs.[19] Social reforms were possible because industrialization had increased national wealth. But the men who laid the foundations for the new order were incapable of understanding modern economic disorders, and many even denied in the 1880s that a social crisis existed. Typified by the lawyers who held a virtual monopoly over the political process, their attitude toward social issues was characterized by a conservative and juridical approach.[20]

A final consideration is that early French radicalism was neither sterile in its social content nor entirely obstructionist in its political behavior.[21] Further, Clemenceau's leadership of this movement must be seen against the backdrop of the depression of the 1880s and the Radical campaign to effect social and economic reforms. These reforms, which are discussed below, represented an advanced philosophy of social action that, in the words of Leo A. Loubère, "sought actively to lead France in the direction of a welfare State." While Clemenceau was the first to popularize the term "Radical Socialist" during his campaign in Montmartre in 1881, the idea of state intervention on behalf of the lower classes grew out of an old republican tradition, both Rousseauist and Jacobin, that had frequently assailed laissez-faire capitalism and the power of high finance. Radicals in the 1840s had extolled the Republic as the instrument for emancipating labor, and such concepts as the right to work and limitation of hours were inspired by the Radicals. In areas like the lower south, they had called themselves *démocrates-socialiste* and had made little distinction between an advanced democrat and a Socialist.[22]

Labor, in turn, had long viewed the Republic as its best hope for economic freedom. Those craftsmen and skilled workers who were known as cooperative trade Socialists believed that the Republic would help labor by providing public credit and contracts and by aiding the efforts of workers to collectivize industrial capital. The specter that haunted the French bourgeoisie at mid century, Bernard H. Moss has argued, was not Marxism but radical republicanism and cooperation.[23]

Modern historians have increasingly recognized that the working class's alienation from the Republic began during the

1880s as a result of political policies of the Opportunists.[24] The possibility of such alienation was among Clemenceau's foremost concerns. As he had demonstrated during the campaign for amnesty, he knew that the future strength and stability of the Republic depended on its willingness to aid the disinherited. In opposing the war in Vietnam in the 1880s, he also recognized the degree to which colonial diversions and the exploitation of less advanced peoples both wasted the nation's resources and corrupted the spirit of social progress at home.

Several factors, however, have obscured the essentially radical character of his efforts. The first is the sometimes distorted emphasis on his later career, in which he was often at odds with the demands of workers and, as prime minister, frequently used troops to put down strikes. The second is the tendency of some writers to see his ideas as only a rehashing of old Jacobin notions and to dismiss his work on the social question as an effort to woo voters away from the Socialists. The third is the fallacy of judging the ideology of Radical socialism in the 1880s in terms of its outlook in the 1920s, when its concerns in the social domain had decreased and when it was truly "neither Radical nor Socialist." By the latter period, socialism had long represented the idea of collectivism. But as Professor Loubère has noted, in the early years of the Third Republic, socialism represented for many Radicals, not collectivism, but state intervention on the side of the lower classes.[25]

Historians have ignored the merit contained within many of Clemenceau's early ideals. These deserve further investigation not only for their own value as a constructive alternative to Opportunist policies but also for what Clemenceau's inability to get them enacted reveals about the parliamentary leaders who directed the destinies of the nation. Nevertheless, despite the obstacles to reform, his failure reveals much about his own character as well. Not once during the period 1876 to 1893 did he exercise the kind of political power, either in or out of office, that would have enabled him to begin implementing even part of his program. It is true that political office is only one method for effecting social change and that Clemenceau's articulation of social issues enhanced public consciousness and ultimately produced some of the reforms that he desired. Guy Chapman has noted that labor legislation around the turn of the century may have been the product less of the growth of socialism than of increased knowledge about working conditions.[26] In the 1880s Clemenceau was at the forefront of those who were attempting to diffuse such knowledge.

Still, the patterns of his behavior between 1880 and 1893 indicated a contradiction in attitudes. On the one hand, he showed a rare capacity to understand modern social problems, and on many occasions he formulated realistic proposals to solve them. On the other hand, he pursued a course of conduct that could only result in defeat of his ideals, which is why it was suggested earlier that his destructiveness was more inner- than outer-directed and consisted in a form of self-punishment by which he refused to succeed as the champion of his father's ideals.

The remaining chapters of this book will attempt to show how this dualism of character exhibited itself in Clemenceau's early career. At this point it will be useful to note some of those traits that may be interpreted as evidence for this cycle of guilt and punishment. These undermined his capacity to take advantage of certain political possibilities that existed within the system—possibilities whose realization might have either won office for him or at least have enabled him to forge a strong reformist party that could have bargained effectively for legislation.

First, Clemenceau tended to isolate himself from those whose help was essential if he wished to achieve his goals. As I will show in the last section of this chapter, these included not only his fellow Radicals but also many of those deputies who had formed the advanced faction of Gambetta's group before the latter's death in 1882 and who had frequently voted with the Extreme Left on such issues as amnesty, election of judges, the ten-hour day, protection of railroad workers, liberal trade-union laws, and revision of the constitution.[27] In parliamentary debates Clemenceau's own isolation was often accompanied by a needless wounding of the self-esteem of others—moderate republicans as well as monarchists. A recent analysis of one six-week period of debates in 1882 shows that he was the second most frequent interrupter of the speeches of others, and the fear that he inspired among his opponents was a central factor in what one contemporary saw as a "systematic" alienation of others.[28]

Second, while Clemenceau deeply believed in his ideals, his moral perfectionism in the political arena can be viewed as a primary method by which he engineered failure situations. He refused to modify his goals in accordance with the realities of political life, and by doing so, he ensured the defeat of his ideals in advance. He prided himself on "principle" in the unprincipled business of politics, and when he was criticized on specific legislative matters, he frequently adopted a moralizing posture. One example was his response to interruptions in the Chamber during a speech in 1881: "I have been a republican since I took my first breath. I have been in love with the Republic. I have seen my father wounded by the Second of December. Later I have seen my father leave for Africa, chained like a common criminal. There is not an act of my political life in which I have not sincerely tried to serve the republican cause."[29] Furthermore, Clemenceau regarded those who were willing to make compromises in order to exercise power as being tainted with ambition or corruption. In *La Justice* of February 1, 1881, he charged Gambetta with corrupting the republican spirit. To an interviewer who asked why he did not seek office more actively, he replied that he had no desire for the "harassing responsibilities and *corrupting influence*" of power.[30] The self-defeating idealism that was inherent in his campaign against the Opportunists was also evident in his dealings with other Radicals, and as will be demonstrated below, it undermined his efforts to create a reform party that could bargain in Parliament for specific legislative results. Finally, for one who embraced principle as a creed, Clemenceau demonstrated a bizarre capacity to enhance his own vulnerability—and hence that of the principles for which he fought—by linking his destiny with such unscrupulous figures as Cornélius Herz and Georges Boulanger.

THE CAMPAIGN FOR THE DISINHERITED

In this section I will focus on Clemenceau's social and economic ideals and on his campaign in defense of the rights of labor between 1880 and 1885. At the outset it must be emphasized that, following a long tradition in Radical republicanism, Clemenceau believed that political reform was the prerequisite for social change.[31] His platform in Montmartre in 1876, which was similar to Gambetta's Belleville program of 1869, typified the political goals of the Extreme Left during the 1880s. Throughout these years the Radicals proposed a series of bills and amendments, which were usually defeated, that aimed at achieving their maximum program in such areas as the separation of Church and state; free and obligatory education; freedom of speech, press, assembly, and association; the election of judges; the *scrutin de liste;* and constitutional revision. Though of a political nature, these proposals touched on a variety of social and economic concerns and were the preliminary steps for what Radicals hoped would be a more fundamental transformation of French society.

Clemenceau's belief in the separation of Church and state was a case in point. He thought that by destroying the power of the Church in regard to education, the Republic would take the first step toward ending the ignorance and isolation that were responsible for much of the misery of rural life.[32] Educational reform in turn necessitated judicial reform, since some judges blocked educational reform in courts.[33] He stressed these points in his caustic attacks on Ferry's limited moves against unauthorized teaching congregations in 1879 and 1880, describing Ferry's actions as little more than "removing the furniture of the Capuchins" and bemoaning the fact that millions of francs came out of the budget annually to keep France "under the yoke of ignorance."[34] But Clemenceau was not able to change the fact that in the 1880s the Church was still capable of defending its prerogatives in many regions. Republicans had to be content with piecemeal legislation, such as a bill of 1881 providing for free and compulsory education for children. In all, only about a third of the teaching orders were dissolved.

Since Clemenceau believed that political consolidation of the Republic must come before everything else, the only concrete economic proposal in his 1876 platform had been one for income and inheritance taxes.[35] By the beginning of the 1880s, economic matters figured much more largely in his speeches.

At that time, France was entering a new cycle of depression, which was part of a general slump that touched much of western Europe. The depression caused a slackening in the rate of French industrial growth; it also produced widespread unemployment, which, at the height of the crisis, between 1883 and 1886, affected about 10 percent of the total number of industrial workers and especially hurt miners and metallurgical workers. In the cities the price of food offset previous wage increases, while in the countryside, agriculture suffered from both falling prices and an infestation of phylloxera, which gradually destroyed the vineyards. The collapse in 1882 of a new Catholic bank, the Union Générale, compounded the nation's problems.[36]

Clemenceau's early career coincided with what Edward Shorter and Charles Tilly have called "the great mobilization of the working classes."[37] In 1880 the number of strikes and strikers was more than double that of the previous year and reflected a new militancy among workers that was born of their confidence in the social promises of the young Republic. As the depression deepened in 1884, however, strikes became increasingly defensive in character, and the rate of success with them fell.[38] Zola portrayed the growing disillusionment of miners in his novel *Germinal,* which appeared in 1884 and was based in part on what he had witnessed at Anzin. As the voices of protest grew louder and as trade unions, which in that year had only seventy-six thousand members,[39] began to appear, Clemenceau, as leader of the Radicals, had to provide answers to a question that hecklers at the cirque Fernando frequently asked him: What was the Republic going to do for the worker?

His response is best understood when viewed against other reactions on the Left to the crisis of the 1880s. One was revolutionary collectivism, which by the spring of 1880 had been adopted as the official program of Guesde's Parti ouvrier.[40] But the collectivists constituted a minority within the nation as a whole, and throughout the early years of that decade, Radical socialism continued to exercise a powerful influence on workers, much to Guesde's dismay. As noted earlier, the labor movement had long been dominated by the philosophy of cooperative trade socialism, which aimed for collectivization of the means of production through federations of skilled trades and which looked to the social Republic as the instrument for emancipation from the wage system. The first National Labor Congress in Paris in October, 1876, reflected this idea; and well into the mid 1880s, labor leaders at the local level still believed in both republicanism and cooperation.[41]

In Montmartre, Clemenceau found himself in a running fight with the well-organized collectivist minority from 1880 on. For him, collectivism symbolized not only the negation of human freedoms but also the undoing of the Republic itself. Karl Marx, whom Clemenceau met briefly in London in the summer of 1880 and whose son-in-law Charles Longuet was on the staff of *La Justice*, was convinced at one point that Clemenceau had been won over to the cause.[42] But Guesde's followers were under no illusions. Guesde's newspaper, *L'Égalité*, challenged the Radical leader to public debate, and the collectivists frequently assailed him as a "Kalmuck" and a "parliamentary athlete" who was trying to wean the workers away from revolution. Hostile questioners often disrupted his speeches at the cirque Fernando. On April 12, 1880, one asked him what he intended to do for the proletariat and whether he believed that the ballot should be supported by the gun. "We must repudiate all appeals to violence," Clemenceau answered, adding that "political reformation is the instrument of social reformation." Another man tried to pin him down, asking if he supported collectivization of the soil, the subsoil, and machines. "I respond categorically," Clemenceau replied, "No! No! I am for integral liberty, and I would never consent to enter into the convents and barracks that you are waiting to prepare for us." He added that just as France had its black Jesuits, it also had "red Jesuits."[43]

There is no evidence that Clemenceau ever gave serious study to the theories of Marx and Engels; but there were, in any case, certain features in his outlook that prevented him from accepting collectivist notions. For one thing, he understood the importance of French rural society and its conservative peasantry. He elaborated on this theme during an interview with the British Socialist H. M. Hyndman: "Nobody can know them better than my family and I know them. Landed proprietors ourselves, . . . we have ever lived with and among the peas-

antry. . . . I have seen them very close in birth and death, in
sickness and in health, in betrothal and in marriage, in poverty
and in well-being, and all the time their one idea is property.
. . . Preach nationalisation of the soil in a French village, and
you would barely escape with your life, if the peasants understood what you meant."[44]

Clemenceau distrusted grandiose philosophical systems that
isolated one from the realities at hand, and he also disliked the
Marxist emphasis on manual labor.[45] He especially condemned
violence as a force for social change. At the cirque Fernando
he told his audience that he was afraid of Jules Guesde because
of the latter's willingness to use violence in order to achieve
his ends. "Are you ready," he asked one heckler, "to accept the
frightful responsibilities that you would incur if, in healing the
evils that you point out, you were to deliver society over to
worse misfortunes?"[46]

Finally, there was his fear that the individual would be
crushed in a regimented world where freedom was restricted.
This was one reason for his condemning the Social Catholicism
of Albert de Mun, which was based on the old idea of small
corporations of workers and employers. He hated the paternal-
ism and idea of the *état-providence,* which he described as "a
Socialism of oppression" and which he compared to the ideas
of former slaveholders in America, who boasted that Negroes
had been better off when they had masters to feed and clothe
them. By the same reasoning, Bismarck's welfare programs were
little more than "a vast system of charity" that denied freedom
to the worker.[47]

Clemenceau first attempted to enunciate a Radical economic
program in his speech at Marseilles in October, 1880. He declared that the goal of Radicals was "to deliver man from the
chains of ignorance, to free him from religious, political, and
economic despotism, and having freed him, to regulate his freedom of initiative by justice alone." He condemned the law of
1872 that had banned the First International, stressing that victory in the fight for freedom of assembly and association was
crucial in order for workers to organize. He described the
growth of labor organizations as "the proletariat making its
cahiers" and emphasized that freedom of association would

allow workers to solidify their diverse interests by giving birth to other institutions such as consumer societies.

Specifically, he reiterated his demand for the abolition of indirect taxes and for the creation of a progressive tax on income and inheritance, which he believed would counter the forces that were producing an excess accumulation of capital. Other features included credit and insurance; repeal of those sections of the civil code that created inequality between workers and employers; participation of workers in regulation of workshops; a reduction of the hours of labor; and the awarding of public works contracts to workers' associations. He also called for "the liquidation of the great railroad companies, canal and mine companies, and the profitable exploitation of these industries by the whole of those who operate them."[48]

In the eyes of the Guesdists, such proposals on the part of one whom they regarded as an opportunistic bourgeois politician threatened to undermine the creation of a truly proletarian party.[49] The legislative elections scheduled for August of 1881 offered a good opportunity for them to challenge Radical domination over the working classes. In Montmartre, Clemenceau was a logical target. Although he had enjoyed a great popularity here since the days of the siege, he worried over the growth of the Parti ouvrier in his district, which was the major reason in late 1880 for his creating an organization called the Alliance socialiste républicaine. The alliance, which was supported by a few communards such as Alphonse Humbert and Henry Maret, promoted a list of its own candidates, including Clemenceau's friend J. A. Lafont, for election to the Municipal Council in January of 1881. But this organization had little influence, and it soon disappeared.[50]

In the meantime the collectivists had formed a "Workers' Committee" to support candidates for the Chamber in the legislative elections. It was in response to this that Clemenceau's followers created the Comité républicain radical-socialiste du XVIIIe arrondissement, which drew up a list of cahiers des électeurs containing the reforms he had outlined at Marseilles. The term "Radical Socialist" was meant to distinguish the movement from both the old radicalism of such people as Gambetta and the socialism of the collectivists, who nevertheless denounced the phrase as a simple political maneuver.[51]

Before the elections, Clemenceau's eighteenth arrondissement had been divided into two districts—Clignancourt and the Grandes-Carrières Quarter. He stood in both; he was also on the ballot in the southern city of Arles, where he and Pelletan had met an enthusiastic reception the previous year. In Montmarte, Clemenceau won by substantial majorities in both districts, his closest opponent—his old assistant Dereure from the days of the siege—getting only a few hundred votes. In Arles he failed to win on the first ballot, but his opponent, a local politician named Félix Granet, resigned before the second ballot was taken. Clemenceau then decided to take his seat for the Clignancourt Quarter. In the nation as a whole the Guesdists had received only sixty-five thousand votes. The Extreme Left won 46 seats, but Gambetta's Republican Union was the real victor, winning 204 seats as compared with 168 for Ferry's Republican Left.[52]

The elections of 1881 proved Gambetta's enduring popularity and opened the way for his brief ministry, which was formed in November but lasted only seventy-seven days. Although Clemenceau had long admired Gambetta, had worked hand in hand with him during the *seize-mai* crisis, and had even served as his second during a duel with Fortou, minister of the interior, in 1877, he had now become one of his most unyielding opponents. At Marseilles in October of 1880 Clemenceau had been extremely caustic in his attacks on Gambetta, comparing him, in his post as president of the Chamber, to a general who watches the clash of armies from an isolated position on the field. Gambetta had become an "occult power," who was unwilling to come out and fight for the principles of his youth.[53]

Clemenceau's opposition to the Gambetta ministry arose specifically from the issue of constitutional revision, which will be treated in the last section of this chapter. What needs to be stressed here is that despite Gambetta's conservatism and his often clumsy personal response to opposition during his brief time in office,[54] he was one of the few politicians in the early 1880s who might have brought both stability and moderate social reform to the Republic. Despite Sanford Elwitt's argument that the economic proposals of the republicans were designed to enhance bourgeois primacy, within the ranks of the Opportunists the Gambettists showed much more sensitivity to labor questions than did the Republican Left of Ferry and Grévy.[55] It is true that in the late 1870s Gambetta had looked on the social question as merely "a series of problems to solve" and had included both the proletariat and the bourgeoisie in his *couches sociales nouvelles,* which were coming to dominate the new Republic. By 1880, however, he was admitting that class struggle did indeed exist, and in cooperation with Joseph Barberet, a leader in the cooperative movement, he was beginning to aid labor leaders in creating unions that supported the Republic.[56] Gambetta's support of trade-union legislation was instrumental in eventually producing the law of March, 1884, that legalized trade unions. Pierre Sorlin has noted that the Gambettists, especially after the elections of 1881, tried to project themselves to the country as the party of reform whose specific programs contrasted with the vague rhetoric of the Radicals. Gambetta's idea for the creation of a Ministry of Arts, for example, was intended to include the industrial arts and programs for worker education.[57]

The trouble with this approach, Clemenceau believed, was that it did not go far enough. Radical socialism in general argued for a much more active state role in the economy in order to assure, as Clemenceau often put it, that the individual could realize his potential. "It is when all social forces are placed by you in the service of the strong against the weak," he told the Chamber, "that you come to us and say, 'Liberty! That is the solution to all social and economic problems.'" Unbridled laissez faire was "a deceitful liberty that consists in allowing the strong to wipe out those who have no defense."[58]

At the cirque Fernando in 1882 Clemenceau outlined two forms of property. One was the soil, which could be infinitely subdivided and was therefore democratic. The other was the subsoil, which was concentrated, owned by few, and therefore oligarchic. The state was a contracting partner in allowing private individuals to exploit the riches of the subsoil. The state thus had certain rights and duties—primarily regulatory—in assuring that workers and their families were protected from the "financial feudality." The matter was crucial for the future of the Republic, since, in his view, many of the most powerful leaders of the financial world were still hostile to the regime.[59] The rise of revolutionary collectivism also implied new threats from the Left should the Republic stumble in carrying out its duties to the working class. "Be on guard," Clemenceau told the Chamber in 1884, "the economic struggle that is beginning can be infinitely more dangerous for the Republic than the political struggle."[60]

Loubère has treated in detail the specific legislative proposals emanating from the Extreme Left during the 1880s and 1890s. He notes that, though they were invariably defeated, these aimed toward an industrial democracy characterized by producers and consumers' cooperatives, which would be financed by cheap credit, available through a state bank. There were bills to limit the privileges of the Bank of France, which Pelletan described in June of 1892 as being controlled by the two hundred wealthiest families in the country; to nationalize railroads, which touched on the Republic's responsibilities in the areas of national defense, protection of railroad workers, and cheap transport for small producers; and to appropriate some of the southern mines, although Clemenceau's frequent calls for the state to impose a system of profit-sharing in mining illustrated the Radicals' indecision over whether nationalization or regulation was preferable for the mines. In addition, the Radicals proposed bills dealing with unemployment and accident insurance, old-age pensions, industrial safety, limitation of hours, regulation of night work, factory inspection, child labor, and compulsory arbitration in industrial disputes.[61]

These measures echoed Clemenceau's platform in Montmartre in 1881. While he did not always assume the leading role in arguing them before the lower house, *La Justice* proved to be an important instrument for publicizing Radical welfare proposals throughout the country. In addition, he proved on numerous occasions that he understood the complex relationship between the economic crisis and the failure of social institutions. An example was his attacks on the legal system, which, he believed, discriminated against the poor and was thus an integral part of the problem of social and economic inequality.

Clemenceau portrayed many judges as being prejudiced in favor of propertied elements, for they punished as criminal behavior what was in fact behavior that was dictated by social forces over which the offender had little control. Abolition of the death penalty, election of judges, reform of the penitentiary system, and eradication of the system of hiring prison work gangs were included in Clemenceau's platform of 1881. He discussed his views in detail in April of 1883 during an attack on the Habitual Criminals Bill. This bill, which had been prompted by an increase in the number of criminal repeaters, proposed to remedy the problem by transporting these offenders to penal colonies.

He noted that in most European countries, prison reform started with a softening of penalties. In France, however, reform was to begin by transporting five thousand people across the ocean each year. The cost of such an operation, which could be applied to prison reform at home, argued against the measure. He also pointed out that almost every civilized nation had abandoned the practice of transportation for humanitarian reasons. But the worst feature of the bill was that it neglected rehabilitation and failed to attack the forces that produced crime in the first place: economic misery and the penitentiary system itself. The proposed law was especially severe towards vagabonds and beggars, which was a problem that was related to economic dislocation rather than to recidivism. Often these were simply men who could not find jobs—many, in fact were former miners who had been fired for joining unions and were unable to find work elsewhere because of the *livret*. This was the book that employers kept on each worker; along with noting the wages that had been received, it recorded reasons for dismissal and was invariably demanded by prospective employers. As to the charge that habitual criminals were corrupting children in the streets, Clemenceau argued that it was often the children who corrupted other children. In Paris, for example, gangs of young boys ran loose in the streets. Many were already degraded by poverty. Their fathers were in the factories and their mothers in the sweatshops, and the fact that they had been left to their own devices was the result of the government's failure to build schools, workhouses, and programs of professional ap-

prenticeships. Prisons themselves were "schools of demoraliza-
tion," where entrepreneurs, who had no interest in rehabilitation,
exploited cheap labor and where any noble instincts of men and
women who had no training programs and libraries were crushed
out of them.[62]

Loubère has mentioned that our understanding of the early
Radical Socialists has been blurred because of their dual emphasis on both individualism and state intervention. In the context
of the 1870s, however, when their fight against monarchy had
driven them to an insistence on individual freedom that almost
resembled anarchy, this dualism is understandable.[63] While
Clemenceau argued that the "intellectual emancipation" of the
individual was "the true foundation of economic emancipation,"
he also saw the need for a sensitive state, one that would be
sympathetic to the needs of ordinary people and ready to help
them.[64] One of his favorite targets was the French bureaucracy.
"We have in France," he once told the Chamber, "a series of
political, administrative, and scientific mandarins, laboriously
organized, but absolutely useless and all too often harmful."[65]
This point was best illustrated during the cholera epidemic that
struck Marseilles in the summer of 1884. In a situation that is
reminiscent of the one in Albert Camus's *The Plague,* the government did little to ease the situation, even opposing Clemenceau's suggestion that a parliamentary commission be formed to
visit the city and report back with recommendations on cleaning
up the sources of infection. He therefore formed his own delegation from the Extreme Left. At the risk of becoming infected
himself, he toured the deserted city and came back with proposals for containing the disease, but to little avail.[66]

Most of Clemenceau's activities in the social domain
throughout the early 1880s were devoted to the rights of labor—
specifically its right to organize and to strike. Trade unions,
which had been dispersed by Thiers following the Commune,
had emerged again in 1876, although they had no legal basis.
In July of that year Édouard Lockroy presented a bill in the
Chamber to legalize unions of both workers and employers, with
the stipulation that the names, addresses, and numbers of all
union members be registered with government officials. Clemenceau was listed third among the twenty-four cosponsors of

Lockroy's bill.[67] The workers' congress meeting that October strongly opposed the registration requirement, and in any case, the events of *seize-mai* postponed further consideration of the measure. By 1880 a majority in Parliament was inclined to grant legal recognitions of unions. In November of that year the government itself, with Gambetta's support, presented a modified version of Lockroy's original proposal. It stipulated that only officers of unions, not the entire membership, had to register. This measure was reported out by the Gambettist Allain-Targé in May of 1881.

In the meantime, Clemenceau had changed his mind on two points of the original Lockroy bill. First, he wanted to include the right to unionize under a more general law on freedom of association; he supported an amendment to this effect, which was proposed by the Radical Félix Cantagrel during the first deliberations on the government's bill. The amendment was defeated by a vote of 215 to 168, with about half of the Radicals, fearing that the amendment would recognize clerical associations, either voting against it or abstaining.[68] Second, Clemenceau now worried that unions that refused to register would be suppressed by the courts under provisions of the penal code. For this reason *La Justice* advocated a simplified measure that would recognize the right of each worker, alone or in concert with others, to negotiate contracts as he wished.[69]

Between 1881 and 1884 the government's bill passed back and forth between Chamber and Senate—the upper house attempting to incorporate articles that would ban not only unions that refused to register but also federations. The intervention of Waldeck-Rousseau won over the Senate to the idea of federation, but continuing disagreement over the status of unregistered unions brought the bill back to the Chamber in March of 1884.[70] In January of that year, Clemenceau had already voiced his fears that the law would leave unregistered unions, which were presently tolerated, at the mercy of the police. He stressed this point again during the final reading in March. While admitting that the law had some strong points, especially in its authorization of federations, he argued that the registration provision was a "law of guarantees against liberty," since it would result in having police dossiers on union organizers. By limiting freedom of association, it would also stir defiance in the working classes, whom, the Opportunists claimed, they were trying to help. He and most of the other Radicals then supported an amendment, which failed by a vote of 277 to 198, that would make the registration requirement less strict.[71] The Chamber then approved each article of the new labor law by voice vote.

Clemenceau's fear that the registration provision would alienate working-class leaders proved to be justified. A workers' congress at Lyons in 1886 condemned the new law, which continued to be a source of controversy for years.[72] Moreover, long before the law was passed, Clemenceau had already discovered that employers had their own means for dealing with union agitators and that the state, the supposedly "neutral" protector of order, tended to favor employers throughout the industrial strife that characterized the early 1880s.

In December of 1881, for example, several coal companies in the Gard Basin began to fire workers who had joined unions. Strikes broke out at the mines of Bessèges, Molières, and Grand'Comb. The director of Grand'Comb then appealed to the prefect on the grounds that the strikers were planning to block mine ventilators in order to keep out nonunion workers. The government of Gambetta responded by sending in troops, who crushed the strike within two days and dispersed the "Study Circles" that the miners had organized.

In early February of 1882, Clemenceau and others on the Extreme Left met in Paris at the Palais Bourbon to hear testimony from a miners' delegation from Grand'Comb. The Radicals decided to send their own delegation to study conditions in the pits firsthand. As part of this group, Clemenceau traveled on the nineteenth to the little town of Alais, near the mines, where he talked with the mine director (who was also the mayor and who admitted that the troops had been placed at his disposition) and where he visited the pits and heard complaints from the miners. Clemenceau could find no evidence that the strikers had planned to commit any acts of violence, and he was angered by the way in which the government had favored management throughout the strike.[73] Thus, on March 9 he launched an attack on Freycinet, who had succeeded Gambetta.

Under the Empire, he said, republicans like Gambetta had denounced the use of troops to break strikes. Gambetta had changed, but the mine owners had not. Most had been good Bonapartists then, browbeating their workers and forcing them to support official candidates. Since the victory of the Republic, they had shifted to republicanism, but the truth was that they were still reactionaries. Although the state was a contracting partner in granting them concessions to exploit the subsoil and thus had a duty to protect the rights of workers, it had instead sided with the owners by sending in troops. Knowing that it could always count on such assistance, management was thus more determined than ever to reject the legitimate demands of the workers.

Clemenceau noted that events in industrial disorders always followed the same pattern, and he rejected the defense that soldiers were merely defending freedom of work: "Just go and talk about freedom of work to a laborer suspended from a mine in the Gard because he belonged to a circle or to a trade union. Just tell him that he is free to work when his *livret* shows a secret mark, a note of infamy that prevents him from being hired by a mining company in the Loire or Nord." The fact was, Clemenceau said, that the company was master of the worker's life and labor. The worker lived in a company house and got his food, clothing, and medicine from the company store. The bosses kept his first month's salary as a "guarantee," and by the time the worker received his wages, he was already in debt. At stake for him was nothing less than the bread with which to feed his family; yet, it did not matter if he had worked for twenty years, if the company found out that he was involved with unions, it could reduce him to instant misery. This was a "barbarous war" in which the lives of men, women, and children were at stake; and the only response of the government had been to extol the virtues of individual initiative: "Individual initiative! What are you doing to permit its free exercise? The industrial companies suppress it in shackling and suppressing the liberty of the worker."[74]

Clemenceau was correct in arguing that fear of worker violence at Grand'Comb had been much exaggerated. In fact, between 1870 and 1890 only about 3.2 percent of the strikes actually involved violence.[75] When it did occur, as at Montceau-les-mines in the fall of 1882, Clemenceau was quick to condemn it.[76] He showed much more initiative in trying to get to the roots of popular agitation than did Opportunist leaders like Ferry. In January, 1884, for example, he and some of his colleagues on the Extreme Left met with trade-union delegates who had brought a petition summarizing their griefs. The petition claimed that large numbers of craftsmen were being hurt by foreign workers and by overproduction caused by machines.[77] On the thirty-first, Clemenceau initiated in the Chamber a broad discussion of the economic situation, one of the few such debates that one sees in this period.

He argued that France was in the grip of a real crisis, pointing to declining salaries and the growing number of unemployed to prove his point. A depression in the construction trades in the cities, plus the onerous burden of direct and indirect taxes, made the situation worse. The Republic could begin to solve these problems through a more equitable tax structure, credit institutions, and obligatory social insurance. Reform was impossible, however, until the government knew more about the economic situation. Against Ferry's opposition, and by a slim margin of five votes, Clemenceau won approval for the creation of a commission of forty-four deputies, which would gather data about industrial, commercial, and agricultural workers.[78]

The commission started its work at once, despite Clemenceau's complaints that Ferry refused to give it information and that he had packed it with people who were opposed to the idea (in fact, eighteen of its members had voted against the project). Nevertheless, as a member of the subcommittee that drew up a plan of work, Clemenceau infused life into the project. Throughout February and March the commission met with various Socialist and trade-union representatives. On February 14, in company with Richard Waddington, brother of the former prime minister, Clemenceau went to London in order to study the methods used by English parliamentary commissions in investigating labor conditions.[79]

One practical result of Clemenceau's labors on the commission was a detailed questionnaire that attempted to gain information on the worker in both his occupational and familial setting. Composed of three sections dealing with workers in industry, commerce, and agriculture, it contained 241 questions on all aspects of the worker's life: his personal background, the wage levels, working conditions, accidents, public assistance, and his membership in unions, mutual-aid societies, and other organizations. Clemenceau's colleagues on the commission used the questionnaire as a basis for study, printing over one hundred thousand copies, which were then mailed to trade unions, agricultural societies, and Chambers of Commerce. At the cirque Fernando, Clemenceau stressed that before effective social legislation could be written, such information was essential and that the gathering of social statistics was already standard procedure in many countries.[80]

While Clemenceau was working on the commission, a new strike broke out in February of 1884 at the coal mine of Anzin in the Nord. On March 10 he asked the commission, as part of its study, to send a delegation to the mines, but the conservative republican members argued that this would compromise the commission's objectivity.[81] In April, after troops had ended the strike, he spoke to the Chamber, challenging any deputy or minister to prove that any violence had occurred that could justify military intervention: "The truth, and you know it well, is that the soldier in this affair represents the state itself placed at the service of the Anzin company." Certainly there had been threats and harsh words from the miners, but this was because the company had been firing union organizers. Despite the recently enacted law regarding trade unions, workers still had no rights: "While you were making what you thought were serious laws, the companies—and not even private companies, but those holding their powers and almost their fortunes from the state—arrogate to themselves the right of wiping out these laws."[82]

That fall, Clemenceau and Germain Casse traveled to Anzin to study the conditions of the miners and then presented a summary of their recommendations in *La Justice*. The report contended that the company had been determined to crush the unions by firing labor organizers. The report also urged that stiff penal sanctions be imposed for illegal acts against the unions.[83] The next year the Chamber did pass a measure that provided fines and imprisonment for employers who suspended workers for unionizing, but the Senate killed it. The same thing happened in 1890 and 1893. The big companies continued to intimidate and to undermine unions, a fact that must be considered when one seeks to explain the slow growth rate of unions in France.[84] Union membership did grow, climbing to almost a half million by 1893; but this represented a small proportion of an active industrial population that had stood in 1881 at 4,444,-000 and that, if one included workers in service categories, totaled 8,580,000. In addition, after the period 1884 to 1886—which Perrot has called "the end of a reciprocal illusion" between labor and the Republic—the rate of military intervention in strikes rose steadily, always remaining above 10 percent and in 1890 reaching 15 percent.[85]

While in terms of immediate practical results Clemenceau's fight on behalf of workers must be judged a failure, he was at least among the first and most articulate of those in the 1880s who tried to stir public consciousness of the problems that the Opportunists tried to ignore. Both his speeches and his newspaper played an important role in investigating and reporting on the conditions of the working classes. Furthermore, his conviction that the Republic would never win the loyalty of the worker until it fulfilled its obligations in the social and economic domain proved to be correct. In particular, the decline of cooperative trade socialism and the rise of a militant revolutionary syndicalism can be traced to the political failures of the republican bourgeoisie. "The change," says Bernard H. Moss, "occurred in direct proportion to the disappointment experienced with the new Republic, its failure to pass a significant program of social reforms and to deal with the economic depression of the mid-1880s."[86]

THE FIGHT AGAINST COLONIALISM

During the years that Clemenceau campaigned on behalf of labor, he was fighting a battle against colonialism. By the early 1880s he had become the most vigorous opponent in

France to the building of an Empire, a fact for which he has been censured by those who believe that the Empire was a worthy goal and who are impatient with the obstructions that he created.[87] But there was a logic—and a compelling one at that—in his anticolonialism, especially if it is placed against the backdrop of the depression and is viewed as part of his general struggle against Opportunist domestic policies.

Much of the literature on French colonialism has emphasized prestige and the desire to erase the humiliation over the loss of Alsace-Lorraine as the motives that underlay overseas expansion. But patriotic motives were often intertwined with economic ones, and many Frenchmen regarded national honor and commercial advantages as one and the same thing.[88] The drive to realize economic interests abroad also casts light on the attitudes of the republican bourgeoisie toward the social question. Many Gambettists, for example, believed that an active colonial policy would serve as a form of social pacification, since it would both enhance national prosperity and divert discontent outward. Elwitt has made a convincing case that Ferry, who is regarded as the author of the French colonial enterprise and whose outlook reflected that of the textile bourgeoisie of the east, believed that social tensions resulted from crises in production. In Ferry's view, such tensions could be alleviated by expansion of markets and by the creation of a protected "metropolitan-colonial political economy."[89]

The radical antecedents to Clemenceau's opposition to Ferry can be seen in the anticolonial and antislavery traditions of 1789 and 1848.[90] In the 1880s Clemenceau continued this tradition. He attacked racist assumptions, which were often invoked in support of expansionism, and charged that the financial interests that were profiting from colonialism, no matter how they might clothe their intentions in ideas of *mission civilisatrice,* were insensitive to the human exploitation they caused. At the same time he and some of his followers, such as Perin and Pelletan, broadened the earlier moral argument to include questions of national defense: troops should not be tied down in remote corners of the globe at a time when France was still weak on the Continent. In 1884 Clemenceau told the Chamber of Deputies: "Prince Bismarck is a dangerous enemy; he is perhaps a still more dangerous friend. Yes! It was he who showed you Tunis at the Congress of Berlin; it was he who placed you in opposition to England. . . . And while we fritter away our money and the best of our blood in foolish enterprises, he makes the most terrible economic war on you."[91]

But the patriotic argument against colonialism, which was an especially powerful propaganda point, must not obscure an even more fundamental concern of Clemenceau's. This was the Republic's ability to implement social justice at home. Military security was essential in achieving this goal, but it is an error to portray the early Clemenceau as a die-hard advocate of revenge against Germany.[92] While he had no illusions about the Empire across the Rhine, "whose national industry has long been war," he recognized French weakness and believed that the race for colonies threatened to upset the delicate equilibrium that had existed since 1871. "I do not believe that Germany alone is responsible for the precariousness of the peace," he told the Chamber in 1883, "we also must make our *mea culpa,* and others like us."[93] The future of the Republic, moreover, did not depend on military strength alone. Herein lies one of the most important reasons for the bitterness of his fight against colonialism: if the heart and treasure of the young Republic were in overseas ventures, this would result in a weakening of both the will and the resources essential for a creative social program at home.

The first of many clashes between Clemenceau and Ferry came over Tunisia. At the Congress of Berlin in 1878 the British had hinted to Waddington that France could have a free hand in this area, which was nominally a part of the Ottoman Empire. Since then, French leaders such as Gambetta had become increasingly interested in the old lands of Carthage.[94] After Ferry became prime minister in 1880, he began to emphasize the threat of an Italian naval base at Bizerta. He was also responsive to appeals from Frenchmen in Tunisia (all seven hundred of them), who stressed the need to suppress the raids of native Kroumirs across the border into Algeria.

Until 1881 Clemenceau had taken little interest in foreign policy. What he now saw as adventurism on Ferry's part alarmed him. In March of that year, for example, he rose in the Chamber to question Ferry about sales of weapons to the Greek government, and he stressed that Parliament should ensure that France not become involved in foreign dealings that would hurt the national interest.[95] The following month, however, Ferry got parliamentary approval for an expedition to put down the Tunisian tribes that were raiding in Algeria. The troops found few rebels, but they managed to extract from the bey the Treaty of Bardo, by which Tunisian foreign and domestic affairs were placed in French hands. In May, 1881, Ferry presented a draft of the treaty to the Chamber.

Clemenceau denounced the march on the bey's summer palace at Bardo and expressed concern over the alienation of Italy, which had its own visions of a Tunisian protectorate. He also thought that German approval of the expedition meant that Ferry was arriving at some kind of understanding with the Germans. But Ferry's explanations satisfied the Chamber, which approved the treaty by a vote of 430 to 1, with Clemenceau and most of the Extreme Left abstaining.[96] During the summer, while the legislative elections were taking place, the situation in Tunisia deteriorated. Ferry had to mobilize a new expedition to put down the tribesmen, but even this was not enough. Criticized in the press for the way he had managed the affair and recognizing his vulnerability because of the election gains of Gambetta's Republican Union, Ferry decided to resign, but not before explaining his Tunisian policies to the new Chamber.

In a caucus of the Extreme Left on November 3, Clemenceau asked for an investigation of the Tunisian affair and announced that he would demand a full explanation from the government. Debate started in the Chamber two days later, with Ferry arguing that the expedition had been only an effort toward pacification of the Tunisian countryside. He pointed to the economic advantages of the endeavor, and in an appeal to the patriotism of the deputies, he maintained that dissension at home was the real enemy of French efforts abroad. On the ninth, Clemenceau rose to answer Ferry's arguments. "Patriotism," he said, "does not consist in pronouncing excited phrases about the grandeur of *la patrie;* true patriotism consists in saying today that we want the truth."

He used against Ferry the very documents that the latter

had distributed to the Chamber, with which the prime minister tried to prove the economic advantages to be gained in Tunisia. Clemenceau argued that the documents showed only that Ferry had failed to control events and that the French consul in Tunisia, on his own initiative, had committed French honor and resources. What had been the motive? In theory, said Clemenceau, it had been economic development of Tunisia for the good of France. In reality, the consul had been the spokesman for speculators and financiers in Paris. Furthermore, in making war without the consent of Parliament, Ferry had violated the constitution: "The Prime Minister thinks he can close the affair by saying, 'We have not declared war.' But this is precisely our grievance. You have not declared war, but you have made it."[97]

The session of November 9 proved to be one of the most confusing in French parliamentary history. Gambetta's group, which had been victorious during the elections, was determined to get rid of Ferry, but it wished to do so without also rejecting the possibility of having a protectorate in Tunisia. After Clemenceau's speech, six orders of the day, all opposing Ferry, came to the floor from both the Extreme Left and the Extreme Right. At that point, Clemenceau asked for a committee to be formed in order to review the whole Tunisian affair, but this was defeated by a vote of 328 to 161. Then eighteen more orders of the day were presented, but each one failed to win a vote of priority. It was Gambetta who saved the day: he urged the Chamber to approve the Treaty of Bardo while simultaneously expressing no confidence in Ferry. The motion passed by a vote of 355 to 68, with most of the opposition coming from the Extreme Left and the Extreme Right. On the next day, November 10, 1881, Ferry sent his resignation to President Grévy.

Disagreement over colonial matters was a significant factor in Clemenceau's attack on the Gambetta ministry that was formed afterwards. In this case the country was Egypt, where Gambetta believed that France had vital economic interests. Shortly after becoming prime minister, he had become alarmed over the growth of a nationalist antiforeign party there. Since Britain and France jointly headed an international commission to administer Egyptian debts, he had persuaded the British to join him in support of the khedive. But Gambetta was overthrown in the Chamber before the issue could be resolved. His replacement, Freycinet, hesitated to take decisive action, agreeing only to send a naval squadron to join British ships off Alexandria. This show of force failed; the result was a massacre of foreigners in the city on June 12, 1882. The vacillating Freycinet withdrew the French squadron, but in July he agreed to a British request for a joint landing and occupation.

Clemenceau was suspicious of this latest adventure, which he blamed on Gambetta.[98] A caucus of the Extreme Left declared itself "for a policy of peace," and as a member of the parliamentary commission that had been formed to consider Freycinet's request for eight million francs for the navy, Clemenceau condemned the proposed expedition, which he compared to Napoleon's methods. France was strong only when it exported the ideas of justice that it had inherited from the French Revolution. It should be trying to help the peasants of Egypt, not substituting itself for the exploiters of them: "Just be sure that if you march with England, the first interest that will be attended to will be that of the bankers, who have only one goal and could never have any other, to exploit the country for their own profit."[99]

When debate on the naval credits began on July 18, Gambetta criticized Freycinet for doing too little to protect French interests. He also ridiculed those who were defending the Egyptian rebels: "It has been discovered that these people, who have been enslaved for forty centuries, are on the eve of finding the principles of 1789 in the hypogea of the pyramids!"[100] Clemenceau's response came the next day. He emphasized that he favored a friendly policy toward England. He was not willing to make any sacrifice, however, in order to maintain an accord with England, which in any case could protect the Suez Canal alone. Besides, the French economic interests in Egypt that had been proclaimed by Gambetta were largely fictional and "not worth a drop of French blood."

France, Clemenceau said, would serve its true interests through a policy that "attaches more to moral conquests than to material ones, that believes war is an economic heresy where the vanquisher suffers as much as the vanquished." A superior civilization that imposes itself on a primitive one should seek to create an order "founded on the principles of Right and Justice" rather than one based on exploitation of man by man. He lashed out against those who argued that certain races were incapable of improvement and therefore needed the tutelage of "superior" peoples:

> This is precisely why I requested the floor, to protest against this theory that consists in introducing into humanity, at the moment when it is disappearing from science, the principle of the immutability of species.
>
> Is it not strange that people are starting again to speak of races at a time when they are mixing more and more and when the unity of their character appears singularly compromised? The truth is that there are people who dream of universal domination, either by the propaganda of ideas, or by material conquests. There is pan-Germanism, pan-Slavism, pan-Islamism; there is the theory of the Latin races. . . . Many Englishmen are convinced of the superiority of the Anglo-Saxon race to the point of believing that they alone are capable of liberty and that other races should be delivered over to different forms of despotism. . . . Someone mentioned Canada. I have gone to Canada, I have lived there, and I have seen Englishmen who call the French the vanquished and inferior race.[101]

Clemenceau indicated that he would vote to approve Freycinet's request in order not to leave the navy in the lurch. The credits were approved, but on July 29, when the prime minister brought a request for credits of nine million francs for the army, Clemenceau went on the offensive again. This time he hit hard on the matter of French security in Europe. France might become bogged down in Egypt and even find itself in conflict with England, and all the while it would be ignoring its security on the Continent: "Europe is covered with soldiers; everyone is waiting. The Powers are reserving their liberty of action for the future. Let us reserve the liberty of France!"[102]

Many writers have credited Clemenceau with toppling the government on this occasion, and in his memoirs, Freycinet himself blames this speech for causing his downfall.[103] What this view overlooks is that the credits were rejected by an overwhelming vote of 416 to 75 and that several other speakers from

the Right and from the Left Center also argued against the
expedition. De Marcère, in particular, raised the issues of the
safety of French troops in Egypt and of the possibility of a
wider war. Gambetta himself wished to get rid of Freycinet
because he believed that the prime minister had bungled the
Egyptian effort. Thus, Opportunist support for Freycinet was
weak from the start, with only a few prominent figures such as
Jules Ferry, Alexandre Ribot, and Sadi Carnot voting in support
of him.

The last phase of Clemenceau's anticolonial campaign occurred between 1883 and 1885, during the French conquest of
Indo-China. In opposing this conquest, he invoked many of
the arguments that he had used against the Tunisian and Egyptian interventions, although after 1883 one sees in his speeches
a greater emphasis on the economic damage that was being
wrought by colonialism. The conquest of Indo-China coincided
with some of the worst years of the depression, and workers
sometimes complained to him about the irony of France's vigorous overseas expansionism in contrast to its policy of social
neglect at home.[104]

It was Ferry who led France along the paths to colonial
glory. Gambetta died in December, 1882, and many of his
followers drifted to Ferry, who took office the following February with a relatively stable coalition of Left and Left Center.
One of his most significant achievements over the next two
years was the building of the Empire. From the start, both the
vagueness of his goals and his secretive attitude toward Parliament aroused Clemenceau's ire. In July of 1883, for example,
Clemenceau questioned Ferry's request for an appropriation of
four and a half million francs for construction of a railroad in
Senegal. He promised that the Radicals would vote the credits
if French soldiers were endangered, but he sugested that the
request for four million would soon be one for ten million. The
argument that "we are engaged" would be repeatedly used, but
towards what goal no one could say.[105]

Indo-China, the area comprising modern Laos, Cambodia,
and the two Vietnams, had long been an object of interest to
France. In 1859 the Second Empire had acquired a protectorate
over Cambodia. Then, in 1874, France had signed a treaty with

the Annamite Empire that in theory provided for a protectorate over Annam, which possessed Tonkin. The latter region included the rich Red River Delta around Hanoi plus the port of Haiphong. China never did recognize this treaty; and China, at the request of the emperor of Annam, who was a vassal of China's, sent troops into Tonkin when France tried to consolidate its control over this area in the early 1880s. France found itself fighting both Chinese regulars and the guerillas known as the Black Flags. In the spring of 1883, after the death of the French commander Henri Rivière, Parliament unanimously approved an expedition to disperse the guerillas. By August, after a brief bombardment of Hué, Ferry extracted a new treaty, which guaranteed French rights in Tonkin and a protectorate over Annam. Still, China refused to recognize the treaty, and the fighting went on.

During an interpellation by Granet in October, 1883, Clemenceau criticized Ferry for the way in which he had handled the affair. He accused the prime minister of aiming toward a protectorate all along, even though Parliament had not authorized him to do so. Clemenceau stressed the danger of waging a protracted war against China's "inexhaustible reservoir" of men. Such a struggle would consume the sons of France, and even if victory were achieved, the economic gains would be minimal. He ridiculed Ferry's suggestion that what was at stake was a ready market of four hundred million consumers in China. During the twenty years that France had engaged in sporadic fighting with China, Chinese exports had increased, whereas French trade with China had remained at the same level. Continuing the war was thus contrary to economic logic. Clemenceau also noted that the race for colonies was whetting the appetites of the Great Powers and that France's greed in Tonkin, like that of England in Cyprus and Egypt or of Austria in Bosnia and Herzegovina, would ultimately work to the benefit of Germany. Bismarck knew that the most important colonies were those that were won or lost on the battlefields of Europe. France, thus, should aim for a policy of "European solidarity" in place of antagonistic competition.[106]

Ferry defended the protectorate as being a great gain for France. All "industrial races" were engaged in a competition for outlets in Africa and Asia and especially in the vast Chinese market. To deny the Republic a colonial policy would work against the future of France. For the moment a majority approved Ferry's actions by a vote of 328 to 185.[107] In early December, after the government had requested new appropriations of nine million francs for Tonkin, Clemenceau resumed the attack, arguing that war with China would break out in full if French troops continued their march on the village of Bac-Ninh, which was north of Hanoi. He asked the Chamber to vote against the ministry; but the credits were approved, and Ferry received another vote of confidence.[108]

The conflict in Indo-China dragged on throughout early 1884, with victory eluding French expeditionary troops in the rugged terrain north of Hanoi. By March the town of Bac-Ninh fell to the French, but contrary to Clemenceau's prediction, no major war with China ensued. By June, Ferry finally received Chinese recognition of France's rights in Tonkin, but a palace coup in Peking brought to power a new emperor, who was hostile to the French. The fighting in the south went on. A skirmish near the village of Bac-Lé resulted in the deaths of eighteen Frenchmen and the wounding of seventy-five more. Ferry denounced the incident as an ambush and demanded that China evacuate Tonkin and pay an indemnity of two hundred million francs. When China refused to comply in full, he ordered the shelling of Foochow and a blockade of Formosa.

In October, 1884, Clemenceau questioned Ferry during a meeting of the parliamentary commission that was examining a new request for Tonkin appropriations. He was especially concerned over the diplomatic situation in Europe, but Ferry would respond only that French security was "total and complete" and that the military situation in Tonkin had never been better.[109] In the Chamber on November 21, Ferry assailed Clemenceau's "campaign of insinuations." Complaining that the delicate state of negotiations with China prevented him from giving details, Ferry condemned Clemenceau for attacking him "personally and perpetually."[110]

But Clemenceau was unsparing of the man who he believed was wreaking disaster on the Republic. On November 27 he told the Chamber that the actual military situation was "in flagrant contradiction to ministerial optimism." He noted that in April of the previous year, Ferry had declared that no Chinese troops were in Tonkin and that French military operations were almost finished. Such self-delusion had led to the Mexican disaster and to Sedan in 1870. As for the famous "ambush" at Bac-Lé, Clemenceau charged that it had been caused by a French officer who exceeded his orders, not by Chinese treachery. In any case, China had offered to pay reparations of three and a half million francs, but Ferry had insisted on the original demand for two hundred million. Clemenceau continued:

> And now, I declare that up to that point you had made many mistakes, you had transgressed by an unbelievable negligence and inexcusable thoughtlessness, and these accumulated errors could assuredly constitute a heavy responsibility. But on this last occasion—I must say it—you committed a veritable crime. . . . The men who died at Bac-Lé, those who are dying heroically in the Tonkin combat, die by your mistake. . . . It is your work and yours alone, since in refusing an honorable peace you have decreed a useless war.

The Chamber was in an uproar, and the president warned Clemenceau about his language. But he went on, noting on a map, which Ferry had distributed, that the Chinese had already penetrated the interior of the delta and that French forces were on the defensive as fighting continued thirty kilometers downstream on the Claire River. Ferry countered by saying: "At ten kilometers only. The action took place in a town whose name is not on the map." But Clemenceau objected: "I regret exceedingly, Mr. President of the Council, to point out to you that the name of the town is certainly on the map which you have distributed to us. It is the town of Hung-Quan. You haven't looked at the map—that's your excuse."[111]

Despite this blistering attack on the government, the Chamber voted the credits for Tonkin and gave Ferry another vote of confidence by 295 to 196. Ferry still had a majority, but he knew that the longer the war went on, the more precarious his position would become, particularly since many of the deputies were already concerned that an increasingly unpopular war would hurt them in the next elections.

By January, 1885, new negotiations were begun with China. While these indicated that France would get its maximum demands, the delicate nature of the talks prevented Ferry from mentioning them in public in his own defense. Thus, any new military difficulties in Asia might doom his ministry. On March 27, Paris newspapers reported that there had been a French defeat near one of the hamlets of Tonkin. Granet launched an interpellation on the matter, and on the twenty-eighth, Clemenceau rose with a new denunciation of "this eternal question of Tonkin." Was Ferry going to declare war or not? For years, Clemenceau said, Ferry had misled the country. Faced with a limitless force, which was armed with the latest rapid-fire weapons, French soldiers were being beaten. He asked Parliament to reassert its control over the power to make war and warned that a new vote of confidence would allow Ferry to go on doing as he pleased.[112]

Ferry got a vote of confidence, but by a close vote of 259 to 209. The next day he received more bad news. Gen. Brière de l'Isle cabled to Paris that his troops had taken a beating at the town of Lang-Son on the Chinese border and that he and his men were in retreat. This defeat, as it turned out later, was not as great as the message implied; but this was not known at that time in Paris. Soon the news was out, and there were demonstrations in Paris, denouncing the defeat as a new Sedan.

Clemenceau is often portrayed as the chief architect of Ferry's downfall during the events that followed the incident at Lang-Son. Clemenceau certainly aimed to see the ministry defeated; moreover, he wanted to see Ferry put on trial. But the collapse of the Ferry cabinet resulted from several factors, of which Clemenceau's intervention was only one. The hostility of the Right over anticlerical legislation was one factor, but a more important one was that a substantial number of deputies on both the Left and the Left Center feared that an unpopular war would weaken them in the approaching elections. On the morning of March 30 a delegation representing the two groups of the Opportunist majority went to see Ferry and asked that he resign before Parliament convened later in the day. The prime minister rejected this advice and told his cabinet that he would go to the Chamber and ask for funds to avenge the defeat.[113]

When Ferry appeared before the Chamber, he was greeted with silence. In a brief statement he asked the deputies to grant new appropriations. Clemenceau walked to the tribune, "overwhelming in his contempt and bitterness," as the correspondent for the London *Times* wrote.[114] He came quickly to the point:

> Gentlemen, I do not come to respond to the president of the Council. I consider that at the present hour no debate can any longer take place between the ministry of which he is the leader and a republican member of this house. . . . Yes, all debate is finished between us; we do not wish to hear you any longer, we can no longer discuss with you the great interests of *la patrie*. (Very good! Very good! Applause from the Extreme Left.)
>
> We no longer recognize you. We do not wish to recognize you any more . . . . these are no longer ministers I have before me, these are the accused! (New applause at Extreme Left and Right.)

At these words, Ferry laughed, thus infuriating many of the deputies. Amidst the tumult, Clemenceau continued the attack: "These men are accused of high treason, upon whom, if there exists in France a principle of responsibility and justice, the hand of the law will not be slow in falling!" He asked the Chamber to vote all the funds needed to aid French soldiers in Asia while at the same time replacing Ferry with a responsible prime minister with whom the Chamber could work in deciding what to do about Tonkin.

Clemenceau's dramatic speech is often quoted in accounts of this episode, but little attention has been given to the speech that followed by Alexandre Ribot, who, like de Marcère during the debates over Egypt in 1882, best reflected the feelings of moderates and whose words spelled the end for Ferry's cabinet. Ribot charged that the ministry was too weak to deal with the Tonkin situation; he noted that this was the first time a ministry had ever asked for money without also asking for a vote of confidence. "At the moment you have no choice but to resign," he told Ferry, "you owe it to the Republic on which you have just inflicted the first humiliation, and finally and especially you owe it to France." The credits were then rejected by a vote of 306 to 149. A motion by the Extreme Left to bring Ferry to trial failed by 287 to 152, which best reflects the number of votes that Clemenceau would have been able to muster against Ferry without the support of the moderates.[115]

Ironically, Ferry got word the next day that the negotiations had been completed. The treaty was signed in April, with China recognizing France's rights in Annam and Tonkin and with France agreeing to forgo any indemnity claims because of the Bac-Lé incident. By the summer the deputies had approved the treaty, their main concern having been to get rid of Ferry rather than Tonkin. Clemenceau supported the treaty because he believed "it augments the chances for peace," but he also described the treaty as a "false peace" because the questions of how long the occupation would continue and whether it would involve greater expenses in administration had been left unresolved. With the elections approaching, most deputies wanted to postpone a consideration of such problems, and it was not until December that the Chamber, by a narrow margin, approved thirty million francs for proceeding with the conquest of Indo-China.[116]

No doubt, Clemenceau was brutally unsparing in his attacks on Jules Ferry. The latter is often pictured as being a victim of popular passions, who, in refusing to divulge information on the state of negotiations with China, sacrificed his career on the altar of national interests. Yet, Clemenceau's arguments were not without merit; his fears for the future not without justification. The treaty of 1885 did not end the fighting. The struggle against the Tonkin guerillas went on for years afterwards. While a tentative pacification was achieved by 1897, the last chapter in this story would not be written until the middle of the twentieth century. And after all the expenditure in blood and money, the economic gains in which the whole nation was to have shared remained—except for a few big companies and a professional cadre of administrators—largely a myth of colonial propaganda.[117]

The dubious character of Ferry's economic goals became apparent when he tried to defend his policies in detail before the Chamber on July 28, 1885, four months after his fall. He argued that colonial expansion was "a political and economic system" necessary for those "industrial races" that were searching to obtain export markets. Such nations as Germany and the United States were becoming protectionists, keeping out French exports while pouring their own goods onto French markets. In addition, France needed coaling stations because of the new conditions of naval warfare. It was through colonies, Ferry said, that France could exercise its influence over Europe. To critics who charged that imposing civilization by cannonballs was just another form of barbarism, Ferry answered that "superior races have rights over inferior races."[118]

Clemenceau responded on July thirtieth. First, he stressed that the volume of colonial trade—with Algeria and Cochin-China, for example—was negligible and that even if one excluded the initial cost of conquest, the cost of administration meant that France lost far more money than it gained. Good markets could not be opened with cannons, for one had to work at developing a market by preparing buyers and sellers alike. Thus far, the principal export to colonies had been the billions of francs that they cost, money that should have been used for reform at home. In fact, French citizens paid for these colonial adventures, thus diminishing their own purchasing power. Second, Clemenceau rejected the theory that failure to obtain colonies would mean decadence for a Great Power: "This is the first time that anyone has recommended to a people, as a system, a policy of continuous warlike expeditions." Peace was the true condition for progress.

Finally, while Clemenceau admitted that the struggle for life on this globe was "a fatal necessity," he rejected any attempt "to dress up violence in the hypocritic name of civilization." Colonial conquest was "the pure and simple abuse of the force created by a scientific civilization over rudimentary civilization":

> Superior races! Inferior races! That's sooner said than done. For my part, I have singularly reduced my claims after seeing German scholars demonstrate scientifically that France had to be vanquished in the Franco-German war because the French were an inferior race to the Germans. Since then, I avow, I look twice before turning to a man

or a civilization and saying, "inferior race." The Hindus! With this great refined civilization that was lost in the night of time, with this great effervescence of art, of which we still see today the magnificent vestiges. An inferior race, the Chinese! With this great civilization whose origins are unknown and that appears to have been pushed from the very beginning to the extreme limits.[119]

The debate was a postscript to Ferry's career, for he was never able to recover from his defeat. But Clemenceau continued to be bitter against him, blaming him for the initial monarchist gains in the elections of 1885 and always holding him responsible for a policy that, he believed, had damaged the Republic.[120] In particular, Clemenceau's confidence in the reforming capacities of the Republic appears to have been dampened by the war in Tonkin. In December of 1885 the diplomat Paul Cambon paid him a visit in his Paris apartment. He found him brooding over the "inextricable" Tonkin situation. A complete occupation of Indo-China, Clemenceau told Cambon, would be an abyss. Total evacuation would "dishonor those who do it and perhaps lead to catastrophes." Tonkin would be a "ball and chain" on any future cabinet, which "will always be at the mercy of a futile incident and will be unable to concern itself with either our internal affairs or the organization of the army." He added that the results would be a move to either the Extreme Left or the Extreme Right and that "we are heading toward an anarchy the likes of which no one shall have ever seen in our history."[121]

The foregoing analysis of Clemenceau's social and economic ideals and the relevance of his anticolonial campaign to them will hopefully place his activities during the years 1880 to 1885 in better perspective. In the last two sections of this chapter, I have tried to show that his vision of a just social Republic was a worthy one and that his capacity to empathize with the weak and oppressed—whether the miners of Anzin or the peoples of Egypt and Tonkin—was an important part of his psychological makeup. It is necessary now to turn to a more negative aspect of his character, which was his inability to work in harmony with others toward the practical realization of his ideals. This study suggests that his inability to do so resulted from the psychological inhibitions, noted earlier, that tended to preclude personal success, at least as it is usually defined in the world of politics. These inhibitions become especially evident after the Radical victories in the elections of 1885, but they are also apparent in the way in which he reacted to the challenge of creating an effectual reform party in France.

FAILURE TO BUILD A REFORM PARTY:
THE REVISIONIST CAMPAIGN AND THE ELECTIONS OF 1885

In a speech at Bordeaux in the summer of 1885, Clemenceau advocated the creation of a progressive party and a conservative party along Whig-Tory lines. A progressive party, which could constitute a reforming majority in Parliament, would respond to the fundamental need for change in a democratic society. A conservative party, which would accept the Republic as the definitive form of government, could, when necessary, slow the pace of reform without threatening the regime itself.[122]

Despite the many forces that undermined the development of disciplined parties, the creation of a more unified reform movement was not beyond the realm of possibility. The most natural grouping would have been a coalition between Radicals and advanced moderates (the addition of reformist Socialists such as Paul Brousse after 1885 would have been possible but difficult).[123] Clemenceau possessed the talent and the requisite vision to lead such a coalition, but the task required flexibility, compromise, and the ability to be a follower as well as a leader. In this section I will try to demonstrate how Clemenceau responded to the political options that were available to him and how the flaws of his own character helped to ensure his failure. In order to develop this argument it is necessary to examine some of the long-range trends on the French Left during the years 1876 to 1893.

The steady growth of the Radical faction in the Chamber of Deputies until 1889 is evident during these years in the composition of each legislature:

1876–77: Radical, 11 %; Republican, 53 %
1877–81: Radical, 12 %; Republican, 48 %

1881–85: Radical, 14 %; Republican, 69 %
1885–89: Radical, 20 %; Republican, 44 %
1889–93: Radical, 16 %; Republican, 45 %; Socialist, 2 %[124]

Shifting personal alignments and the practice of dual registration in parliamentary groups make it difficult to use the term Radical with any precision in describing many deputies. Charles Floquet and Germain Casse, for example, were grouped in the Extreme Left in 1876, but they gradually moved toward a more moderate position. Indeed, the Radical wing of the republican movement contained many tendencies. Loubère delineates the basic three: the hard-core Radical Socialists, who included Clemenceau and whose voting record on legislation of an advanced social and economic nature attained around 90 percent; the Radical Socialists, who had a record of about 75 percent; and the Social Radicals—many of whom joined a new group called the Gauche radicale in 1881—who had a record of about 60 percent.[125]

Gambetta's Republican Union, which was more politically advanced than Ferry's group and which won 204 seats in the elections of 1881, was the key to any successful forging of a reformist group. Clemenceau had essentially two choices: he could have modified his planks on constitutional and economic reform and tried to rally some of the Radicals to support Gambetta in an effort to achieve a limited program; or—and this was the more logical course, given his own ideals and the dislike for Gambetta on the part of many of his Radical colleagues— he could have sought to rally the advanced faction within the Republican Union to a more moderate Radical program. There were many within this advanced Gambettist faction who sympathized with Clemenceau's goals and who had voted with the Extreme Left on such issues as amnesty, prosecution of the officials involved in the *seize-mai* affair, abolishing the immovability of judges, protection of railroad workers, the ten-hour day, a liberal trade-union law, and revision of the constitution.[126]

The consistency between the views held by many Radicals and advanced Gambettists is evidenced by the fact that *La Justice* itself included voting records on these issues as a standard by which to judge candidates during the elections of 1881.[127] The possibility for greater cooperation between these two factions was especially present after Gambetta's death in December, 1882. Prost and Rosenzveig have demonstrated that a common admiration for Gambetta was the bond that held the Republican Union together; when he died, his followers dispersed toward the Right and the Left.[128]

In trying to fill the void left by Gambetta's death and to create a true Progressive party, Clemenceau envisioned a three-pronged strategy. This involved the imposition of unity and discipline on the parliamentary Radicals, effective organization at the local level that could produce winning candidates, and an organized drive to revise the constitutional laws of 1875. France's Senate constituted one of the prime obstacles to reform legislation. No matter how strong radicalism might become, experience had taught that the upper house, as the bastion of conservative and rural interests, could always frustrate the intentions of the Chamber of Deputies.[129] Nevertheless, Clemenceau's pursuit of this strategy displayed tactical and personal weaknesses that invariably resulted in failure.

First, although he saw the need for unity among the Radicals, his own personality traits tended to alienate others on the Extreme Left, a group described by Le Temps on November 6, 1881, as "an aggregate of more or less brilliant personalities, but without cohesion, without unity of views." He often isolated himself from others, confiding in and relying on only his closest followers such as Stéphen Pichon or Georges Laguerre. He could also be dictatorial when he perceived any betrayal of ideals on the part of fellow Radicals. He virtually excommunicated from the Extreme Left one of his own early collaborators on La Justice, Jules Roche, who disagreed with him on the matter of the election of judges.[130] Among Radicals such as Casse, Lockroy, Floquet, Barodet, and Naquet, there was respect for Clemenceau, but few close bonds with him. Jacques Kayser has correctly noted that, for Clemenceau, organization was "the very opposite of action, a paralysis," and that his radicalism "excluded all party life."[131]

It was suggested earlier that his embracing of a rigid idealism was the primary method by which he ensured failure. His inflexibility was just as apparent in his dealings with fellow Radicals as in his dealings with Opportunists. This tendency can be seen in his attempt to organize the Extreme Left after the elections of 1881. At this point the Extreme Left, as a formal group, numbered forty-six deputies, but this figure would have been larger had Clemenceau been willing to permit double inscriptions on the part of those Gambettists who wished to belong both to the Extreme Left and to the Republican Union. In broader terms the debate was over whether the Extreme Left would be "pure" in its adherence to principles. In a meeting of that group in December, Clemenceau argued that the Extreme Left should be closed and that one could not be a true Radical unless he were formally pledged to the programs of that faction. He won the argument, but the vote to reject double inscriptions was a close one—22 to 21—with such notable Radicals as Germain Casse, Madier de Montjau, Édouard Lockroy, Paul Ménard-Dorian, Alfred Naquet, Jean Turigny, Clovis Hughes, Émile Brelay, and Camille Laisant in the opposition.[132]

What was at stake was the choice between systematic opposition and the possibility of contracting electoral alliances in which advanced republicans could help to form cabinets. The result of Clemenceau's attitude was a split in Radical ranks and the creation of another group that called itself the Gauche radicale. It initially comprised about seventy-five members and included Floquet, Lockroy, Allain-Targé, and Casse—men who had worked with Clemenceau and respected his integrity, but who were unwilling to accept a political leadership that seemed to be doomed to failure. The leaders of the Gauche radicale stressed that while they would defend their principles, they would be willing, when necessary, to modify their views in the interest of achieving results. Creation of this new group was a blow to the Extreme Left, which, in addition, lost to it at least twelve deputies who had pledged themselves to the programs of the Extreme Left during the elections.[133]

Clemenceau's exclusion of moderate Radicals did not eliminate all dissent within the now-closed Extreme Left. As early as the fall of 1881 Le Temps noted the presence of two distinct factions that grouped themselves around Clemenceau or Madier de Montjau. The latter group advocated a more advanced economic program, although what this was remained vague and, as Le Temps indicated, ranged from Jacobin to collectivist

ideas.[134] The split became evident among Radical candidates
in Paris during the legislative elections of 1885. Clemenceau
consistently refused to assume the presidency of the Extreme
Left, even though in caucuses he was generally able to overrule
opposition viewpoints. When he was elected to this office in
1884, he sent a note to the outgoing president, Barodet, refusing
the post without giving any explanation for doing so. *Le Temps*
speculated that his refusal stemmed from a conflict between
his followers and de Montjau's.[135]

A second factor that undermined Clemenceau's hopes for
a reform party was his weakness with regard to local organization. In general, he viewed his political role only in the highest
moral terms, far removed from the mundane business of organization, visiting of constituents, and dispensing patronage. As
noted earlier, his Alliance socialiste républicaine in Montmartre
had only a brief existence. Outside of Paris, the departments of
the Mediterranean south offered the most realistic possibilities
for effective organization. The Pyrénées-Orientales, Aude,
Hérault, Gard, Bouches-du-Rhône, and the Var had strong
Radical movements dating back to 1848. In the 1880s these
areas were hard hit by the phylloxera, and their volatile population of wine growers and workers was generally more sus-
ceptible to new ideas than were other areas.[136] In both 1881
and 1885 these departments fell just behind Paris and the department of the Seine in their contribution to the Radical representation in the Chamber.

In 1881, southern Radicals looked to Clemenceau and Pelletan for leadership. In that year, Clemenceau campaigned at
Arles in the Bouches-du-Rhône and won a victory on the second
ballot. Although he kept his Paris seat, he visited the lower
south frequently over the next four years, and in 1885 he was
a candidate in the Var, delivering speeches at Draguignan and
in other towns in the region. Radical lists were completely victorious in the Var (as well as in the Bouches-du-Rhône and
Pyrénées-Orientales), with Clemenceau and Camille Raspail
winning seats along with two incumbents from Toulon, Honoré
Daumas and Auguste Maurel. But Clemenceau was not a true
méridional like the Radicals Ferdinand Théron or Émile Brousse,
who spent much of their time among constituents, defending

local interests and building a personal following. For all the enthusiasm that he generated when he traveled to the lower south, Clemenceau remained a "true Parisian" and a part of what Loubère has called the Paris "brain trust."[137]

The difficulties in local organization are related to another weakness. This was the absence of any forms of patronage by which Clemenceau could have built a larger following. There were a few cases in which he was able to dispense political favors, as that to Félix Granet, who lost to Clemenceau at Arles in 1881 and who apparently agreed to join the Extreme Left if Clemenceau would keep his seat in Paris, thus clearing the way for Granet's election at Arles. With Clemenceau's backing, Granet became minister of posts and telegraphs in 1886. But such examples were rare and reflected the inevitable weaknesses of a minority party that had few favors to hand out to the faithful. While some deputies enjoyed limited patronage powers by holding local offices after being elected to the Chamber—a practice known as *cumul*—Clemenceau condemned such methods as being an outrage to "public morality."[138]

A third area that illustrates Clemenceau's weakness in organization was the campaign to revise the constitutional laws of 1875. It is instructive to examine his activities in this regard, for they again show how his grasp of an issue was not equaled by the tactical ability to achieve his goals. He recognized that the constitutional laws formed a barrier to social legislation; yet, the manner in which he pursued revision of them indicated that he preferred failure to compromise.

Clemenceau favored the concept of integral, or total, revision of the constitution. At the cirque Fernando in April, 1880, he had described the present regime as "a Republic hemmed in by monarchist institutions." He believed that the presidency always posed the threat of a deadlock with Parliament; but it was the Senate, which was chosen by about forty-six thousand electors, that prevented France from having a true democracy. Not only did the Senate veto social legislation; its very existence meant that the lower house could never deal with reform on its own merit but had to deal with it on the basis of whether the Senate would approve it.[139] In 1881, he reminded the Chamber that in choosing the senators, a commune with fewer than one hundred electors had as much weight as Paris, Lyon, or Marseilles. The resistance of the Senate, he said, was the reason that men such as Gambetta had abandoned their earlier commitment to an income tax.[140]

Clemenceau would have liked to abolish the Senate or, if this proved impossible, to provide for its election by universal suffrage. A constituent assembly was necessary in order to effect such changes.[141] Gambetta, on the other hand, saw the Senate as a balancing force in French democracy and termed it "the great council of the departments." When he took office in the fall of 1881, he presented a modest plan for revision that included the proposal that senators for life who died or retired be replaced by new ones who had been elected by a national assembly. He also wished to reapportion the number of electors in municipal councils according to the population of the commune and to secure the financial and budgetary rights of the lower house.[142] In order to strengthen party discipline, he called for adoption of the *scrutin de liste*, or voting by list, a reform that Clemenceau had also urged.

Clemenceau viewed Gambetta's revisionist plans as insignificant and saw inclusion of the *scrutin de liste* at this point as a shift of emphasis from reform of the upper house to reform of the only body that represented the popular will. Nevertheless, Gambetta's plans represented a start in the right direction; furthermore, Clemenceau knew that the Senate would never agree to a meeting of a national assembly if the agenda included a proposal to abolish the upper house. Clemenceau stubbornly refused to take such realities into account. When Gambetta appeared before the Chamber in November, 1881, Clemenceau and Barodet attacked the new prime minister's idea of a "wisely limited" reform of the constitution and argued that a national assembly was a sovereign body that could discuss whatever it pleased. But a motion of the Extreme Left that there be a meeting of the National Assembly the following January with an open agenda received only 120 votes.[143]

Clemenceau was courting failure. Not once did he provide a convincing response to Gambetta's argument that the Senate would never agree to its own dismantling. In addition, Clemenceau himself later admitted that of the 557 deputies in the legislature of 1881, only 80 or so were in favor of the kind of integral revision that he wished.[144] He refused, however, to concede the necessity for compromise, and he continued to proclaim that Gambetta had betrayed his principles. There was a danger here, too, for his caustic attacks on the prime minister were bound to alienate many deputies in the Republican Union who sympathized with Clemenceau's political goals but who, like Scheurer-Kestner, idolized the hero of 1870 and were offended by Clemenceau's treatment of him.

On January 23, 1882, for example, Clemenceau led the attack on Gambetta in the parliamentary commission that had been formed to consider the cabinet's proposals for revision. He queried the prime minister about what the government would do if the National Assembly departed from a restricted agenda. Gambetta answered that such a move would be revolutionary and would therefore require the intervention of President Grévy. This response started the absurd rumor that Gambetta had threatened to stage a coup d'état.[145] By this point an incoherent majority, which included moderates as well as the political extremes, had solidified against the ministry. A conflict between parliamentary and ministerial autonomy, plus that localism that caused deputies to be fearful of any changes in the system under which they had just been elected, played a major part. On January the twenty-sixth, Gambetta failed to persuade a majority to agree to retain the *scrutin de liste* as part of his proposed constitutional revisions. The vote was 268 to 218 against the government, with Clemenceau and the Radicals being opposed to Gambetta. The entire ministry resigned, having lasted only seventy-seven days.[146]

It is possible that Gambetta's reforms with regard to both labor and the constitution might have laid the groundwork for the kind of more thorough reforms that Clemenceau wanted. But Gambetta's successors had even less of a chance; indeed, Gambetta's fall helped to clear the path for Ferry, who had little patience with Radical revisionist schemes. In early March, 1883, after the Chamber had again taken up Barodet's motion for revision, Ferry urged that the discussion be postponed for eighteen months, promising that he would take the matter up before the next renewal of one-third of the Senate. Clemenceau objected, arguing that delay would harden the resistance of the senators. He stressed that the worsening economic crisis demanded a quick solution to the problem of the Senate's vetoes of social measures: "I know that many of you are not afraid of social reforms. I know that a great number of you are disposed to begin them . . . but you need to know that your discussions are not academic ones." Ferry replied that social change was possible in cooperation with the Senate, and he reminded the Chamber that the upper house had approved the educational reforms, which he termed "the greatest reform accomplishment in this century." A motion of support for Ferry, which was presented by Sadi Carnot, then passed by 302 to 166 votes.[147]

It was at this point that Clemenceau made his most significant attempt to forge the reformist majority that would be essential if his aims were to be realized. This was the Ligue revisionniste, which he helped to create in March, 1883; its aim was to put pressure on Parliament and the cabinet in order to achieve meaningful revision of the constitution. The league proclaimed as its goal "the organization of the Republic on the basis of universal suffrage," and it began organizing local groups and distributing revisionist propaganda. The bylaws were drawn up by Pelletan, Barodet, and the Radical senator Labordère. These provided for an executive board consisting of a president, a bureau, and a central committee, which in turn was composed of deputies, revisionist senators, municipal councillors, and other local officials. The league's funds were to come from contributions.[148]

The initial response appeared promising. Within less than a month after the creation of the league, Clemenceau's newspaper was claiming the support of sixty-three deputies, five senators, sixteen Parisian and fifty-seven provincial newspapers, four municipal councils (including that of Toulouse), and assorted republican societies throughout the country. Pelletan reported to officials of the league in June that the organization was active in a third of the departments, especially in the lower south. Such writers as Charles Longuet compared the league with the earlier Anti-Corn League in England and expressed hope that the French organization would serve as a vehicle for future reform after revision of the constitution had been achieved.[149]

Even had the league held such promise, Clemenceau's activities were not calculated to help it realize its potential. He did participate in the campaign by the league to sponsor revisionist orators throughout France, his most important speech being delivered at the industrial city of Lille in May, 1883. Here, in the Lille Hippodrome, he made an address to five thousand people, in which he emphasized that the Senate was preventing the enactment of liberal trade-union laws that would "free these important associations from all shackles."[150] He reiterated this idea at the cirque Fernando in May, 1884. But speechmaking was no substitute for the firm political leadership that the league required in order to become an effective force for change. Clemenceau isolated himself from his own collaborators and generally refused to become personally involved in the organizational details of the league. One senses on his part a bizarre lassitude when confronted with specific challenges that had to be met in order to achieve any success.

He was not present, for example, at some of the most important meetings of the league, particularly the first ones at which decisions were made that eventually crippled the organization. These included the decision to eschew all electoral activity, to rely on contributions instead of dues, and to give almost complete autonomy to local groups. While Clemenceau did serve as a vice-president of the national bureau of the league and was a member of the executive committee of the organization in the Seine, most of the work was done by his old friend Laurent-Pichat, who served as president, and by the secretaries Pelletan, Laguerre, and Laisant. What was equally important, Clemenceau made few efforts to enlist the Gauche radicale, most of whose leaders, such as Floquet, remained skeptical about the league.[151]

Ferry, meanwhile, had convinced the Senate to agree to a meeting of a national assembly by promising that no effort would be made to alter the Senate's equality with the Chamber in legislative matters. His reforms, which he made known in March, 1884, were minimal, providing only for the gradual elimination of the senators for life. *La Justice* called his plans "laughable."[152] In June the Extreme Left presented a counter-proposal, which called for unlimited revision and a constituent assembly. The majority defeated it. On July 3 Ferry's proposals passed the Chamber by a vote of 403 to 106. Clemenceau, sensing the inevitability of defeat, nevertheless voted in favor of the proposal (unlike Madier de Montjau and a few other Radicals). His motive, he claimed, was "to see the senators more closely" and to show in open debate that they were the chief obstacle to reform in France.[153]

At a caucus of the Extreme Left on August 1, Clemenceau was hard pressed in persuading some Radicals such as Barodet not to resign should the upcoming National Assembly fail to call for a constituent assembly. There was agreement on the need for cooperation with the Gauche radicale, but Clemenceau's previous attitudes had done little to make such cooperation effective.[154] When the National Assembly finally did meet between August 4 and 13, all the Radical proposals for revision were voted down. On the last day of the congress at Versailles, Clemenceau made an impassioned speech in which he charged that in rejecting constitutional reform, the "bourgeois aristocracy" had failed to perceive even its own interest. "You have presented a spectacle," he told the senators and deputies, "that has no analogy in any other country of the world in any era."[155] Ferry's constitutional measures were then approved by a vote of 509 to 172.

The failure of constitutional reform and the implications of that failure for the social goals of the Radicals must be kept in mind when examining the subsequent crisis of Boulangism. For the first followers of Gen. Georges Boulanger were disaffected Radicals, and one of their primary goals was constitutional revision in which a more powerful executive could effect changes where squabbling and ineffectual parliamentarians had failed. This was not the kind of revisionism that Clemenceau had wanted; he had hoped for peaceful institutional changes that would facilitate the implementation of programs designed to strengthen the Republic. It was for this reason that he often portrayed the obstinance of the Senate on social legislation as "a permanent danger toward revolution."[156]

Clemenceau cannot bear all the blame for the absence of a

reform party in the early Third Republic. As we have seen, the obstacles to party discipline were formidable, and on the whole, the bourgeoisie that dominated French institutions tended to be unyielding in its social attitudes. But even this system offered certain possibilities had Clemenceau been willing to compromise his principles and to work in harness with others—if not with Gambetta in 1882, then at least with those of his followers who had often voted with the Extreme Left and who, after Gambetta's death, might have been convinced of the need for cooperation with many Radicals on social legislation. But they were unwilling to accept the kind of inflexible and erratic leadership that Clemenceau offered, which to them spelled impotence.

"I never look behind me, only before me," Clemenceau told someone in 1885.[157] Such is not the attitude of an individual who is trying to learn from experience in order to avoid defeat. Those traits that led him to inevitable failure were apparent to his contemporaries. The correspondent for the London *Times*, who thought that Clemenceau delivered the best speech at the Versailles Congress in 1884, observed that while his tactics made sense when his rival Gambetta was still alive, "the qualities of a statesman and ability in the selection of men and means" were now lacking in the leader of the Radicals. Since Gambetta's death, the correspondent wrote, "M. Clemenceau has only associated himself with causes which had little chance of success."[158] Although Clemenceau told an interviewer in 1885 that he was willing to take office, he stipulated that the Radical program would have to be accepted along with him.[159] The chances of Grévy's asking him to do so under such conditions, as he surely realized, were minimal. Clemenceau's habit of undermining his own potential in the political arena makes sense only when one grasps the idea that success in the form of ministerial office was not the standard against which he weighed his actions. First and foremost was his drive to satisfy deep-rooted psychological needs arising from his father identification. One of his chief satisfactions in politics, he told an audience in the Var during the elections of 1885, was *"the indescribable joy of serving the most noble cause without exhaustion and without self-interest."*[160]

Clemenceau's ambivalence toward success became even

more apparent after Radical gains in the elections of 1885 had strengthened his position in the Chamber of Deputies. The campaign was a difficult one for him, and the apparent revival of monarchism was a matter of deep concern. The republican majority, which had finally agreed in March of that year to adopt the *scrutin de liste* during the elections, entered the campaign divided and leaderless after Ferry's fall. Monarchists and Bonapartists, on the other hand, managed to forget their differences and joined together in a Conservative Union in order to present common electoral lists.

Clemenceau stood in both Paris and the Var. He had great difficulty in the capital in trying to control all the squabbling Radical factions. In June, 1885, he had called a meeting of Radical deputies at the lodge of the Grand Orient,* which resulted in a manifesto known as the Program of the Rue Cadet. Rejecting a "uniform formula" for republican views, this program attempted to rally all Radicals by means of a platform based on anticolonialism, constitutional and financial reform, separation of Church and state, reduction of military service and abolition of exemptions for seminary students, and laws for the protection of labor. Seventy-nine Radicals signed this manifesto.[161]

The studied vagueness of these points did not please such men as Madier de Montjau or Henri Rochefort, who subsequently formed rival electoral groups such as the Central Committee of Radical Socialist Republicans of the Seine. Clemenceau countered with a group called the Radical Socialist Departmental Committee. On September the twelfth this group published in *La Justice* a more detailed economic platform, fifteen of its twenty-five articles dealing with economic reform. By late September, representatives of the most important Radical newspapers in Paris had abandoned their efforts to unite the two factions, though nine of them, including *La Justice,* formed the Union of the Radical Socialist Press and published common electoral lists.[162]

---

* The Grand Orient was the most important headquarters of Freemasonry. Clemenceau was not a Freemason, though many Radicals were and though the Grand Orient was often the scene of meetings that he addressed.

In the Var, hecklings and disruptions of Clemenceau's meetings were often worse than those that he had encountered at the cirque Fernando. The situation became worse after his opponents dredged up his old Bordeaux speech of 1871, in which he had advocated the separation of Corsica from France. At the little town of Dole on September 17 the Opportunist mayor prevented him from speaking in the town hall, and in other places, fights often broke out during and after his speeches. Clemenceau usually countered with humor and, according to the reports to *La Justice,* managed to win over the crowds.[163]

The first balloting took place on October 4. The votes indicated that republicans were facing a disaster. The Rightist coalition received 100,000 more votes than the republicans, raising the number of conservative seats in the Chamber from 80 to 180. The republicans, including the Radicals, captured only 138 seats. In the Var, the Radical list headed by Clemenceau outdistanced Opportunist and conservative lists; but lacking an absolute majority, he was forced into a second balloting, which was scheduled for October 18. The same was true in Paris, where he got 202,543 votes, which was short of an absolute majority. He was bitter over the initial monarchist triumph, for which he blamed the Tonkin adventure, but he realized that now was not the time for recriminations. "All divisions disappear in face of the common enemy," he wrote in *La Justice.*[164] He urged that republican candidates step aside in favor of other republicans who had won more votes on the first ballot.

Such cooperation between moderates and Radicals paid off on the second ballot. The Right gained only 22 additional seats, while republicans of all shades went from 138 seats to 374. After by-elections a few months later, and after several monarchists had been denied seats in contested areas, the final composition of the Chamber showed 183 on the Right, 279 moderate or Opportunist republicans in the Center and Left-Center, and 122 Radicals, including both the Extreme Left and the Gauche radicale, the latter with about 40 members.

Clemenceau won in both Paris and the Var and elected to take his seat for the latter. By choosing the Var, he was ridding himself of the problem of an increasingly strong Socialist opposition in Montmartre, which promised to make life difficult for any noncollectivist representative. His change in constituency, however, did not indicate any lessening of his parliamentary influence. The increase in seats for both parliamentary extremes meant that his power in the lower house would have to be dealt with by any cabinet. In November the diplomat Paul Cambon wrote to a friend that "everyone trembles before Clemenceau" and that if the Radical leader so much as lifted his finger, "the débâcle will be almost immediate."[165]

Our study will now focus on Clemenceau's activities between 1885 and 1889 and will attempt to show how those psychological drives that had previously inhibited and weakened him became, under conditions that enhanced the possibility of success, more pronounced than ever.

FOUR

Suffering & Expiation
1885-1893

CLEMENCEAU AGAINST HIMSELF

Watson has observed that after the elections of 1885, Clemenceau's career was marked by a new moderation. His speeches decreased in number, and his actions lacked the vehemence that had characterized his earlier assaults on the Opportunists. Watson offers a political explanation for this change: Clemenceau was seeking a place in government, knowing that because of a reduction in their numbers, the Opportunists would be forced into coalitions with either the Left or the Right.[1]

In this chapter I will suggest a different thesis in trying to explain this change in Clemenceau: first, that his inactivity on the political front signified a desire, not to achieve a ministerial position, but to avoid it; second, that his quiescence denoted not only a new psychological reaction against his role as the defender of his father's ideals but also a recurrence of the cycle of fatigue, depression, and withdrawal that had been evident in 1865 and again in 1877; and finally, that both his private and public behavior were symptomatic of what Piers and Singer have termed "guilt-engendered activity,"[2] whose unconscious aim was self-punishment for his inability to throw off his father identification. In particular, throughout the Boulangist and Panama affairs, Clemenceau's behavior showed a bizarre tendency to pursue courses of action that enhanced his vulnerability to defeat.

Psychologically, through punishment it was possible for Clemenceau to expiate the guilt that he felt toward himself; but as Piers and Singer have stressed, the process is a difficult one that often produces frustration and rage, which in turn feed more guilt into the system. Despite all his frenetic efforts on behalf of his father's ideals, and despite the new parliamentary power that he enjoyed as a result of the Radicals' electoral gains, the Clemenceau of 1885 was an increasingly bitter man. Middle-aged, balding, slightly overweight, still exceptionally nervous, he had yet to achieve the sense of his own identity and the capacity for true intimacy with others that he had desperately craved as a youth. Emotionally, he tended to remain fixated at an earlier developmental level, unable to achieve what Erikson has termed "ego integrity."[3]

Below are examined some of the patterns of Clemenceau's political conduct between 1885 and 1893 that lend support to the theory of guilt and punishment as the dominant drives in his unconscious motivation. First, it will be helpful to note those forces in the mid 1880s that were creating intensified psychological strains in his life and that aid us in understanding the self-restrictive patterns of his political conduct. One of these forces grew out of his relationships with the financier Cornélius Herz. The other involved his private life and the collapse of his marriage.

Clemenceau had met Herz in the early 1880s through the editor of *Le Temps,* Adrien Hébrard. Born of Jewish parents in Bavaria in 1845, Herz had studied medicine in the United States and had returned to France to serve as a medical officer during the Franco-Prussian War. Later he had struck it rich in the developing electrical and telephone industries; he had also invested in Algerian real estate with such financiers as the Baron Jacques de Reinach. A perpetual schemer, Herz began developing friendships in the political world that could serve his own interests. His influence helped him to climb the ranks in the Legion of Honor: a chevalier in 1879, an officer in 1881, a commander in 1883, and a grand officer in 1886.

Clemenceau developed a close personal relationship with Herz, often entertaining him in his home, even entrusting the upbringing of his children to him at the time of his tour of the cholera-stricken areas around Marseilles in 1884. In addition, Herz took on Clemenceau's younger brother Paul as a protégé in the electrical industry. There is no question but that Clemenceau received money from Herz for the support of *La Justice.*

As Clemenceau told Georges Wormser in a conversation in 1927, "Why should I have refused his funds? They were for a useful struggle. Moreover, I completely paid him back."[4] How much money he received is not known. The journalist Henri Rochefort claimed that Herz told him that he had given Clemenceau between three million and four million francs.[5] Even if one grants the unreliability of Rochefort's testimony, the amount must have been significant. Between 1881 and 1883 La Justice survived only because of Herz's advances. Clemenceau then consolidated his loans, ceding to Herz half the shares in the newspaper. But in April of 1885 Clemenceau finally began to realize that Herz's well-known dealings might compromise him. By borrowing from friends, he managed to buy back Herz's shares, though it plunged him into debt to do so.

The matter was not to end here, however. For Herz was also friendly with both Georges Boulanger and the politician Félix Granet who, as we have seen, apparently promised Clemenceau that he would join the Extreme Left in exchange for the Arles seat in 1881. Granet, who became minister of posts and telegraphs in 1886, looked with favor on Herz's ambition to acquire a monopoly over the Parisian telephone system. In a parliamentary commission, however, Clemenceau voted against the concession, which the Council of Ministers finally rejected. Nevertheless, newspapers were already raising questions on the Clemenceau-Herz-Granet relationship, and on December 4, 1886, Clemenceau inserted the following statement in La Justice:

> M. Herz is not a *commanditaire* of La Justice. He was a shareholder from 26 February 1883 to 15 April 1885. On February 26, 1883, M. Clemenceau ceded to him half of the paid-up shares in payment of sums put in by him from 31 March 1881 to 16 June 1883.
>
> On 15 April 1885 M. Clemenceau bought back M. Herz's shares.
>
> M. Clemenceau has never recommended M. Herz to any minister, nor to any person for any transaction or any favor.
>
> Finally, in the matter of the telephones, M. Clemenceau rejected, by his vote in the budget commission, the proposal for a concession.

There was nothing unusual in the fact that a newspaper of small circulation had to depend on outside funds. Nor, contrary to what his enemies were to charge during the Panama affair, was Clemenceau guilty of any wrongdoing in accepting Herz's money. Yet, the above disclaimer did not tell everything about his relationship with the financier. Herz lost at least two hundred thousand francs in supporting *La Justice,* and he remained banker for the newspaper until September, 1886. Even after the severing of their business relations, Clemenceau occasionally saw Herz, for example, in London in 1891 when he dined with him and Rochefort.[6] Was the fatal flaw in Clemenceau's character only that he was a poor judge of other men? The patterns of his private and political relations after 1885—with Herz, Boulanger, Granet, at times even with such irresponsible people as Henri Rochefort and Paul Déroulède—suggest something more. This was Clemenceau's strange willingness to associate with those who could only weaken him and whose own ideals proved to be the antithesis of those to which he had devoted his life.

Aside from Herz and the financial problems of *La Justice,* there was another factor that both intensified the strain in Clemenceau's life and made this man of principle vulnerable in the eyes of Frenchmen. That was his private life, about which little is known and which his disciple-biographers have jealously protected. His father appears to have remained the one great emotional cathexis of his life, and he often visited him at L'Aubraie. In his advanced years, Benjamin had grown more misanthropic and solitary than ever; and his wife spent much of her time away from home, taking care of their daughter Adrienne.[7] According to Clemenceau's son Michel (who as a child supposedly had serious emotional problems of his own and who had a stormy relationship with his father in later years), Benjamin "divided his time between his library, his stables, and his garden. He did not modify his attitude of reserve except when his son Georges was there. Then there were great conversations on great subjects."[8] This impression is confirmed by Gustave Geffroy, who visited L'Aubraie with Clemenceau in 1882. He was struck by the old man's "fixed character" and his "persistent fervor for the goddesses of Liberty and Justice," but he also noted that "the totality of his judgments on humanity was that of a solitary man who suffered from the disparity between reality and the ideal."[9]

Geffroy believed that Benjamin had given to his son a love for the most noble ideals of the human elite; but others viewed the Clemenceau of the 1880s as a callow and irresponsible politician, a habitué of the Opéra, who, though married, spent his evenings in the company of his mistress Léonide Leblanc, who was perceived to have great influence over him.[10] One of his grandsons relates that he led an active night life; and family friends constantly conveyed to his wife the names of his latest lovers. As was noted earlier, Mary had endured this situation for years. Then, according to some accounts, in the early 1890s she began seeing a young man, and Clemenceau discovered them together. One story that circulated at the time, which was later related by Edmond de Goncourt, claimed that the suspicious Clemenceau, on the advice of one of his daughters, had had Mary's lover followed in order to catch them together.[11]

Despite his own infidelities, Clemenceau flew into a rage and managed to get a divorce within days. Even this was not enough to appease his anger. His grandson tells us that because French law was in his favor, he had her threatened with imprisonment and finally had her escorted by two policemen to Boulogne-sur-Mer, where she was put aboard a ship bound for Boston. At home he packed her belongings in a trunk and sent them to her sister. He took a hammer and smashed a marble statue of Mary that he had kept in his study, and he destroyed everything else that reminded him of her, including photographs and paintings.[12] Was it only wounded vanity that produced this reaction? The full story will never be known. But it is possible that his rage fed on an even deeper source of bitterness, for the total and irrevocable failure of his marriage may have unconsciously symbolized the total and irrevocable failure of his one effort to assert ego autonomy during his psychosocial moratorium in America, of which the marriage had been the chief handiwork.

The above sources of tension interacted with Clemenceau's longstanding identity conflicts and help us in understanding a larger pattern of self-defeating drives that were evident in his political activities after the victories of the Radicals in 1885. Had he truly been interested in achieving a place in government, he would have been compelled to assuage the doubts of moderates (as well as those of President Grévy) by evincing a willingness to compromise his principles, especially on the issues of constitutional revision and the separation of Church and state. He also needed to demonstrate responsible statesmanship in directing the Radicals, particularly during the third Freycinet ministry, between January and December of 1886. An examination of the evidence shows that Clemenceau followed precisely the opposite course of action.

Clemenceau was certainly aware of his increased influence, and he hoped to exercise it in some manner. He assumed too (as his young lieutenant Stéphen Pichon expressed it on December 31, 1885, in *La Justice*) that the moderates would never dare form an alliance with the Right and that, thus, no new ministry was possible without the cooperation of the Radicals. Yet, when Freycinet was attempting to form a new cabinet after the resignation of Brisson in December, 1885, Clemenceau made no systematic effort to acquire a ministerial position. He did meet privately with Freycinet in early January of 1886; and while *La Justice* denied that negotiations had faltered because of Clemenceau's refusal to compromise his program, he had made it clear in the past that he would not accept office unless his program were accepted with him.[13] An interview that he gave shortly after the fall of Ferry throws some light on his attitude in this regard: "Surely I cannot say, 'take me,' but I have always declared my readiness to accept office. A politician in opposition who is not ready to accept office, if offered it, is not a serious man. I do not refuse, for my cabinet would be speedily formed; *but my programme, which is no secret, would of course have to be accepted with me.*"[14]

After a decade in Parliament, Clemenceau was certainly aware that the moderate republicans would never be willing to accept the total Radical program. He must have been equally aware of the glee with which many of his enemies read a satirical pamphlet entitled *Le Ministère Clemenceau,* published in 1885 by the Opportunist deputy Joseph Reinach, which described, tongue in cheek, an imaginary Clemenceau ministry that manages to change nothing.[15] Moreover, Clemenceau's stance of intransigent opposition was not motivated by any larger strategy by which he hoped to achieve either a cabinet post for himself or even a workable coalition. During each of the five cabinet crises in the legislature of 1885–89 he failed to pursue those political possibilities that were available, and in general, he offered little constructive counsel to Radical caucuses. The absence of effective and consistent leadership on his part is especially noticeable during the political debates on the Radical Left that followed each cabinet turnover.

The collaboration of Radicals and moderates on the second ballot in 1885 had produced a republican majority of 380, which included, on the Left, roughly 120 Radicals (80 in the Extreme Left and 40 in the Gauche radicale) plus a dozen or so independents and Socialists. The old majority in the previous legislature had reconstituted itself as the Union des gauches, which numbered around 200, but this group was far from united and contained an advanced faction whose support was essential for the cabinets of René Goblet (December, 1886, to May, 1887) and Charles Floquet (April, 1888, to February, 1889). These two ministries had a Radical orientation; and in the votes of confidence that eventually toppled them, both enjoyed a significant degree of support from the Union des gauches.[16]

As we have seen, however, in his earlier relations with the advanced Gambettists, Clemenceau repeatedly bungled the opportunities to provide direction to the fragmented republican Left. Isolated and psychologically incapable of using flexible tactics that might compromise his ideals, he showed little openness toward moderates or even toward many fellow Radicals. After the collapse of the Rightist-backed cabinet of Maurice Rouvier in November, 1887, the Radical deputy for the Gard, Fernand Crémieux, asked Clemenceau, during a caucus of the Extreme Left, if he did not think it advisable to call a general meeting of all Radicals in order to decide on a course of action. Clemenceau opposed the idea.[17] To Goblet, who in a parliamentary session of March 30, 1888, had warned that Pelletan's move for immediate debate on constitutional revision would result in the fall of P. E. Tirard's cabinet, Clemenceau responded: "You are turning your back on the true principles of the Republic, and you are asking us to turn our backs with you. We will never do it!"[18] *Le Temps* quoted one of Clemenceau's frustrated supporters as saying: "I am beginning to believe that Clemenceau does not want a majority in the Chamber."[19] But it is in Clemenceau's role during the third Freycinet ministry of 1886 that one sees this pattern of self-defeating drives most clearly, for here the leader of the Radicals chose to exercise his influence through Gen. Georges Boulanger, whose brief political career almost ruined Clemenceau's life and severely undermined the strength of early French radicalism.

Boulangism was initially a movement of the Left, a protest against the failure of the Opportunist Republic to confront the economic problems of the 1880s. Even after certain forces of the Right sought to exploit the general for their own ends, key elements in the Boulangist program continued to be formulated by a group of Radicals.[20] As early as 1882 *La Justice* had begun publishing biographical sketches and excerpts from the speeches of Boulanger, who claimed to be a republican and who had the ability, which was sadly lacking among the politicians of the Republic, of stirring the imagination of his countrymen.[21] A graduate of Saint-Cyr, he had seen action in Italy, Africa, and Cochin-China and had been wounded early in the war against Prussia. By 1880, with the help of the Orleanist prince, the duc d'Aumale, he had become the youngest brigadier general in the army. He renounced his Catholic and conservative background; and when he became the director of infantry two years later and championed reforms for the common soldier, his reputation among Radicals increased. In January of 1886 he became minister of war in Freycinet's new cabinet. Two other radicals, both of whom were Clemenceau's friends, were also included: Granet as minister of posts and telegraphs and Lockroy as minister of commerce and industry.

While Freycinet has denied in his memoirs that he took on Boulanger as the price of support from the Radicals, many observers at the time viewed the new minister of war as Clemenceau's puppet.[22] Clemenceau was often seen at the Ministry of War, and there were messengers, such as a certain Lieutenant Jubault, who constantly scurried back and forth between the ministry and Clemenceau's newspaper office.[23] It is significant

to note that not once during the later passion of the anti-
Boulangist campaign did Clemenceau deny the widespread
charge that it was he who had been the general's most powerful
backer. One thing is clear: the leader of the Radicals at first
gave full support to the new minister of war and hoped to use
him for his own purposes. His motives in doing so have never
been completely clear. Some contemporaries believed that he
was trying, as Gambetta had done, to gain a personal following
in the army.[24] The evidence indicates, however, that Clemenceau hoped to use Boulanger as a tool in order to implement
republican principles in the army, which he believed was still
monarchist in outlook. Specifically, in 1886 Clemenceau was
concerned with two aspects of army reform.

The first one involved the officer corps, whose personnel
had not been purged during the military reorganization measures of the early 1870s.[25] Although the army had since accepted
its role of being the instrument of the regime in power, Clemenceau believed that certain monarchist generals had been
ready to carry out a coup d'état in 1877. Furthermore, for a
long time he had believed that republican officers were often
being bypassed for promotions. In supporting the Senate candidacy of a former colonel named Labordère, who had publicly
protested against orders that he had received at Limoges during
the *seize-mai* affair—orders that supposedly implied a coup—
Clemenceau emphasized that military discipline must be based
on "absolute respect for law."[26]

The second aspect concerned a proposed law that would
have reduced the term of service from five to three years and
would have eliminated exemptions for teachers and students of
the priesthood. The measure, which had been proposed first by
the Radical Camille Laisant in 1876, had gained support only
after the Tunisian expedition.[27] By 1885 it had passed a second
reading in the Chamber. Clemenceau was especially anxious to
eliminate exemptions for students of the priesthood, believing
that his ideal of the army as the democratic instrument of the
Republic was impossible so long as certain privileged classes
were excused from duty. "Equality of sacrifice for *la patrie*,"
he told the Chamber in 1887, "will result in making ourselves
stronger against the enemy." He told the deputies: "We wish

to give to the national army its maximum power. . . . We do not have the right to ask the father of a family to give up his son as long as he can answer back, 'I give my son to *la patrie,* I send him into battle to defend national soil, but why is my neighbor's son, who wears the habit of a seminarist, exempt from military service?' "[28]

Again, one is faced with the contradiction between Clemenceau's ideals, which had merit, and the methods that he employed in order to achieve them. For one thing, any sentiments that he entertained regarding his ability to control the flamboyant young general should have been dispelled by the fact that Boulanger was acquiring a reputation as a troublemaker. In 1884, for example, Boulanger, as commander of the army in Tunisia, had locked horns with the civilian resident, Paul Cambon. The conflict stemmed from the general's foolish order of the day, which instructed his men to use arms in any conflicts with foreigners. By 1885 both men were back in Paris plotting against each other, Boulanger relating his version of the squabble to political friends such as Granet, Naquet, and Clemenceau. Furthermore, there is evidence that Clemenceau recognized Boulanger's superficiality from the start. He did tell Rochefort that Boulanger was "the only truly Radical republican general in the army."[29] At the same time, however, he was privately contemptuous of the officer's intellectual abilities and mockingly called him "Boul-Boul" behind his back. In a letter of 1885 Cambon noted that Clemenceau had referred to his protégé as a *farceur,* or joker.[30] Again, only by reference to Clemenceau's psychological tendency to create failure situations for himself may one fully understand why he was willing to entrust both his reputation and his most sacred ideals to the hands of a "joker," even given any naïve calculation on his part that he could control him.

Clemenceau soon discovered, for example, that his influence mattered little on issues involving the rights of labor. In late January, 1886, a strike broke out at Decazeville, and the miners murdered one of the more hated company engineers. The Freycinet government ordered in troops, despite Clemenceau's warnings that he could not support a cabinet whose actions threatened "to massacre citizens." But Boulanger saved the day for the ministry (and won applause from many Radicals) when an interpellation on Decazeville reached the floor on March 13. He assured everyone that keeping order was his only concern: "Perhaps, at this very moment, each soldier is sharing his soup and bread ration with a miner."[31]

Clemenceau refrained for the moment from further attacks on Freycinet, hoping that the military reforms that had been initiated by the new minister of war could be carried out. During the first half of 1886 Boulanger prepared a total of 217 proposals for military reform. In order to facilitate this more thorough plan of reorganization, President Grévy withdrew from the Senate agenda the bill that would have reduced the term of military service to three years (it was passed only in 1889, with the exemptions retained, after a long battle between the Chamber and the Senate).[32] In the meantime, Clemenceau hoped that his protégé could attack the problem of royalist influence in the army. He supported Boulanger when the latter removed from Tours a royalist regimental commander.[33] This act touched on the larger question of the royal princes still living in France, who, at least in Clemenceau's mind, were plotting a restoration.

The chance to strike at them came in May of 1886, when the comte de Paris gave an extravagant reception in Paris for his daughter, who had just become engaged to the crown prince of Portugal. Using the reception as an excuse, the Radicals pressured Freycinet to bring in a bill to expel from France all claimants to the throne. The law became effective in June, and in the Chamber debates that followed, the Right pictured Clemenceau as being the moving force behind the bill and taunted him over his past defense of liberty for all. He answered that the bill had "stripped away the mask" and that now one could be aligned only to the cause either of the Republic or of the monarchy.[34] Boulanger began applying the measure to the officer corps and to those who already held commissions, which included his old mentor, the duc d'Aumale. On July 13 Rightist speakers in the Chamber reminded Boulanger that the duc d'Aumale had helped him to get his promotion. Boulanger denied this, but during the next few days the press published some of his earlier letters of appreciation to d'Aumale.

Clemenceau remained silent about these letters, his news-paper publishing them without comment on August 4. But the general's increasing popularity in the country, and especially among some prominent Radicals, concerned him. There was Camille Laisant, who was a graduate of the École Polytechnique, and Ferdinand-Camille Dreyfus of *La Lanterne*. Others in-cluded Clemenceau's own disciple Georges Laguerre and Alfred Naquet, who was the author of the divorce law of 1883. In 1886 these men had begun to nurse schemes that they hoped the general would help them to realize. On one occasion at Durand's Restaurant (Clemenceau, Naquet, Granet, Laguerre, Laisant, and others sometimes dined there with the general), Naquet spent the evening beside Boulanger, berating the social failures of the Republic. At one point Naquet suggested that a coup might be necessary. That remark stung Clemenceau: "The Republic is very sick and I certainly don't like its diet," he an-swered, "but the eventualities that you consider, Naquet, would be frightful."[35]

Two additional figures often joined this group, though what they had in common with the Radicals was little more than a hatred for the Opportunists. One was Paul Déroulède, founder of the League of Patriots. The other was the journalist Henri Rochefort, who saw in Boulanger a tool against the system that he hated. In his memoirs, Rochefort claims that it was Clemen-ceau who acted as intermediary between him and Boulanger, after Rochefort had written an article criticizing the minister of war for receiving reactionary deputies and army officers.[36]

Freycinet managed to withstand the attacks of the Right with regard to Boulanger's indiscretions. But by the fall of 1886 Freycinet was in trouble with the Radicals, whose support was essential if his ministry were to survive. The problem in-volved a projected deficit in the next year's budget and the opposition of the minister of finance, Sadi Carnot, to a plan that had been advocated by the Budget Commission, of which Clemenceau was a member, for an income tax and a raising of taxes on alcohol. In an unexpected development on December 3 the Radicals joined the Right in supporting a proposal to abolish subprefects, which passed by a vote of 262 to 249. Frey-cinet resigned, despite Grévy's belief that the vote had been based on a misunderstanding and that Freycinet should continue in office.[37]

While condemning Freycinet's failure to enact reforms, Clemenceau admitted that the overthrow of his ministry had not been intended.[38] Nevertheless, he opposed those in both the Extreme Left and the Gauche radicale who wanted a reconciliation with Freycinet. In a meeting of both groups on December 6 he argued that "our role is finished," and in a separate meeting of the Extreme Left he told his colleagues that they should wait until a new ministry had been formed before deciding what to do.[39] In the meantime, Grévy had prevailed upon René Goblet to form a cabinet, after Floquet had rejected an offer to do so despite Clemenceau's urging.[40] Since Goblet had the reputation of being a moderate Radical and since Boulanger was retained as minister of war, the new cabinet was temporarily safe from Radical attacks.

Clemenceau, however, was exploiting Radical strength in Parliament with less skill than was necessary in order to achieve any legislative goals. He lacked long-range plans either for making himself acceptable for office or for creating a coalition that could bargain for such measures as an income tax or military reform. Two days after Goblet and his new cabinet appeared before the Chamber, Clemenceau complained that the real reason for the ministerial crisis had been that no one knew how to "elicit from the national representation in this assembly a governmental majority." But this was only blaming others for what was in part a result of his own bungling. By March 30, failing to see immediate reforms on Goblet's part, he was reverting to earlier patterns of political behavior: "The day you win the confidence of the Right you will lose ours," he told Goblet, "there can be no compromise between them and us, either on political matters or the social question."[41]

At the same time, any influence that Clemenceau had had over the minister of war was disappearing, although the liability of his initial sponsorship remained. In early 1887 France experienced a war scare with Germany over the latter's arrest of a frontier official named Schnaebele. Boulanger argued for sending an ultimatum to Germany, which Grévy opposed, and wisely so, since the crisis died down after Bismarck ordered that Schnae-

bele be released. Clemenceau knew that France was not prepared for war with Germany, as he had often made clear during
the Tonkin debates. Furthermore, the general's brashness could
not fail to upset him. It was during this crisis that Clemenceau
is supposed to have coined his famous aphorism, "War is too
important to be left to the generals."[42]

Moderates and conservatives were even more agitated by
Boulanger's behavior. Grévy insisted on getting rid of Boulanger, but the moderates realized that in order not to make him
a martyr, the entire Goblet cabinet would have to go. In one of
the stranger episodes of this affair, Ferry and others who were
in league with the baron de Mackau, president of the Union
of the Right, plotted to get a new cabinet led by the moderate
Maurice Rouvier. Rouvier planned to pay for Rightist support
by easing up on anticlerical policies. During a budgetary
squabble on May 18 the Goblet ministry fell under an attack
by moderates and conservatives; Clemenceau and about half
the members of the Extreme Left also voted against Goblet,
thus unwittingly aiding the designs of both Grévy and Ferry.[43]
By the thirtieth, Rouvier was in office, his cabinet being the first
in the history of the Republic in which republicans looked to
the Right for support. The new ministry assigned Boulanger to
a remote command in Clérmont-Ferrand, hoping that he would
soon be forgotten.

Clemenceau was indignant about the perfidy of a republican cabinet that rested on monarchist support. Learning that
General Ferron—a man whose career he had furthered in cooperation with Boulanger—was taking over the war ministry,
he refused to shake hands with him outside the Chamber of
Deputies. "Albe has named you," he said, taking a line from
Corneille, "I don't know you any more. . . . Twenty times I've
heard you say that the *Tonkinois* were miserable men, and here
you are their associate."[44] On May 31 *La Justice* published
Boulanger's last order of the day, in which he thanked his supporters and promised "to set an example of this dual military
and republican discipline." Rochefort, meanwhile, was waging
a campaign to have the general retained in the Rouvier government, and Déroulède was organizing a demonstration to prevent
Boulanger from leaving Paris. At the Gare de Lyon on the

evening of July 8, some twenty thousand of the general's supporters gathered at the station, blocking the tracks, and Boulanger had to take an alternate route.

Three days later a subdued Clemenceau rose in the Chamber and spoke in such a low voice that the deputies had to ask
him to repeat his words: "Very well, yes! This popularity has
come too fast for someone who likes noise too much, or, to be
more just, who does not elude it enough." For the first time,
France heard the expression "Boulanger question" from the
mouth of the man who had been his strongest backer. He
condemned the mob scenes at the Gare de Lyon, but he had
a ready explanation for the behavior of the Parisians: "I say
that this popularity was served by the events in Alsace-Lorraine.
. . . The German press systematically attacked General Boulanger . . . . in such a way that some superficial spirits saw in
him the incarnation of *la patrie*. Finally, the Right, out of spite
because of the decision taken against the Orleanist princes,
attacked him with such extreme violence that many who witnessed him being attacked systematically by the enemies of the
Republic saw in him the incarnation of the Republic." Boulanger had brought élan to the army and had introduced reforms
for which the nation hungered. The glory bestowed on Boulanger would fall instead on Parliament if it were willing to
embark on a program of reform.[45]

Clemenceau's speech, which was one of several delivered
by Radicals during an interpellation of Rouvier, did not end his
relations with the general. He still referred to him as his friend,
and shortly afterwards the two effected a temporary reconciliation. Clemenceau's failure to effect a clean and open break
with Boulanger at this point, especially after he had seen firm
evidence of the general's character, was a serious political error.
But it was consistent with those psychological drives that often
seemed to lead Clemenceau into untenable situations, particularly those in which he occupied the role of a sufferer who, in
the uncompromising defense of ideals, is caught between two
extremes. For moderates regarded him, and could not help but
continue to regard him, as the maker of Boulanger; the view of
some contemporaries that the whole affair had begun to erode
Clemenceau's position as an occult power in Parliament was

not without foundation.[46] Equally important was the attitude of men such as Déroulède and even Clemenceau's disciple Georges Laguerre, who later could not forgive him for what they believed was a betrayal of their hero.

THE APOGEE OF BOULANGISM AND
THE WEAKENING OF CLEMENCEAU'S INFLUENCE

The two years that followed Boulanger's ouster as minister of war witnessed the growth and collapse of the movement that bears his name. The following section will examine Clemenceau's conduct during the unfolding of the crisis and will show that despite his growing hatred for Boulanger and the threat that he posed to the Republic, Clemenceau's actions on behalf of his own reputation and career were aimed less toward achieving personal success as the defender of his father's ideals than toward enhancing his own role as a sufferer. To a taunt from the benches following Boulanger's electoral victory in Paris in January, 1889, Clemenceau replied: "I ask to be counted among the defeated. I claim my place among those who have suffered this glorious defeat."[47] The damage that was dealt to Clemenceau's prestige and the split that Boulangism produced in the highest circles of Radical leadership figure among the most significant causes for the weakening of early French radicalism. Equally relevant was the fact that as a protest movement against the social failures of the Republic, Boulangism attracted the support of many disillusioned citizens who had once supported the Radicals and who, after Boulanger's eclipse, would look increasingly to socialism.[48]

Soon after Boulanger had departed from office, a scandal erupted in Paris that discredited the parliamentary regime and hence worked in his favor. The scandal involved President Grévy's son-in-law, Daniel Wilson, who, after his marriage to the president's daughter, had established a business office at the Élysée to oversee his newspaper interests. Wilson, who was also a member of the anti-Opportunist Left in the Chamber of Deputies, had long bought favors by means of Legion of Honor decorations. But it was only after a parliamentary investigation of corruption in government had exposed his misdeeds in early November, 1887, that a public outcry ensued.

Clemenceau realized that the scandal provided a chance to destroy Rouvier's conservative coalition. He feared, however, that the Right would use the scandal to discredit the Republic. That was why he suggested to his old enemy Ferry that republicans should not allow divisions among themselves to redound to monarchist credit. His remark was published in the press, and Rochefort charged that it was evidence of a plot to cover up official graft. Clemenceau denied this in his newspaper.[49] As if to prove his point, he took Rouvier to task in the Chamber on November 19, admitting that he should have spoken up earlier since the prestige of the Republic was at stake. He noted that newspapers were preoccupied with the affair and that the public was asking whether any citizen was above the law. He urged a full and open discussion. Rouvier, pointing to pressing financial matters, requested a delay. But the majority, fearing that it would be compromised by a vote of confidence, supported Clemenceau. Rouvier and his cabinet thereupon resigned.[50]

Grévy refused to disassociate himself from Wilson, and he tried to persuade Freycinet and then Goblet to form a new ministry. The latter urged him to invite Clemenceau to do so. Grévy, who desperately wanted to stay in office, finally agreed. But the leader of the Radicals had exhibited little interest in becoming prime minister under these circumstances. To the defeated Rouvier he had said that the only solution to the crisis was for Grévy to "give his resignation and admit that he does not associate himself in any way with the acts of his son-in-law."[51] Nevertheless, on November 21, for the first time in his career, Clemenceau was called to the Élysée. Grévy made his offer, but Clemenceau answered that the present crisis was a governmental rather than a ministerial one. Grévy became emotional, pounding his fist on the table and even offering Clemenceau a free hand in the selection of both a cabinet and a program. Clemenceau suggested, instead, that another meeting be held, with himself, Grévy, Floquet, Freycinet, and Goblet in attendance. Together they would work out an arrangement in which the president could leave office with dignity. For the moment, Grévy agreed.

That evening the deputies told him what the "honorable conditions" of his retirement would be: Grévy would resign and would go out with the praise of Parliament, while the Chamber would try to end any further prosecution of Wilson. Still Grévy hesitated, and the next day he tried to persuade Brisson and then Ribot to form cabinets, but to no avail. He was bitter over Clemenceau's refusal: "He'd better watch out. . . . If he makes me leave and Ferry succeeds me, what will he have gained with the change?"[52]

One may sympathize with Clemenceau's reluctance to assume office under such conditions. His actions during the next few days, however, make it doubtful that he wished to be a minister under any circumstances. Certainly he was waking up to the danger of a Ferry presidency; Clemenceau detested *le Tonkinois,* and he also believed that a Ferry election might result in an outbreak of violence in Paris.[53] But the evidence does not suggest that in opposing Ferry, he was aiming toward a replacement who would look more favorably on a Clemenceau ministry. In a series of meetings that began on November 28 at the lodge of the Grand Orient in Paris, the Radical leadership attempted to forge a strategy to deal with the crisis. In these meetings one sees several traits in Clemenceau's behavior that betray a fundamental ambivalence with regard to the matter of proving himself to be a serious contender for power. One was his inability to provide constructive leadership, particularly in the matter of electing a president. Another was his willingness, however reluctant at first, to treat with such individuals as Rochefort and Déroulède on political matters that affected his own role as leader of the Extreme Left.

The "historic nights" (as some writers have pretentiously called them) began with a meeting of Clemenceau, Pelletan, Pichon, Perin, Révillon, Granet, Laisant, Millerand, Dreyfus, Mayer, Simon (of *Le Radical*), and Rochefort. Granet warned the group that Ferry was promising the Right that he would ease up on the laic laws if it would help to get him elected president. The Radicals should therefore try to keep Grévy in office, even if it meant forming a ministry. Everyone agreed except Pelletan and Perin, who contended that the Radicals would be discredited if they stuck by Grévy. Clemenceau took

little part in the discussion. Finally, he informed the group that
while he shared Granet's views, the very fact that Pelletan and
Perin were opposed was an indication that the nation might not
understand such a Radical maneuver. "The operation is a failure," he said, "let's not discuss it any more."[54]

Clemenceau left the meeting, but both Laguerre and Mayer
were angry that the Radicals' hands were tied just because two
of Clemenceau's lieutenants had expressed opposition. Joined
by Granet and Laisant, the two headed toward the offices of
La Justice to discuss the matter again with Clemenceau, who
agreed that something might yet be done, although he told them
that he could not talk then because he had a midnight rendez-
vous with "Boul-Boul." Laguerre expressed surprise, not knowing that Boulanger had just come to Paris on military business
and that Laisant had arranged a dinner between the two men.
Clemenceau then invited his visitors to join him and the general.

The group met Boulanger at Durand's. Rochefort and
Déroulède dropped by shortly afterwards. The men decided
to attempt to persuade either Freycinet or Floquet to form a
ministry. Although Clemenceau had already refused Grévy's
offer under identical circumstances, he agreed to go with Rochefort and Mayer in order to convince Floquet. Laisant and
Déroulède went off to visit Freycinet. But both Freycinet and
Floquet, each of whom was convinced that he had a chance of
becoming the new president, rejected the offer of the Radicals.
Laguerre and Granet, who had remained behind with Boulanger,
were disappointed. They were convinced that Boulanger's presence would be essential in any new cabinet, as a counterweight
to Grévy's unpopularity, and they had hoped that some scheme
could be worked out in which the general could return to the
Ministry of War. Now the radicals were back where they started.
Such were the events of the first "historic night," less important
for what happened than for the insight that they provide into
Clemenceau's own attitudes and the thinking of some of those
who had been his closest collaborators.[55]

The next night the group met again at Laguerre's house on
rue Saint-Honoré. Laguerre revealed that he had talked with
Grévy during the day and that the old man had pleaded with
him to find a prime minister with "great authority" who could

overcome the difficulties of the moment. Laguerre proposed that Clemenceau take office, with Boulanger at the Ministry of War. The new ministry could either prorogue the Chamber or convince the Senate to dissolve the Chamber should the latter prove to be hostile. Mayer added that force might be necessary, and Déroulède proposed that the League of Patriots be mobilized to march on Parliament.

Rochefort later recalled that such talk distressed Clemenceau, who, pretending to ignore what was being said, chatted with Madame Laguerre and took little part in the conversation.[56] At last he made it clear that he would not support the idea of a Clemenceau-Boulanger ministry. The general likewise said little; around midnight a messenger called for him, and he was gone for two hours. Unbeknownst to the Radicals, he had left in order to talk with the royalist Mackau and his friend the comte de Martimprey, who wanted to make a deal with him whereby they would support his reappointment to the Ministry of War if he would support the restoration of the monarchy. These nocturnal schemes came to nothing, although Boulanger had apparently agreed to them and had offered the support of the army. Returning to Laguerre's house, he found the discussion still raging. The argument centered on the possibility of dissolving the Chamber and the dangers that this would entail. "I see Augereau clearly enough," Clemenceau said, "but afterwards, what will the garrison of Paris do?" "It will stay in its barracks," Boulanger answered.

Augereau had been the Napoleonic officer who had purged the legislature in 1797. For a few moments after Boulanger's remark, Clemenceau stared at his former protégé. Then he walked into the kitchen with Madame Laguerre, where he said: "To think that a French general is listening to everything we are saying!"[57] Andrieux, the former prefect of police whom Laguerre had also mentioned as a possible prime minister, arrived at 3:30 A.M., but he also rejected the Radical offer on the grounds that the appointment of Boulanger would mean a fight with the Chamber. On the next day, Laguerre reported his failure to Grévy, who finally gave in and resigned.

A meeting of a national assembly was scheduled for December 3 at Versailles to elect a successor. On the morning of

December 1 Rochefort visited Clemenceau at *La Justice,* where the latter said, "We are lost" and observed that the "hideous misfortune" of a Ferry presidency was all but certain. According to Rochefort, Clemenceau, searching for the names of others who would have an outside chance, was the first to mention that of Sadi Carnot, a grandson of the Organizer of Victory of the Great Revolution. In the polling for a new president at Versailles, the candidates were Ferry, Freycinet, Brisson, and Carnot, Clemenceau having already persuaded Floquet to withdraw in favor of Freycinet. After two ballots in the plenary meeting of republicans, Freycinet failed to gain ground against Ferry. It was at this point, over the objections of Laguerre, that Clemenceau decided to muster support for *l'outsider,* Carnot. "Carnot isn't very strong, and what's more, he's a perfect reactionary," Clemenceau had told Rochefort earlier, "but he carries a republican name, and besides, we don't have anything better."[58] By early afternoon, Carnot was catching up with Ferry, and by six o'clock the strategy had paid off with a victory for Carnot.

There are some curious features about Clemenceau's decision to throw Radical support to a man like Carnot, especially in light of our earlier comments regarding Clemenceau's tendency to create failure situations. For he recognized Carnot as a reactionary and had already seen him, as minister of finance in 1886, oppose the Radicals' hopes for an income tax. Furthermore, shortly after Carnot's election, Clemenceau admitted to a newspaper reporter (one senses almost with relief) that Carnot's views differed from his own and that there was no chance that he, Clemenceau, would be called upon to form a ministry.[59]

Had there, in fact, been no alternative to Ferry's election other than that of Carnot? The confusion of the voting permits no definitive answer, but it might be noted that on the first two ballots of the plenary session, Ferry had outdistanced Freycinet by only seven and twenty votes respectively. The one historian of this affair, Dansette, has observed that Ferry's support was deceptive, being essentially the votes of a listless Center for a man who had already been abandoned in 1885.[60] Even ruling out Freycinet, a successful Brisson candidacy was not out of the question; and for all his weaknesses, Brisson, as a moderate Radical, would probably have been more receptive to a Clemenceau ministry than was Carnot. Yet—and this is a crucial point—Clemenceau had been focusing his attention on Carnot since the meeting with Rochefort on December 1, two days before the balloting started. In an article in *La Justice* of September 1, 1890, Clemenceau tried to play down the importance of this meeting, but he never denied the details as they were given by Rochefort. Whatever the truth may be, one thing is certain: Clemenceau had no friend in the presidency in Carnot, who a few days later asked P. E. Tirard to form a cabinet.

In Clérmont-Ferrand, meanwhile, Boulanger was toying with numerous schemes for returning himself to power. Alfred Naquet encouraged him in his plans, as did two new members of his entourage—an old classmate from Saint-Cyr named Count Dillon and a Bonapartist journalist named Georges Thiebaud, who was looking for someone to fill Napoleon's boots. In December, Boulanger slipped back into Paris for further talks with Mackau and Martimprey. His courting of the Right went even further in early 1888, when he traveled incognito to Switzerland to visit Prince Jerome Bonaparte, who encouraged Boulanger in his plans to wage a campaign for revision of the constitution by means of a plebiscite, a Bonapartist device. The idea of constitutional revision had long been part of the Radical platform. But in the case of Naquet and Laguerre, who were now serving as the theoreticians of the movement, a fundamental change was evident: unlike Clemenceau, they had come to accept the view that a strong man could be an instrument of progress as well as of reaction. Boulanger himself never spelled out his plans for revision explicitly, other than by saying that he wanted to strengthen the executive power. The ultimate plans of the increasing number of royalists in Boulanger's camp were likewise never made clear, aside from their wish to use the general as a tool against the Republic and to capitalize on his popularity by running candidates on lists that would be headed by his name.[61]

By February of 1888 the government had proof that despite his denials, Boulanger had encouraged his friends to enter his name in several by-elections scheduled for April. Clemen-

ceau recognized these tactics for what they were—thinly veiled
plebiscites to test the general's popularity. On March 16 *La
Justice* also publicized the report of General Logerot, minister
of war, to President Carnot which revealed that, contrary to
orders, Boulanger had left his post at Clérmont-Ferrand on at
least three occasions. On March 17 Carnot ordered the general
to turn over his command. Laguerre immediately formed the
Committee of National Protest, which issued a pro-Boulangist
manifesto signed by ten Radicals. Clemenceau countered with
his own statement, signed by fifty-one Radical deputies, which
condemned the intrusion of military leaders into politics as
being a menace to free institutions.[62]

In the Chamber on March 20, Laguerre reminded his
former mentor about his past defense of men who had been
unjustly vilified. Clemenceau answered that Boulanger had been
guilty of breach of discipline in leaving his post. He also criticized his former "colt" Laguerre for gloating over the fact that
Parliament was unpopular in the nation. While accepting his
share of the blame for reproaches aimed at the "babblers" in
the Chamber, Clemenceau again contended that Boulanger's
popularity arose from the fact that Opportunist governments
had failed to satisfy hopes that the Republic would solve the
nation's social and economic problems. He then proposed a
motion: "The Chamber, deciding to maintain discipline in the
army, ascertaining the impotence of government, and convinced
that only a policy of reform can put an end to agitation in the
country, passes to the order of the day." But several deputies
objected that such an admission of weakness would only help
Boulanger, and Alexandre Ribot retorted that the real problem
of the French government came from the fact that it was perpetually being assaulted by Clemenceau. The motion did not
reach a vote.[63]

It mattered little, for Clemenceau's speech did no damage
to the former minister of war. Although Carnot put Boulanger
on the retired list on March 26 (a foolish act, since the government no longer had any control over him), Boulanger had already entered his name in by-elections scheduled for April 8
in Dordogne and the Nord, where Rochefort, Déroulède, and
Laguerre were busy campaigning for him. A new Boulangist

newspaper, called *La Cocarde,* spelled out his program: *Dissolution, Revision, Constituante.*

Ten days after Clemenceau's skirmish with Laguerre in the Chamber, the Tirard cabinet fell over its resistance to a new Radical proposal for constitutional revision. Clemenceau, showing the same uncompromising adherence to principle as always, was in the forefront of those speakers who attacked the ministry.[64] Floquet vacated his post as president of the Chamber in order to form a new cabinet, which included both Goblet and Freycinet. In the closest that he was to come to occupying an official position during his early parliamentary career, Clemenceau allowed his name to be placed in nomination for Floquet's old post, which was an important one in overseeing and influencing the flow of legislation. After three ballots, Clemenceau and Jules Méline were tied, with 168 votes each. Méline was declared the winner on the basis of age.

Why was a tie for the presidency of the Chamber the most that Clemenceau was able to achieve for himself after all his years in politics? A story that is frequently related is that he killed his own chances by playing an untimely practical joke on a deputy for the Yonne named Casimir-Laurent Michou.[65] Even if the story is true, the fact remains that Clemenceau had already hurt his chances for the support of the moderates because of his past actions, including his treatment of Tirard a few days earlier. On April 4 *Le Temps* noted that the deputies of the Center and the Right had rallied to Méline because they wanted to stop Clemenceau; there was some opposition to the latter's candidacy even among such Radicals as Madier de Montjau. In short, Méline was chosen over Clemenceau for the same reason that Floquet was chosen over him to be prime minister. Only Floquet, as Freycinet has noted in his memoirs, was capable of forming a ministry with a Radical orientation, for he had the support of both Radicals and moderates who believed that he would exercise prudence in office.[66] "You always lose by excess of youth," Ribot said perceptively to Clemenceau.[67]

After his defeat, Clemenceau turned his attention to the task of creating an organized anti-Boulangist campaign, prodded by the general's easy victories in Dordogne and the Nord on

April 8 and 15. Working with Arthur Ranc (who represented the moderate republicans) and with the Socialist Jules Joffrin, he called a meeting for May 23 at the Grand Orient of several hundred deputies, senators, municipal councillors, and journalists. In a speech to this gathering, he stressed that while Radicals supported revision of the constitution, they could not support "its exploitation by a general who poses as a pretender." He labeled Boulangism a "new attempt at dictatorship" and suggested, as a means to defend the Republic, that they establish a new "Society analagous to the great political associations of the French Revolution."[68]

Thus was born the Society of the Declaration of the Rights of Man and the Citizen, with Clemenceau as its first president. The members of the provisional committee that was charged with organizing the society in Paris and the provinces included the Radicals Pichon, Révillon, Labordère, and Pelletan, and the Socialists Jules Joffrin, Eugène Fournière, Jean Allemane, and Paul Brousse. The effort at first had all the affected grandeur of the days of the great Committee of Public Safety, but in fact the new society had little success in injuring Boulanger's cause. Most of the Socialists soon withdrew, and the anti-Opportunist tone of the society's propaganda left many moderates cold. Membership in it never rose above nine hundred.[69]

The importance that Clemenceau attached to the society can be judged from the fact that he left most of its work to lieutenants such as Pichon. Therefore there is little evidence to support the impression that it was Clemenceau who destroyed the Frankenstein that he himself had created. Indeed, throughout the early spring of 1888 the Boulangist movement appeared to be irresistible as the general continued his tactic of running in one by-election, resigning, then running in another. But for both Opportunists and Radicals there still remained two effective weapons that were capable of destroying the man and the movement: the power of ridicule and the power of the state.

On June 4 Boulanger took his seat for the Nord and, in the face of laughter and interruptions, tried to read his prepared statement. He claimed that his victories proved that the country was disgusted with a parliament that had become the "servile agents" of party interests. "Parliamentarianism is very seducing in theory," he said, "but it is a mistake to view it as the exact expression of self-government." The Opportunists had treated France as if they owned it, and this was why the first remedy for the "material and moral malaise" of French society was the revision of the constitution, which was neither democratic nor monarchial but was "oligarchic."

Clemenceau struck back. He defended what some saw as political squabbling as being invaluable attempts to seek out truth. "Glory to the country where one speaks," he said, "if it is free discussion you think you are stigmatizing under the name of parliamentarianism, then know this—it is the representative system itself, it is the Republic on which you dare to lay a hand!" But it was Floquet who delivered the most telling blows at Boulanger. Poking fun at the idea that the French people were children who needed leadership from a new Man on Horseback, he said to him: "At your age, General Boulanger, Napoleon was dead." The proposal for constitutional revision was rejected by a vote of 377 to 186.[70]

Undaunted, the general came back on July 12 with a motion asking Carnot to dissolve the Chamber. New insults exchanged between Floquet and the general led to a duel, with Clemenceau and Perin as seconds to Floquet and with Laguerre and Laisant as seconds to Boulanger. The duel took place on Bastille Day in Count Dillon's garden. Boulanger, lunging at his opponent, literally fell on the sword of the short, near-sighted Floquet. For a time it appeared that Boulanger might die, if not from the wound in his neck, at least from the humiliation of being beaten by the little civilian. Yet, within a few weeks, Boulanger was back on his feet. Using money provided by such supporters as the duchesse d'Uzés, he began campaigning again, still gaining new victories in by-elections in the Nord, the Somme, and Charente-Inférieure. What must have been frustrating to the Radicals was that he was deriving some of his strength from those who had formerly been attracted to Radical programs. While it is true that he made great gains in such Bonapartist strongholds as the Dordogne, he made a respectable showing in the industrial complex that is formed by the cities of Lille, Roubaix, and Tourcoing. Among farm workers in the Somme, who had been hard hit by the decline in the prices paid for sugar beets, he attracted much support, while the strike-torn city of Amiens voted heavily for him.[71] The republicans had one last hope: Boulanger had entered his name in a by-election in Paris that was scheduled for January 27, 1889. Here, in industrial, republican, revolutionary Paris, he could surely be stopped. Both Opportunists and Radicals staked their hopes on a republican named Jacques.

Boulanger's victories had deeply embittered Clemenceau, to whom the general represented a threat to the Republic and hence the negation of what the French Revolution had accomplished. With such issues at stake, personal friendships were of little consequence. Since making his first attacks on Gambetta, Clemenceau had come to believe that the loss of friends in politics was inevitable for one who stood by his principles. When Laguerre, who was now his enemy, referred in the press to the matter of Herz's influence on *La Justice,* Clemenceau demanded formal explanations, indicating that however painful it would be, he was still ready to defend his principles on the field of honor, even against one of his former disciples.[72]

But for the Clemenceau of 1888—as for the young student of 1862—there was inner satisfaction in being cast in the role of sufferer for a cause, and in his campaign against Boulangism he frequently defined this cause in terms of the most noble ideals he had inherited from his father. During a tour of the Var in October, he asked: "Is it not shameful, citizens, that in the Republic today a republican speaking to republicans is obliged to discuss the Boulanger question? What could be more humiliating? Should this great revolutionary movement that began in '89 and that has made France the emancipator of the peoples of Europe end with Boulanger? If our fathers were placed on the scaffold, if they were prescribed, if they struggled without respite, was it all just for Boulanger? No!"[73]

Clemenceau now rested his hopes on the city of Paris, which since his childhood he had believed to be the citadel of freedom. It was a bitter campaign, and on the evening of election day, Clemenceau walked the boulevards with an English friend, visiting polling places in his old district in Montmarte, sensing the pro-Boulangist mood of the crowds. As the final returns rolled in, Boulanger had captured 245,000 votes, the

republican candidate, 162,000. Boulanger, Rochefort, Dérou-
léde, and others celebrated the victory that night at Durand's,
cheered on by a crowd of some thirty thousand. But the old
story of a coup that failed because of Boulanger's faint-hearted-
ness has been convincingly laid to rest by Seager; for Boulanger
had every reason to believe that universal suffrage would enable
him to achieve power, and he viewed the real day of reckoning
as being the legislative elections which were scheduled for the
fall.[74]

Such was Clemenceau's fear, as he admitted to the Chamber on January 31 that the defeat of the republican cause had
been a convincing one.[75] But from this point on, he himself
played no further role in the events relating to Boulangism as
the government took steps to rid France of the troublesome
general. First, it was essential to abolish *scrutin de liste* in order
to prevent Boulanger from running in several departments and
carrying his supporters with him. Although Clemenceau wished
to prohibit multiple candidacies, he was opposed to a return
to single-member constituencies. When a bill to do so came
before the Chamber on February 11, 1889, he and about two-
thirds of the Extreme Left voted against it; nevertheless, it
passed by a vote of 268 to 222.[76] Two days later the Right
joined the moderates in overthrowing Floquet, who had hoped
to steal the Boulangist thunder by a new effort to revise the
constitution.[77] His replacement was Tirard, whose clever and
unscrupulous minister of the interior, Ernest Constans, soon
dragged Laguerre, Naquet, and Déroulède into court for sub-
versive activities. Next he prepared action against Boulanger,
building a flimsy case, based on a plot against the state, and
circulating the rumor that Boulanger would be hauled before
the Senate to stand trial. The ploy soon had an effect, and on
April 1 General Boulanger fled to Brussels.

Clemenceau's newspaper gloated over Boulanger's abrupt
flight. In August the Senate sentenced Boulanger, Rochefort,
and Dillon to deportation. The three were already safely abroad,
which could not have pleased the government more. Above all,
Constans had tried to keep from making the general a martyr.
Clemenceau expressed no qualms about Constan's tactics. Indeed, he compared the Senate, when constituted as a high court

to protect the Republic, to the great Revolutionary Tribunal of 1793, despite the fact, as he later admitted, that "we delivered up politicians to other politicians who were their enemies and condemnation was assured in advance."[78] But Clemenceau himself was now a marked man in the eyes of the distraught Boulangists, who saw him as a traitor whose jealousy of the general had wrecked their plans. The Boulangist journal *La Cocarde* warned that Boulanger's return "will mark the end of Clemenceau." The journal described the "ex-leader of the Extreme Left" as a man in failing health with shattered nerves: "In his most intimate entourage he sees Boulangists."[79]

Clemenceau knew that the Boulangists were planning to oppose him in the fall elections with one of their own candidates. Having decided to stand in the arrondissement of Draguignan in the Var, he campaigned in this area throughout late August and early September. His Boulangist opponent was named Ballière, and there were two other candidates who called themselves Radicals. On the first ballot on September 22 Clemenceau placed first, with 7,510 votes to Ballière's 3,583. The other candidates polled 4,343 and thus forced Clemenceau into a runoff by denying him an absolute majority. The two Radicals then withdrew in his favor, and on October 7, with Boulanger's followers boycotting the elections, Clemenceau defeated Ballière by 9,363 to 272 votes. In the nation as a whole the first ballot put an end to any lingering hopes on the part of the Boulangists, since only some 38 were elected, taking their place on the Right. The final composition of the new Chamber also included 172 monarchists and Bonapartists and 366 republicans, the latter containing 216 moderates and 114 Radicals.[80] France had given a vote of confidence to the Republic.

For Clemenceau it was a different matter. Despite his reelection, he continued to be, in the eyes of many Frenchmen, the creator of Boulanger and the one whose initial bad judgment, in making him a minister, had set the stage for the crisis. According to *Le Temps*, it was a common sentiment that Radical policies had been "one of the first causes of the Boulangist movement."[81] Now almost fifty years old, Clemenceau found himself more isolated and more alone than ever. During late 1889 and all of 1890 he did not make a single speech in or out of Parliament, but as we shall see in our last section, this did not indicate any new flexibility in his goals or any weakening in his determination to prove to the world that he was willing to suffer for his ideals. He was to have one last opportunity to do so during his early career, for a new crisis was brewing that, in the words of the Socialist leader Jean Jaurès, would deliver Clemenceau up "to all the surprises of fate, to the violence of blind passions and the treachery of party hatreds."[82]

THE PANAMA SCANDAL

The conclusion of Clemenceau's first career was a time of private and public tribulation for him. His marriage was in ruins, his credibility damaged, his authority as leader of the Radicals undermined. At *La Justice* the "family" of which Geffroy had spoken during the glory days of combat a decade ago had broken up. Millerand was drifting toward socialism, while Laguerre, who was in despair after Boulanger committed suicide in Brussels in 1891, eventually renounced politics and turned to alcohol for solace. Of the three "colts," only Pichon remained faithful to the end. In the eyes of many Frenchmen, including some Radicals, Clemenceau was a voice of the past, incapable of adjusting to new realities. Charles Benoist summed up this attitude in 1891, when he noted that Clemenceau's politics "rest upon abstractions, aspirations, principles—not facts. M. Clemenceau is a theologian of a theology without God." Benoist believed that what motivated Clemenceau's behavior was an exaggerated view of his own value: "If his self-love is bruised, he is incapable of pardon. No one, at any moment, has the right of forgetting that he exists."[83]

What Benoist saw as an exaggerated self-love may also be interpreted as a desperate attempt to reclaim a lost self, to achieve, through suffering, not success in life, but a sense of personal identity and the mitigation of inner guilt. For all the emotional pain that his involvement in the Panama affair was to bring him, it is possible that the role of combative sufferer and object of scorn that he was able to play was to have a salutary and ego-liberating effect on his life. This point will be examined more closely in the concluding chapter of this study.

Before turning to the events of Panama, it is necessary to consider some of Clemenceau's other activities that had further weakened his position in the public eye even before the scandal erupted. His interventions in the legislature of 1889 to 1893, which was a generally conservative body,[84] were relatively rare; but on those occasions when his principles were at stake, he was able for brief periods to rekindle the moral fervor that had characterized his career just after the founding of *La Justice*. While some on the Left were willing to adjust their goals to the growing conservatism of the era, he remained faithful to the principles that he had preached since his Latin Quarter days. In January, 1891, after several deputies had attacked government censorship of *Thermidor,* an anti-Robespierre play at the Comédie-Française, Clemenceau rose in the Chamber to defend the action. "Whether it shocks us or not," he said, "the French Revolution is a block . . . , a block of which one can destroy nothing because history does not permit it." To those on the Right he said: "You have remained the same. We have not changed. The struggle must thus continue until the day that victory is definitive for one of the two parties."[85]

By this reasoning, Clemenceau rejected any compromise with the movement for reconciliation between Church and Republic known as the *ralliement.* He viewed it as an effort on the part of the Church to obtain by stealth what it had failed to achieve in open combat with the republicans. In February, 1892, after Freycinet had proposed a new bill to regulate the orders, Clemenceau attacked him for his refusal to commit himself to total separation of Church and state. He asked republicans to remember what had happened in the past when governments had found themselves in alliance with the Church: "You say that a hand is held out to you? Put yours in it. It will be so firmly grasped that you cannot get loose." Clemenceau's speech helped to bring down the fourth Freycinet cabinet.[86]

If there was now an arid quality about Clemenceau's determination to fight the battles of his youth, there were nevertheless a few last occasions on which he exhibited the compassion for the oppressed that we have seen in the early 1880s. In the spring of 1891 new labor disorders plagued the country.

When May Day demonstrations at Fourmies in the Nord turned into riots, soldiers fired into the crowd, killing ten people and wounding many others. Perrot has termed the shootings at Fourmies "the first great massacre of the Third Republic."[87] Clemenceau was among the most prominent politicians who raised their voices against what had happened. In the Chamber on May 8 he asked for an end to the prosecution of labor leaders and reminded his colleagues that all republicans must recognize a new historic force. This was the proletariat, which was claiming for the first time the political and economic rights that had been laid down by the French Revolution. He warned that an "inevitable revolution" was coming and that France could receive it either with open arms or with violence and civil war: "Look out the window. See all the peaceable people who work and ask nothing of you except conditions of order and peace that will allow them to work and to prepare the regime of justice. . . . Save the Republic that has promised justice to the oppressed, as the Great Revolution promised liberty! Save the home, save *la patrie!*"[88]

He repeated his appeals for amnesty in the fall, at the same time denouncing the actions taken by the companies during a new strike of thirty thousand miners in Pas-de-Calais. In the summer of 1892 there were new disorders in the Carmaux mines in the Tarn, where the army had been sent in to break up a strike. Many union leaders were fired or jailed. Finally, Prime Minister Loubet agreed to the Radicals' demands for arbitration. Clemenceau, Pelletan, and Millerand acted as representatives for the miners and throughout the fall pressed for the release of those who had been jailed and the rehiring of those who had been dismissed. Eventually the government promised to grant pardons, and the company agreed to rehire its former employees. On October 31 Clemenceau went to Carmaux and spoke to the miners, proclaiming the strike a victory and urging them to accept the accord, which they did.[89] It was a modest achievement, but Jaurès, for one, saw it as a victory for labor.[90]

Another issue—this one outside the realm of domestic policies—absorbed much of Clemenceau's attention in the early 1890s. This was the growing alignment between France and Russia, a development that he abhorred because he feared that

Russia could not be counted on in the event of war. He recognized the danger to France if it had to face Germany alone. In 1891 and again in 1892 he warned the Chamber that the nation was not ready for war, while he chided the government for the lack of rapid-fire cannons for the navy.[91] Though he had never been a part of those forces advocating revenge and had often preached the need for peace, the possibility of a new German attack was never absent from his thinking. Buried deep in his mind were the memories of 1871 and a lingering resentment against the civilization to the east, where, as he had reminded the Chamber in 1883, military leaders like von Moltke had declared that "peace is only a dream and not a noble dream."[92]

Clemenceau's solution to the problem of French weakness and isolation was what he termed an entente cordiale with England. In July, 1891, with the knowledge of unnamed members of the French government, he spelled out some of his ideas to Joseph Chamberlain during a visit with his friend Admiral Maxse in London. Clemenceau told Chamberlain that anti-British feeling in France would disappear if the two countries could reach an accord. As a start, he suggested that in return for a free hand in Egypt and the elimination of French rights in Newfoundland, Britain should support French diplomatic efforts to persuade Germany to neutralize Alsace-Lorraine. He also raised the possibility of a treaty that would bind England to neutrality in case of a Franco-Italian war. Chamberlain, while agreeing about the need for Anglo-French understanding, replied that British pressure on Germany would have little effect and that in the case of Italy, England would not permit an alteration in the balance of power in the Mediterranean area. He did report the conversation to Lord Salisbury, who, being suspicious of French ambitions, was opposed to any new commitments on the Continent.[93]

Clemenceau's efforts did not receive any real backing from the French government, which was still concentrating on Russia. In July, 1891, a French squadron visited the naval base at Kronstadt and was met by Tsar Alexander III. The French public greeted these events with enthusiasm. On August 12, 1891, Clemenceau wrote to his friend the comte d'Aunay, who was France's ambassador to Denmark:

I find that everyone is getting a little bit carried away. I
hope it's not the result of some furious growth of chauvin-
ism among us. To be sure, the tsar's standing up to hear
the *Marseillaise* is something out of the ordinary. . . We
must try to keep calm. We've got to repair our fleet, which
has none of those rapid-fire cannons that the decks of other
fleets are crowded with. And we've got to have generals,
which we do not have.

Will something be signed with Russia? Everyone
thinks so, and I know that people are working on it. It's
a lot of foolishness; hence, there's a chance it will be done.
. . . Be sure to tell your little secretaries not to fall in a
faint before the tsar and to remember that they have the
honor—perhaps unmerited—of being citizens of the French
Republic.[94]

In another letter of October 22 he wrote to d'Aunay again:
"Now we have on our backs the enemies of Russia as well as
our natural enemies. Formerly friendly Austria has become
nervous and bitter. England bluntly threatens to enter openly
into the Triple Alliance if we sign with Russia. Add to this that
Russia can't be of *any* help to us materially."[95]

Clemenceau's opposition to an alliance with Russia created
still more enemies, who thought that this English-speaking,
English-loving politician was endangering French security to
the profit of perfidious Albion. This theme also played into the
hands of the Boulangists. In September, 1892, the marquis de
Morès, a Boulangist adventurer whose chief claim to fame was
that he had killed a young Jewish captain in a duel, published
a letter in Drumont's newspaper, relating a conversation that
he had had with Baron de Mohrenheim, Russia's ambassador
to France. Morès claimed that the ambassador had told him
that he doubted the possibility of a Franco-Russian alliance,
since the Jews and the English controlled the press and since
leading politicians such as Clemenceau "openly attack the
Russian alliance in the corridors of the Chamber." Clemenceau
denied this in a letter to Mohrenheim, noting that it was not
his place to discuss the political consequences of the rapproache-
ment and that he was happy to see a friendship develop between
the two peoples.[96]

Clemenceau's pro-English sympathies were to damage him during events relating to the Panama scandal. This affair was one of the most complicated and acrimonious episodes in the history of the early Republic. It had begun in 1879, when Ferdinand de Lesseps, the builder of the Suez Canal, resolved to crown his life's work by constructing a sea-level canal through the Isthmus of Panama. Poor management plus engineering problems prevented him from completing it, and after several public subscriptions had been raised, popular enthusiasm waned. By 1885 de Lesseps had decided to entice the public with a lottery loan, which needed the approval of Parliament. The company spent millions of francs for publicity, which often included the bribing of journalists and politicians. In charge of this operation was Baron Jacques de Reinach, who sought the help of Cornélius Herz in an effort to influence the Radicals through Clemenceau. In April, 1888, the Chamber approved the lottery scheme, but graft and incompetence further weakened the Panama Company. In February, 1889, the Tribunal of the Seine dissolved the company and appointed a liquidator.

Clemenceau originally supported the Panama enterprise. In July, 1885, de Lesseps and his son Charles, who had been warned by the minister of finance that Parliament might oppose the lottery scheme, visited Clemenceau as part of a general lobbying effort. Clemenceau promised his cooperation, but over the next two years he began to have doubts after he had seen documents indicating that the canal would not be completed on time. In late 1887 he related his doubts to Charles de Lesseps; but the latter, who was now directing the operation, assured him that everything would still work out. The following April, Clemenceau voted in favor of the lottery.[97] Shortly afterwards, Herz, who in 1885 had promised Charles de Lesseps that he would help him to get approval of the lottery in return for ten million francs, began to demand his money, even though his agreement with Reinach had stipulated that he would be paid in full only if the lottery raised all the desired revenue. Herz's pressure turned into blackmail as the result of some secret hold that he had on the baron. Reinach began paying him from his own pocket. At the same time Reinach pressured Charles de Lesseps to give him ten million francs in order to pay Herz, threatening to expose the bribery of journalists and politicians if de Lesseps refused to pay.[98]

Clemenceau learned of Reinach's threat, and on July 12, 1888, he and Ranc visited Freycinet, who was then minister of war, urging him to use his influence in order to calm the situation. That night, Freycinet saw the younger de Lesseps and advised him to get his affairs in order. Afterwards Charles de Lesseps spoke again with Clemenceau, who wanted to learn what the former knew about Reinach's threats. Responding with a torrent of abuse against the baron, de Lesseps claimed that Reinach was extorting money from him. "The nervous, irritable state of de Lesseps," Clemenceau later testified, "inspired me only with the desire to get away as quickly as possible."[99] De Lesseps then saw Floquet, who gave him the same advice as had Freycinet. On July 17 Charles de Lesseps handed over five million francs to Reinach. The next day, Reinach began to pay off Herz, who still demanded, and got, an additional two million.

There was another piece in this bizarre puzzle. Possibly to protect himself against future incrimination, Reinach in 1888 dictated to a secretary named Stéphan a list of politicians whom he had bribed. Reinach foolishly showed the list to Herz, who copied it and showed it to Louis Andrieux, a former prefect of police. Andrieux later claimed that there were 104 names on this list, including those of such prominent people as Albért Grévy, Antonin Proust, Jules Roche, Léon Renault, and Maurice Rouvier. How many politicians had been bribed is unknown, though in 1892 investigators found proof that at least twenty-six politicians and journalists were guilty on the basis of stubs of checks that had been drawn by Reinach. Clemenceau's enemies were later to charge that it was he who showed the list to Andrieux in the hope that the two of them could discredit the Opportunists. Such was the view of Maurice Barrès in *Leurs Figures*. Ernest Judet, who was editor of *Le Petit Journal* and a Clemenceau hater, even claimed that the Radical leader had offered him the list in order to gain his support in crushing the Opportunists and in preparing the way for a Clemenceau cabinet.[100]

There is no evidence that Clemenceau had ever seen this

list. He vehemently denied the testimony of Reinach's secretary Stéphan that he had brought it to Clemenceau. He was also able to prove that the secretary's testimony was contrived, since Stéphan had told some friends that he was going to "rile the deputy." Stéphan finally confessed to having a "bad memory."[101] In any case, the significance of these dealings lay less in who had or had not seen Reinach's list than in Clemenceau's relations with Herz. Two questions thus deserve attention. By intervening with Freycinet and de Lesseps, was Clemenceau trying to do a favor for his old friend Herz? Did he receive any of the money that Reinach paid to Herz?

It should be made clear that Clemenceau was never among those who were charged with accepting bribes for support of the lottery scheme in 1888. Herz had been unable to make good on his assurances to Reinach in 1885 that his political connections could swing support for the scheme; three years elapsed between the Herz-Reinach pact and the vote, the success of which had been assured more by the efforts of Reinach than by those of Herz. Furthermore, Clemenceau claimed in 1893 that he had turned down an offer of fifty thousand francs from a certain Charles Bäl for "special publicity" in La Justice in favor of the lottery.[102] No doubt, Herz had lost money by supporting Clemenceau's newspaper, but this did not mean that in going to see Freycinet in 1888 Clemenceau was acting on behalf of his former financial mentor. The later testimony of both Charles de Lesseps and Freycinet agrees on essential points with Clemenceau's account. While de Lesseps said that he had had a general feeling that he was being pressured on Herz's behalf, he added, "Never for an instant did I think that M. Clemenceau was capable of obeying a secret influence."[103] Finally, the later accusation that Clemenceau received a kickback from Herz—namely, the extra two million that Herz had demanded from Reinach in 1888— is utterly without foundation. Herz himself revealed that this money had gone into real estate. Why, then, had Clemenceau interjected himself into the affairs of the Panama Company?

One motive might have been to attempt to control the situation and hence to defend himself on the matter of Herz's past involvement with La Justice; for if scandal came to light involving Herz and the Panama Company, Clemenceau's name would be dragged into it. Another explanation is one that Clemenceau himself gave: with the anti-Boulangist struggle going on, he feared that a new scandal might undermine the Republic.[104] Yet, his actions were questionable and indicated a shabby effort to hush up a scandal. Once more, the man of principle was pursuing a course of action that would make him still more vulnerable in the eyes of his enemies. By the fall of 1892 it was apparent that such efforts had been futile.

On September 10 the first of a series of articles detailing the inside story of political corruption in the affair appeared in Drumont's *La Libre Parole*. Reinach began to supply more information to the newspaper on condition that his name be kept out of it. On November 10 the minister of justice prepared summonses against the board of directors of the company and against Reinach, who was warned of his impending arrest through his nephew Joseph. At the same time, the Boulangist *La Cocarde* began to print attacks on Reinach, who believed that their source was Herz and Constans, the former minister of the interior who had received yet another list of incriminated politicians from a panic-stricken director of the company in early 1892. Reinach asked Rouvier, who was now minister of finance and who knew that his own name was on the list, to accompany him to see Herz. Rouvier agreed, on condition that they have a witness. Reinach suggested Clemenceau, and that afternoon in the lobby of the Chamber, Rouvier implored Clemenceau to go with them on the grounds that it was "a matter of life and death." Clemenceau agreed to do so.

This was foolish on Clemenceau's part, especially since he would have a difficult time explaining his presence at these meetings if word of them leaked out. Why he was willing to involve himself on Reinach's account at this point remains a mystery. Barrès was convinced that Clemenceau wished to retrieve Reinach's list from Herz in order to use it against the Opportunists. There is no evidence that Clemenceau had seen this list; but if he had known about it and wished to use it to this end, it seems logical that he would have wanted Herz to go ahead with publishing it. Nor do we know exactly what occurred in the meetings of the three men that night. According to Clemenceau's subsequent account, the meeting at Herz's house lasted only ten minutes, with Herz telling Reinach that it was beyond his power to help him. Rouvier then left, and Clemenceau agreed to accompany Reinach to see Constans, who likewise told them that he had no influence over the people who were leading the campaign against Reinach. This meeting was also brief. Outside, Reinach's last words to Clemenceau were, "I am lost."[105]

The next morning the baron was found dead in his home. The official explanation was "cerebral congestion," but rumors circulated that he had killed himself or that someone had poisoned him. That same day, Herz fled to London. On November 21 the Boulangist deputy Jules Delahaye rose in the Chamber to denounce the fraud and deception involved in the Panama business, and the Chamber agreed to his demand for a parliamentary investigation of the affair. One week later, Prime Minister Loubet fell because of his reluctance to order that an autopsy be performed on Reinach's body. "Suspicion is everywhere, and everyone is looking out of the corner of his eye at everyone else," Clemenceau wrote to d'Aunay, "it seems to me that this absurd situation is too painful to be able to last long."[106]

On December 12 *Le Figaro* revealed that on the last day of Reinach's life, Rouvier and Clemenceau had gone with him to see Herz. The next day, Clemenceau published his version of that meeting in *La Justice*. Both Rouvier, who resigned as minister of finance, and Constans gave similar accounts. But the new parliamentary commission wanted to know more, and on December 14 it called Clemenceau to testify. Some members of the commission were especially interested in Clemenceau's earlier financial dealings with Herz. He explained that Herz, who had been a "silent partner" on *La Justice,* had lost two hundred thousand francs in the venture, and that he, Clemenceau, had lost fifty thousand.[107] That afternoon in the Chamber, an exchange took place in which Clemenceau again found himself on the defensive:

Freycinet: It has been insinuated that under pressure from politicians I decorated M. Cornélius Herz.

Clemenceau: I have never recommended Herz for a dec-
             oration.
Millevoye: He won't come back from England to con-
             tradict you!
Clemenceau: Consult the dossiers. You won't find my sig-
             nature there, and no minister can say that I
             verbally recommended M. Cornélius Herz to
             him for a decoration![108]

A few days later came the discovery of the twenty-six check
stubs, bearing the names of ten senators and deputies, half of
whom were former ministers. On December 20 parliamentary
immunity was waived for the accused deputies, and the session
was suspended around three o'clock. When deliberations resumed three hours later, Paul Déroulède climbed to the tribune
for the ostensible purpose of asking the government what disci-
plinary actions the grand chancellor of the Legion of Honor was
going to take against Herz, who refused to come back in order
to testify. First he attacked Herz, "this foreigner who crossed
the sea with his fortune" and who had become one of the most
important men in France. How had Herz risen so fast?

> Who thus among us came proposing to make a place
> for him in our midst? Who, little by little, yet at the same
> time so fast, thus introduced, patronized, nationalized this
> foreigner in France? For you yourselves can attest to the
> fact that he was not presented all alone, that it wasn't even
> another foreigner who took him by the hand and thrust him
> among us. A Frenchman was necessary, a Frenchman who
> was powerful, influential, audacious, who was both his client
> and his protégé, his introducer and his supporter.
>
> Without patronage or patron, this little German Jew
> could not have made such strides along the road to honors,
> could not in so few years have risen so completely, so bril-
> liantly from the bottom of the ladder. I repeat, he had to
> have had someone to represent him, an ambassador to open
> for him every door and every circle, especially political
> circles. He had to have a most obliging and a most devoted
> friend to enable him to meet, on equal terms, as hail fellow
> well met, at one time ministers of state, at another, directors
> of newspapers, at another even, I admit it, General Bou-
> langer himself.

Now, this obliging, devoted, indefatigable intermediary, so active, so dangerous, you all know who he is.

His name is upon your lips, but not one of you will name him, for there are three things about him you fear—his sword, his pistol, and his tongue.

Well, I brave all three and name him.

He is Clemenceau!

There was an uproar in the Chamber, and Floquet tried to reprimand the speaker. Clemenceau stared calmly at his accuser, but he was shaken by the attack and occasionally uttered an almost inaudible no to the succession of charges. But Déroulède had not finished:

What passed between this foreigner and this politician so that there would be no trace of any interchange of good offices? What? Did one give all and the other nothing? Would this German without an interest, without an object, without a view to gaining something, have piled up all these repeated and redoubled payments? Whom will you get to believe that, Monsieur Clemenceau?

We must ask ourselves whether what he expected, if not demanded, of you was not precisely the overthrow of these ministeries, all these attacks on all men in power, all the trouble caused by you and your great talent in all the affairs of this country and of Parliament.

It is to destruction that you have dedicated your efforts.

The things, the men you have crushed!

Your career is built on ruins!

Here Gambetta, there another, and then another—all devoured by you.

Certainly I am opposed to the parliamentary system, but I don't think any man in France has given it ruder shocks or more severe wounds than this so-called parliamentarian. How Dr. Cornélius Herz must rejoice over this ever recurring spectacle!

Clemenceau rose to answer the charges. He admitted that he had not been prepared for such an indictment and that he was in a difficult situation, for he could prove the purity of his motives only by calling as witnesses his own conscience and intentions:

For the twenty years I have sat in political assemblies, those who have seen me at work day by day, my collaborators, my friends who sit upon these banks . . . can testify to the inspirations that have always guided me. For myself I have no more to say. I deliver over my political life to Déroulède. I deliver myself to him. He can analyze, discuss, dissect, incriminate everything I've said and done. That is his right. There is only one right that he does not have, and that is to pour out on me, in a spirit of Boulangist malice, the most odious calumnies. This was to hurl at me the supreme injury that one Frenchman can address to another. This injury, you who inflict it, you know I do not deserve it. You know that it constitutes an odious slander, an abominable lie.

. . . What is there left for me to do? What slanderous imputations remain for me to answer? I search and find nothing, except this supreme injury . . . that I betrayed the interests of France . . . that I introduced in this Chamber a foreign influence whose agent I was . . . that I sought to injure my country.

Gentlemen, to this last accusation there is but one answer.

M. Paul Déroulède, you have lied![109]

Few deputies were willing to believe that Clemenceau had been a foreign agent, but many seemed to be pleased by Déroulède's attack, as if Clemenceau's tyranny over the Chamber had been broken[110] After the session, Clemenceau sent his seconds, Gaston Thomson and Stéphen Pichon, with a challenge to Déroulède, who accepted it. The duel was set for the afternoon of December 22 at the St. Ouen race track. Parisians sensed that it would be a fight to the death, since both men insisted on three shots apiece at twenty-five paces.

On the appointed day, Clemenceau spent the morning with his mistress, Suzanne Reichenberg; then he went to the offices of *La Justice* to instruct the staff on what to do in the event of his death. At two o'clock he arrived at the race track, where a crowd had gathered; within an hour, both men were ready. The first shots were wide of their mark. The two men fired again, but there was no hit, Déroulède saluting his opponent after each try. Then a bystander rushed onto the field and begged them to stop. Both refused, then fired a third time; again both shots missed. Clemenceau was known as an expert marksman, which he had proved in target practice the day before. Had he deliberately missed Déroulède, as some people claimed at the time? No one will ever know, but the importance of the duel lay in the fact that both in the Chamber and in the field, Déroulède had laid to rest the myth of Clemenceau's invincibility.[111]

On Christmas day, Clemenceau wrote to d'Aunay: "I console myself in thinking that the squall is surely not over. And to think that anyone curses the Terror! The guillotine was more suitable." Shortly afterwards he wrote again: "All the blackmailers in Paris are in a flutter, and certain politicians are gathering strength to destroy *at any price* anyone who stands in their way."[112] He heard the rumors about him—that he had resigned, that he had taken millions from the Panama Company, that he was about to be arrested. In his newspaper he wrote: "I do not ask where the lies will stop, for I am quite sure that tomorrow something better will be found, if that is possible."[113] On January 23 of the new year he was called again before the parliamentary commission, where he denounced the lies that had been circulated about him, saying that they had been politically inspired.[114]

On February 9 Ferdinand and Charles de Lesseps were each sentenced to five years in jail. Charges against several deputies were dropped for lack of evidence, and in the end, only the former minister of public works was convicted. In the meantime, Déroulède and Judet kept public attention focused on Clemenceau's role. On June 19, as Clemenceau tried to discuss a bill on electoral reform, Déroulède shouted for him to "speak English," while the Boulangist Lucien Millevoye asked: "Don't you sense that you are held in contempt by just about everybody?"[115] Two days later the editor Édouard Ducret announced in *La Cocarde* that some documents had been found at the English embassy proving that certain French politicians were in the pay of the English government. In fact, these documents were crude forgeries, which had been turned out by a disgruntled employee of the embassy named Norton. Déroulède, who probably knew they were not genuine, devised a simple strategy. Since deputies were immune from the libel laws for anything that they said at the tribune, one of them would make general charges but would refrain from producing the documents, which would then be published. The task fell to Millevoye, who evidently considered the documents to be genuine.

When Millevoye rose on June 22 to make his charges, Clemenceau stood up and asked: "Have I sold my country for ready cash? If you have the proof, bring it." Millevoye promised that he would do so later, but several deputies began shouting for him to produce the names. "That will be done before the Court of Assizes," Millevoye answered. "Liar! Liar! Liar!" taunted Clemenceau.

Losing his head, Millevoye began to read pieces from several of the forgeries, which were so inaccurate and bizarre that the deputies started to laugh. Clemenceau was mentioned as having received twenty thousand pounds, and Rochefort, three thousand. The mention of Rochefort brought the house down, and Déroulède, who was incensed at what was happening, left the Chamber. The deputies then passed a resolution condemning the actions of Millevoye and Déroulède.[116] In August, Clemenceau brought Norton and Ducret before the Court of Assizes of the Seine on libel charges. Both were fined and imprisoned.[117] But in the meantime, Clemenceau had been delayed in starting his campaign in the Var for the legislative elections that were scheduled for late August and early September.

Here his enemies were already at work. The marquis de Morès was conducting operations on the scene. With a local monarchist named the comte de Dion furnishing the money, with thousands of copies of Judet's *Le Petit Journal* being mailed to the electors in the Var, and with several local reactionary newspapers on their side, Clemenceau's enemies stood a good chance of beating him. First, they hoped to exploit local prejudices against Clemenceau's status as an outsider. His opponents included a local mayor (a former Clemenceau supporter) named Maurel and a Socialist named Vincent. His most formidable opponent was a Marseilles lawyer and monarchist named Joseph Jourdan, who had grown up in Draguignan. Second, they exploited a longstanding anti-British sentiment in this Mediterranean department, where the British occupation of Toulon during the French Revolution had never been forgotten. Clemenceau's speech at Bordeaux in 1871, in which he advocated the separation of Corsica from France, his opposition to the Tunisian expedition, and his speeches against the occupation of Egypt—all were revived in an effort to prove that he had devoted his career to safeguarding the Mediterranean interests of the British. Morès and Dion distributed fifty thousand circulars in mailboxes, along with copies of *Le Petit Journal*. Placards appeared on the walls of villages, many showing Clemenceau taking orders from Queen Victoria, his pockets stuffed with pounds sterling.[118]

On August 8 Clemenceau arrived at the little town of Salernes, near Draguignan. That night he spoke to some fifteen hundred people in the court of the Café Sigaud, hoping to regain the initiative over those who had organized against him. But his speech at Salernes, which was one of the most effective of his early career, was more than campaign oratory. It was a catharsis in which, for over two hours, a very emotional Clemenceau delivered himself of his feelings as the persecuted sufferer for ideals:

> My dear fellow citizens:
> After a long ordeal I present myself to you.
> It is the fate of politicians—I speak of men of combat— to be exposed to all surprises, to all outrages.
> In the old days they were assassinated; that was the golden age.
> Today, any action that is generally considered ignoble seems to be legitimate against them. Lies become truth; slander becomes praises; treason becomes loyalty. . . .
> I have read that it was an honor to be the object of such attacks, a redoubtable honor, that can be braved only with the armor of high indifference, capable of enduring everything without swooning. . . . Attacked on all sides at the same time, insulted, vilified in the most cowardly manner, disowned, I have not given way. Having submitted myself to these outrages, I stand before you to give an account of myself. . . .
> For more than thirty years I have fought for the Republic.

As a student in 1862, I was imprisoned for the Republic.

Since that time, faithful to the cause, I have stayed in the fight, without rest, without respite, striving to keep the ardor of some under control, pressing, encouraging others, always pointing out the enemy. . . .

Mayor of Paris during the siege, deputy at Bordeaux and at Versailles, president of the Municipal Council of Paris, a deputy again since 1876, I have always publicly served the cause of the people to the best of my ability. Against the monarchists, the clerics, the reactionaries of all names and under all disguises, in broad daylight, in the eyes of the country, for better or for worse, for happiness or for sorrow, I have fought.

He denied being a systematic opposer, for power had been offered to him only once. That was when Grévy had been forced out of office. At that time, Déroulède had pressed him to take power by force, and it was his resistance, Clemenceau said, that had foiled Déroulède's plan to use the League of Patriots against Parliament. He admitted that he had cooperated in making Boulanger a minister, but he had broken with him when he found out that the general was not a republican soldier. Clemenceau also gave details on Herz's relationship to *La Justice,* emphasizing that his newspaper had never been subservient to the monied interests and that since its first victory, the amnesty of the communards, it had "remained faithful to the cause of the disinherited." Point by point he took up the Panama affair, from the original extortion and bribery to the way in which the guilty had escaped punishment. What had happened? He quoted the words of a journalist who had sold himself: "Panama is Clemenceau." Since then the charges had multiplied. Clemenceau went on:

I am supposed to have extorted from M. de Lesseps fantastic sums.

Everything has been revived, my life has been dug into, nothing has been spared.

I had Lecomte and Clément Thomas assassinated.

The post office in the house where I live pays my rent.

A few weeks ago I read in a newspaper that I had a

box at the Opéra, that I spend 200,000 francs a year and that the budget paid for everything. . . .

I defy anyone to find any luxury in my life other than a saddle horse, which costs me 5 francs a day for 9 months, and a share of a shoot that amounts to fewer than 500 francs. . . .

What remains for me to establish? That there is no trace of these millions in my life. . . .

Could I speak of my personal situation?

I have settled the debts of my youth by a loan from a notary in Nantes. The record can be seen, for the debt still exists.

Where are the millions?

I gave my daughter in marriage without a dowry.

Where are the millions?

I have lived for the past six years in my present flat. The furniture dealer and the decorator have been paid in installments. I haven't finished paying them yet.

Where are the millions?

Here is the kind of admission to which disinterested servants of the Republic are reduced. May the shame of this humiliation rest upon those who have rendered this confession necessary.

But these matters were unimportant, Clemenceau went on, compared to the future of the country. Though today the financial world was less interested than ever in social reform, republicans must gear themselves to a new effort in this direction. In place of being the tool of big business for oppressing the weak, the state must assume the role of protecting the individual and preventing man's abuse of man. Approaching the end of his speech, Clemenceau returned to the imperative that had guided his own life, which was the willingness to struggle and to suffer for ideals:

These party struggles in Parliament that people tell you are sterile, let me assure you that they are creative and that if, in the struggle, some are killed or wounded, they at least have the consolation of falling in a great cause. . . . These little fights are grand because of the ideals that are at stake. . . . We have inherited them from the past and we will bequeath them to the future. I ask no truce. It is not my gift to grant it.[119]

The Salernes speech threw Morés and his men into a panic. Their solution was simply to prevent Clemenceau from speaking. From Paris came reinforcements, and in the Var, local toughs were hired to follow him from village to village, heckling him. In the commune of Bargemon they were waiting for him, and from his first words the shouts began: "Oah yes! Oah yes!" The same response greeted him everywhere, and in his most important rally, which had been scheduled for the Grand Theâtre in Draguignan, the hecklers prevented him from speaking.[120]

The voting took place on August 20. Clemenceau captured 6,511 votes, to 4,641 for Jourdan. Having failed to win an absolute majority, he still had to face Jourdan in a runoff. Normally, the other candidates—Maurel and Vincent—would have thrown their support to him, but now his opponents began to court Maurel and to pressure local Socialist groups to join them in defeating this bourgeois Radical. At this point, Jean Jaurès intervened on Clemenceau's behalf, reminding the workers that Clemenceau had exposed himself to the outrages of reaction in going to Carmaux to support the workers' cause.[121] The appeal had little impact, and in the meantime there had been no letup in the activities of Morès's ruffians. At one point, Clemenceau's carriage was stoned in the village of Bagnols.

When the votes were counted for the second ballot on September 4, Clemenceau had been defeated. Jourdan got 9,503 votes to his 8,640. To his electors, Clemenceau wrote: "Of the infamous campaign against me, I will say nothing. But it would be good that you remember it. For if the people wish to be defended, the guard must not be betrayed."[122] Emboldened by their victory, his opponents sought to humiliate him further, and there was even talk of lynching him when he left his hotel at Draguignan. The prefect got wind of these rumors and asked Clemenceau to leave at night in order to prevent any disorders. But at two o'clock the next afternoon, he walked up the main boulevard, past the crowded cafés and past the headquarters of the opposition, and boarded his train at the station.

The elections throughout the rest of the nation had not been nearly so impassioned as the one in the Var. The Right suffered major losses, and the Radicals too lost seats, beginning now to be supplanted on the Left by the Socialists, who gained their most significant victory to date. The victors, for the most part, were the same moderate conservatives who had dominated in the previous legislature. The most talked-about event was the defeat of Clemenceau. With few exceptions, newspapers viewed his elimination from politics as a gain for order and stability.[123]

To the comte d'Aunay, Clemenceau wrote: "I assure you I am taking this whole adventure with a nice tranquility. I have no desire for recrimination, for raving, for letting myself get indignant."[124] He spent a few days relaxing with his friends Gustave Geffroy and Octave Mirabeau; it did not seem to them that he had lost any of his good humor. To a friend named Charles Edmond, however, he said: "I am a stranger in my own home, betrayed by friends, dropped by my party, ignored by the electors, suspected by my country." He added that the creditors of *La Justice* were "beating at my door. I'm riddled with debts, and I have nothing more, nothing more, nothing more."[125]

His life was in ruins, and adding to his isolation was the fact that few of the old comrades with whom he had worked over the years came forth with any solace or encouragement. While publicly lamenting his defeat, some Radicals were no doubt glad to be rid of a man who had become a liability to the cause. But his disappearance from Parliament was to leave the Radicals leaderless, without the old élan and moral fervor that was necessary in order to sustain their spirits in the face of repeated defeats. Yet, no matter how bleak Clemenceau's future may have appeared to himself and to others in 1893, the failure and suffering that he had endured—much of which, it is suggested, had been self-induced by a psychological need to cope with inner guilt—did not really shatter his ego strength and resources. On the contrary, as we shall see in the next chapter, Clemenceau in 1893 had undergone a psychological purging that may have been responsible for his extraordinary burst of new energy and that over the next few years would, at least temporarily, beget a curative measure of ego health and stability.

FIVE

Appraisal of Clemenceau's Later Years In the Light of His Identity Conflicts

The traditional view of Clemenceau's negative role in the development of the early Third Republic was first set forth by the newspaper *Le Matin* after his defeat: "Clemenceau never personified anything but the active impotence and negation that destroyed. . . . He was a man of crisis, never a man of solutions."[1] The theory that his influence was pernicious argues that by leading the Extreme Left to vote with the Right against centrist cabinets, he helped to establish a pattern for French parliamentary democracy that would last until its collapse in 1940.

I hope that this study has been able to modify this view of the early Clemenceau in three important respects. First, in a strictly political sense the evidence does not bear out the legend of Clemenceau as the awesome and powerful "wrecker of ministries" whose actions prevented the creation of a stable government. This is by no means to imply that his role in cabinet turnovers was entirely negligible. We have seen that his actions were significant in determining the fate of the Freycinet, Goblet, Rouvier, and Tirard ministries after 1885. Even before Radical gains in the elections of that year had enhanced his power in Parliament, he and the Extreme Left had been able on occasions to exploit differences and weaknesses within a coalition, as had happened in the case of the Waddington min-

187

istry during the amnesty debates of 1879. Prost and Rosenzveig have demonstrated that during the legislature of 1881 to 1885 the Extreme Left was one of the few groups that had any semblance of voting discipline.[2] In any unstable situation, Clemenceau's ability to wield a block of votes, however small and indecisive they might be in achieving his programs, could always constitute a disruptive force in parliamentary operations. By the same token, his rancorous attacks on Gambetta and Ferry, though not the decisive causes for their downfalls, no doubt inflamed passions and strengthened those destabilizing forces that existed in French political life.

Nevertheless, an exclusive or excessive emphasis on Clemenceau's responsibility in this regard has prevented a balanced assessment of either his own career or the age of which it was a part. It has obscured the very deep political and personality rivalries within the Opportunist majority, especially those between the Gambettists and Ferryists during the years 1877 to 1885. It has also ignored the larger institutional flaws in the early Republic that militated against stability, with or without Clemenceau's presence in Parliament: shifting coalitions, which inhibited the growth of parties; an electoral system that produced individuals who were lacking in national as opposed to regional and local concerns; and most importantly, a static social and economic power structure, whose spokesmen in the Chamber and Senate possessed neither the understanding nor the motivation required for the enacting of social legislation.

Second, while one may justly criticize Clemenceau's parliamentary tactics, the view that he was essentially a destroyer and a political gladiator who was incapable of offering constructive alternatives to the policies that he attacked is an inaccurate one. Both in Parliament and in the press he and his followers fought for programs that were designed to aid the young Republic in solving new and serious problems. John B. Christopher has observed that of all the Atlantic democracies, France experienced the greatest difficulty in adjusting to the realities of modern economic life.[3] Any assessment of contemporary reactions to the problems that these realities created must give Clemenceau credit for perceiving the dangers that lay ahead. His struggle for amnesty for the Communards, for the rights of trade unions, for the protection of workers against the power of big capital, and for judicial and penal reform was motivated by a profound conviction that if the Republic that he loved were to survive, it would have to have a government that was responsive to the needs of all its citizens. On a number of specific issues, time was to prove his analysis to be correct. He foresaw the great cost, both to the treasury and to the spirit of social reform at home, that the conquest and administration of colonies would entail. He correctly predicted that the registration provisions of the trade-union law of 1884 and, especially after the Anzin strike, the bill's failure to protect striking workers from the wrath of the companies would alienate many working-class leaders from the Republic. And in his campaign for constitutional revision, he rightly portrayed the Senate as a major obstacle to reform. When the Chamber finally approved an income tax in early 1896, for example, the Senate moved to overthrow the cabinet of Léon Bourgeois before the measure ever reached the upper house.[4]

Third, though Clemenceau's rate of success was indeed small during the years 1876 to 1893, this does not mean that his concerns were wasted or that his labor did not eventually bear some fruit. Georges Michon has observed that a reform does not spring overnight from the cabinet in power at a particular moment; it is the result of long and persistent efforts to persuade an indifferent or hostile majority that action is necessary.[5] One must remember that in the late 1870s some political leaders denied that a social question even existed, and the gathering of statistical or other types of information about the condition of the working classes was not coordinated and was not in the hands of specialists. This was one of Clemenceau's greatest concerns, as was indicated in his speech to Parliament of January, 1884, and in his fight to create a parliamentary commission to study conditions among industrial and agricultural workers. His newspaper was already investigating and reporting on strikes; and in his speeches to Parliament and in his visits to Grand'Comb in 1882, Anzin in 1884, and Carmaux in 1892, he attempted to get the facts of social and economic inequalities before the public and to enhance the sensitivity of Frenchmen to these issues. This was a difficult task, from which immediate results were unlikely; but as one of the first and most articulate of those who argued the case of the weak, Clemenceau must be credited with at least helping to lay the groundwork for some of the social measures that were passed in the decade or so after his defeat.[6]

Nevertheless, for Clemenceau to have achieved the maximum results possible within this system, he needed to be more than a catalyst or a conscience for his countrymen. He needed political power and a chance to exercise his talents in a position of leadership that would transcend the confines of the Extreme Left—if not as prime minister or a cabinet member, then as the leader of a coalition that might have bargained for piecemeal legislation and cabinet positions. But the early Clemenceau lacked the skills and the intuitions of a true politician. By alienating many who might have helped him and by refusing to bend on his adherence to principle, he repeatedly doomed his efforts to failure in advance and undermined his own capacity for leadership. His intransigent devotion to a "pure" radicalism during the controversy over double inscriptions in 1881, for example, undermined many possibilities for unity and cooperation on the Left. Similar attitudes on his part during the short-lived Ligue revisionniste and, after 1885, during the ministries of Freycinet, Goblet, Tirard, and Floquet showed his inability to exploit any opportunities to work with moderate Radicals. His bitter attacks on Gambetta did Clemenceau and his ideals little good. To have rallied in 1882 to Gambetta's limited proposals on constitutional reform, or at least to have offered proposals of his own—short of integral revision—that could have been the object of serious negotiation between the Extreme Left and the Republican Union, would not have meant abandoning a future possibility for more substantive reform. Equally important was Clemenceau's failure after the death of Gambetta, especially after the Radical successes in 1885, to establish himself as a flexible and effective parliamentary leader in the day-to-day operations of government. Instead, he chose to wield his influence through Boulanger; this, combined with the tie with Herz, raised legitimate questions about his political judgment and helped to discredit him in the eyes of the moderates.

Clemenecau's flaw lay not in his conception of the Republic

but in the execution of his designs, not in his legendary destructiveness of others but in his destructiveness of self. Circumscribed by the psychological traits that he had first developed in the process of father identification, he played the role of sufferer and martyr for the ideals of his youth. Such a role led him to identify with the sufferers and martyrs of all times and places and, by extension, prompted him to fight the cause of the weak and to formulate many constructive proposals for the ills that plagued his countrymen. If there is a single theme that dominates his early career, it is his unceasing defense of the weak—the former slaves of North America, the exiles and victims of the Paris Commune, the miners of Anzin and Carmaux, the peasants of Egypt and Vietnam. No one ever questioned his courage on these matters. But that same role, formulated as an alternative to the autonomous psychological development that had been thwarted in childhood, produced shame reactions in regard to perceived weaknesses of the inner self. It led to an alternating sense of guilt toward his father and toward himself, of which one visible manifestation was the need for failure as a form of self-punishment. At the heart of both psychological affects of shame and guilt lay Clemenceau's early incorporation of an ego-ideal that was based on his father.

POST–1893 PATTERNS OF PSYCHOLOGICAL DEVELOPMENT

At this point it is necessary to ask what accounts for Clemenceau's later political success and to what degree he was able to overcome the psychological problem of identity loss. In order to answer these questions we must glance briefly at his post-1893 career. Two stages of further psychological development are apparent, each of which demonstrates separate emotional reactions to the underlying problem of identity. The first stage runs from 1893 to roughly 1901 and includes two significant events: Benjamin's death and Clemenceau's involvement in the Dreyfus Affair. The second stage covers the period from his election as senator for the Var in 1902 until his death in 1929. In what follows, my remarks are not intended to provide an evaluation of Clemenceau's role in French politics during the post-1893 period but to suggest ways in which the psychological drives that were evident in his early career continued to affect his attitudes and behavior. It is hoped that this approach will help to explain the seeming inconsistencies between his first and second political careers; for while the later Clemenceau no doubt exemplified in part a historic tendency of leftist leaders and movements to grow more conservative as they become outflanked on the Left (in this case by Jaurès and the Socialists), the reversal of some of his earlier attitudes was in many cases abrupt and indicated that there were forces at work in his life that were more profound than external social and political trends.

In the period 1893 to approximately 1901, one sees two psychological dynamics at work in Clemenceau's life. The first may be characterized as a momentary easing of inner guilt as a result of the humiliation and defeat that he had experienced in 1893. As one of the martyrs of history whom he had extolled in his youth, he had now proved himself worthy in regard to the internalized parental ego-ideal. The second was a simultaneous, though ultimately temporary, satisfaction of the demands of his inner self for punishment for his failure to free himself of father identification. Rather than being an end in itself, suffering may have an object in the ego's unconscious wish to free itself of alien and restrictive influences, to exploit latent sources of psychological energy, and to actualize new possibilities.[7] In Clemenceau's case, the year 1893 marked the end of the period of relative withdrawal that had set in around 1885, and there was now a great surge of energy, which was channeled into journalism and literature. Clemenceau's resilience did not go unnoticed by even his harshest critics, such as Maurice Barrès, who asked: "Is Clemenceau seeking anything from literature but a way of dissipating his surplus energy?"[8]

One notes, in this regard, the sheer volume of his post-1893 labors. Between October, 1893, and October, 1897, he wrote almost daily for *La Justice*, where he had taken over from Pelletan as political editor shortly after the elections of 1893. In mid 1894 he began to write additional articles for a Toulouse newspaper, *La Dépêche*, and in mid 1895, for *Le Journal* and

Echo de Paris. After the debt-ridden *La Justice* had ceased publication in the fall of 1897, Clemenceau joined the staff of Ernest Vaughan's *L'Aurore.* Several collections of Clemenceau's newspaper articles in the 1890s were published as books: *La Mêlée sociale* (1895), *Le Grand Pan* (1896), *Au Pied du Sinaï* (1898), *Au Fil des jours* (1900), *Figures de Vendée* (1903), and *Aux Embuscades de la vie* (1903). In addition, Clemenceau wrote a novel, *Les Plus Forts,* which was published in 1898, and a play, *Le Voile du bonheur,* which was first performed in 1901.[9]

Watson has justly noted that, for the most part, these writings are neither great literature nor great philosophy.[10] Our interest, however, is in knowing what they reveal about Clemenceau's post-1893 psychological orientation. His political articles show a continuing concern with the weak and the oppressed, despite the fact that he increasingly formulated his ideas in terms of a Darwinian struggle for survival. Starting with the very first article that he wrote after his defeat—which he entitled "En Avant" and which was a defense of the rights of workers against the companies—he affirmed with renewed zeal his earlier ideas on the social question.[11] The articles that were published in *La Mêlée sociale* two years later denounced the evils of modern industrialism and pictured the clash between capital and labor as the modern version of a historic struggle between the weak and the strong. His notions on the role of government in the social domain were similar to those of Léon Bourgeois's *solidarisme,* but at times they also showed an almost religious emotion in their passion for justice and human charity, or what Clemenceau called altruism.[12] In *Le Grand Pan* he argued that throughout history the struggle between egoism and altruism had formed "the law of all life." His sympathy for the victims of man's abuse extended to animals, to dogs that were used to pull burdens, for example, or to young apes that had been separated from their families and placed in zoos.[13] The Darwinian rhetoric that he often used must not obscure his true feelings; as one reviewer noted, despite his poor philosophy, his works showed "an inexhaustible fund of compassion for the humble and the defenseless."[14]

Similar features are visible in Clemenceau's sketches, short stories, and other fiction. It is risky to derive personal biography from a writer's fiction, but Clemenceau's lack of literary subtlety and his use of characters and situations to mirror his own ideas are fairly obvious. One notes in his stories a preoccupation with those who suffer persecution (a band of gypsies, a Protestant pastor named Johann Stumpf), cynicism toward the institution of marriage, and a disillusionment with the hardness of man's heart and his eternal failure in family and other relationships to be loving and loyal.[15]

Such writings suggest a projection of his own inner frustrations, which were typified by his failure to achieve love in life or by his unhappy dealings with his children, especially with his son, Michel.[16] The novel *Les Plus Forts* portrays a turbulent parent-child relationship in which the father, a nobleman named Henri de Puymaufray (who lives in a château exactly like L'Aubraie and who bears a close resemblance to Clemenceau) fails in his efforts to guide the life of his daughter Claude, whom he has fathered with the neglected wife of a rich industrialist named Harlé. Puymaufray is an angry, bitter man who, at the end, can cling to but one consolation, which is that "out of wasted lives is made, through suffering, the genius of living humanity."[17] In Clemenceau's play, *Le Voile du bonheur*, the central character is a blind, aged Chinese, who by a miracle regains his sight. But the ability to see leads him to discover that his wife and son, who had pretended to love him, actually hold him in contempt. Preferring ignorance to the pain of knowledge, he blinds himself anew.[18]

The psychological attraction of the sufferer in history may also have been an important factor in Clemenceau's campaign on behalf of Alfred Dreyfus, the Jewish army officer who had been condemned for espionage in 1894. There is no question but that Clemenceau genuinely believed in Dreyfus's innocence when he took up the cause in late 1897. But it is possible that the affair, which laid the basis for Clemenceau's political comeback, symbolized for him more than the need to rectify a judicial error or the opportunity to undermine the Right. The outcast on Devil's Island can be seen as a martyr of history, whose fate provided a compelling emotional as well as political motivation for Clemenceau. There were other martyrs in the affair as well—the novelist Zola and the young officer named

Marie-Georges Picquart, who was willing to wreck his career in the interest of truth (Clemenceau rewarded him by making him minister of war in 1906). Clemenceau's articles on the affair kept the moral as well as the political issues before the public, and in themselves they constitute a prodigious accomplishment in modern journalism.[19] His keenest disappointment came in 1899, when Dreyfus accepted a presidential pardon rather than to continue the fight.

The renewed prestige that Clemenceau earned from his role in the Dreyfus Affair is only part of the explanation for his subsequent political successes. From around 1901 on, Clemenceau demonstrated an increasing ability to compromise his earlier principles and to create conditions for personal success. In April, 1902, he agreed to stand for the Var as a candidate for the Senate, the institution that he had long despised and that he now began to defend.[20] Though he remained aloof from the Radical party that was organized in 1901, he proved during his support for the program of Émile Combes between 1902 and 1905 that he was capable of working with others toward achieving specific legislative goals.[21] In March, 1906, he joined the cabinet of Ferdinand Sarrien as minister of the interior. The following October, nearly sixty-five years old and having been in public life since 1870, Georges Clemenceau became prime minister, a post that he was to hold for three years. There can be no dispute that the changes within him corresponded to and reflected new political conditions in the France of the post-Dreyfus era; but developments in his emotional attitudes were also significant in weakening his self-perception as a sufferer and in creating psychological acceptance of a role other than that of being a sufferer for his ideals.

It can be argued that the event that most affected his altered outlook in this regard was the death of Benjamin in July, 1897. This constituted the physical removal of the role model, and this may have contributed to a lessening of psychological tensions within the son and to a further alleviation (though by no means a permanent eradication) of the cycle of guilt that has been discussed earlier. We do not know what his immediate reactions to this event were; his fellow workers at *La Justice* certainly recognized his sense of loss. In a front-page insert they extended their sympathies over Clemenceau's sorrow, noting that despite Benjamin's arrest and suffering in 1858, the proud man had refused the indemnity that the government had offered in 1879 to the victims of the Empire.[22] In accordance with Benjamin's wishes, no announcements of his death or invitations to his funeral were sent out. Gustave Geffroy seems to have been one of the few outsiders who were present when Benjamin was buried on the wooded knoll near a stream at Colombier.[23] Clemenceau revealed some of his feelings on death and the loss of loved ones in a letter of June, 1898, to Lady Milner:

> As to the belief in another life, this can be a consolation only for those who don't dare to look the world in the face. . . . Do you wish survival for yourself and those you love in some sort of blessed rapture, without nobility since it is without suffering? No. Let us return with serenity to the quiet rest from which we came, content with having one day emerged from the ocean of things for seeing, for knowing, for loving, for suffering: such is the resumé of life[24]

Although the shift in Clemenceau's feelings was gradual, Benjamin's death finally enabled him to assert himself against a psychologically restrictive influence. His decision to do so as a member of the Senate, which had always stood in opposition to his most sacred ideals and which he had denounced as late as 1896,[25] may be interpreted as the beginning of an inner revolt against the parental legacy. Thus, both his suffering of 1893 and Benjamin's death in 1897 constituted liberating forces in his life, but again it must be stressed that expiation of inner guilt is rarely permanent and may produce further guilt, frustration, and rage. These points should be kept in mind in viewing Clemenceau's second career and, in particular, the possibility that both success and the gradual abandonment of his role as defender of and sufferer for his father's ideals might produce new guilt. Georg Brandes's observation in 1903, which was quoted at the beginning of this study, is worth repeating: "Even now the son feels as if his father's eye were upon him." Shortly after becoming prime minister, Clemenceau related the story of his father's arrest in 1858 to an audience in the Vendée. Then he said: "I have worked, and today in Montaigu, when I see all the republicans bestowing on me honors that I do not deserve, I cannot stop myself from turning toward him, to whom I owe everything, and saying to you: 'It is he that you should be honoring!'"[26]

It is true that during his first ministry Clemenceau continued to fight for many of his social programs and that he was able to achieve a few reforms, including nationalization of the Western Railway. But it is also true that many of his actions were alien to the spirit of Benjamin's ideals and to those that Clemenceau had served before 1893. No fair comparison of his two careers can fail to take cognizance of the difference in both style and substance—from his support of the Russian alliance to his backing of a colonial policy in Morocco. The change is especially obvious in his attitudes toward the working-class movement. Watson has argued that his policies were designed to undermine extremism in the trade-union movement and that when viewed comparatively, his record on strikes is not a bad one.[27] But any implication that as prime minister he did not abandon many of the ideals of his youth is ultimately misleading. His use of troops during strikes in the northern coalfields in 1906 and 1907, his arrest of labor leaders such as Victor Griffuelhes, his defense of the police after the shooting of strikers at Draveil and Villeneuve-St. Georges in 1908, his use of *agents provocateurs* against the Confédération générale du travail, his rejection of amnesty for arrested strikers—all these actions contrast sharply with those of the Clemenceau of the years 1876 to 1893. Many Radicals, including men like Pelletan, found his actions reprehensible, and in some areas such as the lower South, the events of his second ministry contributed to a further weakening of radicalism.[28]

Thus, in many significant respects, Clemenceau acted in opposition to his pre-1897 role, which is why it has been suggested that he never managed to overcome entirely his identity problems and that the reversal of many of his pre-1897 attitudes constituted the true revolt against his father's empire over him. As such, in the psychological realm, his post-1897 attitude was negative, not positive or constructive. The policies he pursued between 1906 and 1909 were by no means unpopular with many

Frenchmen, and they helped to ensure his success within a political system and according to political methods that he had once denounced. But I suggest that the problem of guilt was never removed and that the revolt against the father compounded and intensified the inner rage and destructiveness that, as we have seen, had long coexisted with his creative drives. He wrecked his own ministry in July, 1909, by a bitter and unwarranted attack on Thèophile Delcassé. His attacks on others before and during the First World War were equally intense— Raymond Poincaré, Aristide Briand, Joseph Caillaux, and Louis-Jean Malvy, to name a few. In the Senate Army Committee, before he had formed his second ministry in November, 1917, he criticized the conduct of the war with extreme emotion and on more than one occasion was in tears.[29] A man of such an apparently harsh and hostile temperament, a man who could proclaim "I make war" as the formula for his domestic and foreign policy, may have been what France most needed in 1917. But character traits that proved useful and necessary for Clemenceau the Man of War were not the ones that in other times could have enabled him to be a creator and a conciliator, working toward the good society that he had envisioned in his youth.

Clemenceau's ultimate inability to emancipate himself in any positive or constructive way from the fetters of father identification seems to be borne out in the last years of his life. After his defeat for the presidency in 1920, he spent much of his time in the Vendée, where he owned a small cottage by the sea. He had a few close friends, including Jean Martet, with whom he often reminisced about his youth and the early days when the Republic was young. He talked a great deal about his father and the debt that he owed to him.

But one senses a touch of melancholy in his reflections. He told Martet that the house of his birth at Mouilleron and the grave where he would be buried beside Benjamin at Colombier marked the limits of "my sad rainbow." Once he showed him the plot and said: "Here is the conclusion of everything you write about me: a hole in the ground and a lot of noise for nothing."[30] He died on November 24, 1929. In his last will and testament he asked that three things be placed in his coffin:

some dried flowers that he had received from the troops on the Western Front, the little box that his mother had given him, and a cane with an iron knob that he had had in his youth.[31] Clemenceau asked that no name be placed on the grave. The only things that marked the spot were an iron railing, a cedar planted by Benjamin in 1848, and a bas-relief by the sculptor Sicard, which Clemenceau had placed there earlier. The bas-relief was of Minerva, the Roman Athena, goddess of wisdom and the martial arts, who had sprung full grown from the head of her father, Zeus.

Notes

The place of publication for all French works that are cited is Paris, unless otherwise indicated. Translations from French sources are the author's.

PREFACE

1. Guy Chapman, *The Third Republic of France: The First Phase, 1871–1894* (New York: St. Martin's Press, 1962), p. 241.
2. Leo A. Loubère's articles, which will be referred to in chapter 3 of this study, include the following: "The French Left-Wing Radicals: Their Views on Trade Unionism, 1870–1898," *International Review of Social History* 7 (1962): 203–30; "Left-Wing Radicals, Strikes, and the Military, 1880–1907," *French Historical Studies* 3 (spring, 1963): 93–105; "French Left-Wing Radicals and the Law as a Social Force, 1870–1900," *American Journal of Legal History* 8 (January, 1964): 54–71; "Les Radicaux d'extrême-gauche en France et les rapports entre patrons et ouvriers (1871–1900)," *Revue d'histoire économique et sociale* 42 (1964): 89–103; and "The French Left-Wing Radicals: Their Economic and Social Program since 1870," *American Journal of Economics and Sociology* 26 (April, 1967): 189–203. See also his *Radicalism in Mediterranean France: Its Rise and Decline, 1848–1914* (Albany: State University of New York Press, 1974).
3. Jacques Kayser, *Les Grandes batailles du radicalisme: Des origines aux portes du pouvoir, 1820–1901* (Rivière, 1962), and Jean-Thomas Nordmann, *Histoire des radicaux, 1820–1973* (La Table ronde, 1974). One might also consult the more general study by Georges Lefranc, *Les Gauches en France (1789–1972)* (Payot, 1973), as well as the older but still useful work by Georges Weill, *Histoire du mouve-*

ment sociale en France, 1852–1902 (Félix Alcan, 1904).
Theodore Zeldin includes a chapter on radicalism in
France, 1848–1945, vol. 1: *Ambition, Love and Politics*
(Oxford: Clarendon Press, 1973), pp. 683–724, which
devotes a good part of its analysis, however, to the later
period of radicalism around the turn of the century.

4. Langer's speech, "The Next Assignment," may be found in
Bruce Mazlish, ed., *Psychoanalysis and History* (Engle-
wood Cliffs, N.J.: Prentice-Hall, 1963), pp. 87–107.

5. Jean-Louis Flandrin, *Familles: Parenté, maison, sexualité
dans l'ancienne société* (Hachette, 1976), pp. 117–28. See
also Edward Shorter, *The Making of the Modern Family*
(New York: Basic Books, 1975), pp. 61–65.

6. Franz Alexander, *Fundamentals of Psychoanalysis* (New
York: Norton, 1948), p. 118.

7. Some of the key works in ego psychology that I have
found useful include the following: Anna Freud, *The Ego
and the Mechanisms of Defence*, trans. Cecil Baines (New
York: International Universities Press, 1946); Heinz Hart-
mann, "Comments on the Psychoanalytic Theory of the
Ego," in *The Psychoanalytic Study of the Child*, vol. 5
(New York: International Universities Press, 1950), pp.
74–96, and *Ego Psychology and the Problem of Adaptation*
(New York: International Universities Press, 1958); Paul
Federn, *Ego Psychology and the Psychoses*, ed. Edoardo
Weiss (New York: Basic Books, 1952); and Gertrude
Blanck and Rubin Blanck, *Ego Psychology: Theory &
Practice* (New York: Columbia University Press, 1974).
Especially helpful for the present study was Edith Jacobson's *The Self and the Object World* (New York: International Universities Press, 1964). The main body of
Erikson's writings includes "Ego Development and Historical Change," which was first published in 1946 and
was reprinted in *Identity and the Life Cycle*, vol. 1, no. 1,
monograph 1 of *Psychological Issues* (New York: International Universities Press, 1959), pp. 18–49; *Childhood
and Society*, 2d ed. (New York: Norton, 1963), which
first appeared in 1950; "The Problem of Ego Identity,"
which first appeared in 1956 and can be found in *Identity
and the Life Cycle*, pp. 101–64; *Identity: Youth and Crisis*
(New York: Norton, 1968); and *Life History and the
Historical Moment* (New York: Norton, 1975). See also

Robert Coles, *Erik H. Erikson: The Growth of His Work* (Boston: Little, Brown, 1970), and Paul Roazen, *Erik H. Erikson: The Power and Limits of a Vision* (New York: Free Press, 1976).

8. Rapaport introduces Erikson's *Identity and the Life Cycle*, pp. 5–17, with a survey of the history of psychoanalytic ego psychology.

9. Roazen, *Erik H. Erikson*, p. 59; Erikson, *Life History*, p. 39; Henry W. Maier, *Three Theories of Child Development* (New York: Harper & Row, 1965), pp. 16–17. Maier provides an excellent synthesis of Eriksonian ideas on pp. 12–74.

10. Rapaport, in his introduction to *Identity and the Life Cycle*, pp. 14–16.

11. See chap. 7, "Eight Ages of Man," in Erikson, *Childhood and Society*, pp. 247–74. See also Maier, *Three Theories*, pp. 31–67; and Lucian W. Pye, "Personal Identity and Political Ideology," in Mazlish, ed., *Psychoanalysis and History*, pp. 150–73, from which the Freudian parallels for Erikson's life stages are taken.

12. Erik H. Erikson, *Young Man Luther: A Study in Psychoanalysis and History* (New York: Norton, 1958), and *Gandhi's Truth on the Origins of Militant Nonviolence* (New York: Norton, 1969).

13. Erikson, *Childhood and Society*, p. 282, and "Problem of Ego Identity." See also Robert W. White, *Ego and Reality in Psychoanalytic Theory*, vol. 3, no. 3, monograph 11 of *Psychological Issues* (New York: International Universities Press, 1963), which stresses that identication is more than imitation of the parental model and that its central feature is the drive for competence.

14. Pierre Lacombe, "The Enigma of Clemenceau," *Psychoanalytic Review* 33 (April, 1946): 165–76.

15. *Journal officiel de la république française: Débats parlementaires, Chambre de Députés,* January 29, 1891, p. 156. Cited hereinafter as *JO, Chambre des Députés.*

16. Georg Brandes, "M. Georges Clemenceau," *Contemporary Review* 84 (November, 1903): 656–74.

17. Erikson, "Ego Development," pp. 79–81. In formulating my ideas concerning Clemenceau's efforts to cope with shame and guilt, I have relied on the insights provided by both Erikson and Edith Jacobson, as well as those of

Gerhart Piers and Milton B. Singer in *Shame and Guilt: A Psychoanalytic and a Cultural Study* (Springfield, Ill.: Thomas, 1953) and of Helen Merrell Lynd in *On Shame and the Search for Identity* (New York: Harcourt, Brace, 1958). I have also used James A. Knight, *Conscience and Guilt* (New York: Appleton-Century-Crofts, 1969); Serge Lebovici, *Les Sentiments de culpabilité chez l'enfant et l'adulte* (Hachette, 1971); Helen B. Lewis, *Shame and Guilt in Neurosis* (New York: International Universities Press, 1971); and John G. McKenzie, *Guilt: Its Meaning and Significance* (New York: Abingdon Press, 1962).

18. Knight, *Conscience and Guilt,* pp. 91–96; and McKenzie, *Guilt,* p. 22.
19. Lewis, *Shame and Guilt,* pp. 11, 44–45.
20. Knight, *Conscience and Guilt,* pp. 106–8, 116–18.

CHAPTER ONE:

IDENTITY QUEST & IDENTITY DIFFUSION, 1841–1870

1. Roy Schafer, "Ideals, the Ego Ideal, and the Ideal Self," in *Motives and Thought: Psychoanalytic Essays in Honor of David Rapaport,* vol. 5, nos. 2–3, monographs 18–19 of *Psychological Issues* (New York: International Universities Press, 1967), pp. 131–74.
2. See the description given by Gustave Geffroy, who often visited the area with Clemenceau in the 1880s, in *Clemenceau: Suivi d'une étude de Louis Lumet* (Paris and Zurich: G. Crès, 1919), p. 22. Geffroy's major work on Clemenceau is a sympathetic biography entitled *Georges Clemenceau, sa vie, son oeuvre* (Larousse, 1932).
3. For the most accurate account of Clemenceau's ancestors see the unsigned article "Les Familles Clémenceau et Gautreau," in *Bulletin de la société de l'histoire du protestantisme français* 78 (1929): 440–44.
4. Jean Martet, *M. Clemenceau peint par lui-même* (A. Michel, 1929), pp. 131–38. Since Clemenceau left no memoirs, Martet's notes on conversations with him are especially useful, and in factual matters, they are generally trustworthy. See also his *Le Silence de M. Clemenceau* (A. Michel, 1929) and *Le Tigre* (A. Michel, 1930). Se-

lected portions of these were published in a somewhat poor English translation under the title *Clemenceau: The Events of His Life as Told by Himself to His Former Secretary, Jean Martet,* trans. Milton Waldman (New York: Longmans, Green, 1930). Georges M. Wormser's *La République de Clemenceau* (Presses universitaires de France, 1961), contains, on pp. 473–74, a genealogical chart for the Clemenceau family. There is also an appendix with some family papers that had not previously been published.

5. Georges Clemenceau, *Figures de Vendée* (Plon, 1930), pp. 1–8, 51–67, 165–75, and *Au Fil des jours* (Fasquelle, 1900), pp. 94–101; Martet, *Silence de M. Clemenceau,* pp. 199–200.

6. An excellent description of Nantes and its commercial and social life during the period of the July Monarchy may be found in Pierre Sorlin's *Waldeck-Rousseau* (A. Colin, 1966), pp. 12–50.

7. Jacobson, *Self and the Object World,* pp. 56–57. What Jacobson terms "the interplay between these double identifications in parental attitudes"—that is, identification with the needs of the child as well as the revival of old identification problems with one's own parents—should be kept in mind in viewing Clemenceau's later life. As I will demonstrate in chapter 2 of this study, there is some evidence that the birth of his son, Michel, in 1875 triggered a new cycle in Clemenceau's earlier identity conflicts.

8. This letter, dated March 21, 1830, is published in Wormser, *République de Clemenceau,* p. 474.

9. Martet, *M. Clemenceau,* pp. 127, 161–62.

10. Geffroy, *Georges Clemenceau,* p. 71.

11. Martet, *M. Clemenceau,* p. 182.

12. Extracts from Benjamin's notebooks, in Wormser, *République de Clemenceau,* pp. 476–77.

13. Geffroy, *Clemenceau,* p. 28.

14. Georges's brother Paul became an engineer, marrying Moritz Szeps, daughter of the publisher of the leftist Viennese journal *Neues Wiener Tageblatt;* Paul eventually rose to the presidency of the Cie Française de Dynamite. Albert became a lawyer, marrying the daughter of the writer Paul Meurice and gaining some national fame in 1898 as a defender of Georges's newspaper *L'Aurore* in the trial of Émile Zola during the Dreyfus Affair. Except for Adrienne,

who suffered a physical infirmity, the daughters were married—Emma to a naval engineer named Léon Jacquet, Sophie to a journalist named Bryndza. For further information on the family members see Henry Coston, ed., *Dictionnaire de la politique française* (Publications H. Coston, 1967), pp. 253–57.

15. Léon Treich, *Vie et mort de Clemenceau* (Éditions des Portiques, 1929), p. 285, and Martet, *M. Clemenceau,* pp. 181, 185.
16. Martet, *M. Clemenceau,* p. 295.
17. S. Posener, "Clemenceau père et la revolution de Février," *Mercure de France* 234 (February 15, 1932): 253–54. See also Sorlin, *Waldeck-Rousseau,* p. 39.
18. Wormser, *République de Clemenceau,* p. 10.
19. Martet, *M. Clemenceau,* pp. 185–86.
20. Erikson, *Childhood and Society,* pp. 247–58; and Jacobson, *Self and the Object World,* pp. xi, 54, 62. The difference between ego and self, or between self-image and self-representation, is discussed at the beginning of Hartmann's essay "Comments on the Psychoanalytic Theory of the Ego." For further discussion on this definitional problem see Arthur H. Schmale, Jr., "Needs, Gratifications, and the Vicissitudes of the Self-Representation," in *The Psychoanalytic Study of Society,* vol. 2 (New York: International Universities Press, 1962), pp. 9–41; Joseph Sandler, Alex Holder, and Dale Meers, "The Ego Ideal and the Ideal Self," in *The Psychoanalytic Study of the Child,* vol. 18 (New York: International Universities Press, 1963), pp. 139–58; and David Beres, "Ego Autonomy and Ego Pathology," in ibid., vol. 26 (New York: Quadrangle Books, 1972), pp. 3–24.
21. Robert W. White, *The Abnormal Personality,* 3d ed. (New York: Ronald Press, 1964), p. 149.
22. Such was the characterization given by *Le Temps* on November 29, 1929, and by the former deputy for Charente-Inférieure, Eugène Réveillaud, in "Les Familles Clémenceau et Gautreau."
23. Martet, *M. Clemenceau,* p. 187. See also the letter from Clemenceau to Auguste Scheurer-Kestner of February 9, 1864, in Correspondance Clemenceau–Auguste Scheurer-Kestner, Bibliothèque Nationale, MSS Nouvelles Acquisitions Françaises (hereinafter such references are abbrevi-

ated to Bib. Nat., NAF), 24409, no. 17. The contents of the box were mentioned in *Le Temps*, December 4, 1929. In his last will and testament, Clemenceau requested that one of the things that should be placed in his coffin was "the little casket of goatskin in the left hand corner of my wardrobe, with inside it the little box placed there by the hand of my dear mamma." The will was published by *L'Illustration*, November 30, 1929, p. 42.

24. The early photograph appears in William Morton Fullerton, "Georges Clemenceau, Prime Minister of France," *Everybody's Magazine* 16 (February, 1907): 214–23. See also David Robin Watson, *Georges Clemenceau: A Political Biography* (New York: McKay, 1976), p. 393; and Georges Clemenceau, *Lettres à une amie, 1923–1929* (Gallimard, 1970), p. 45.

25. Martet, *Silence de M. Clemenceau*, p. 53.

26. Geffroy, *Clemenceau*, p. 22; "Familles Clémenceau et Gautreau"; and Martet, *M. Clemenceau*, pp. 127, 161.

27. Martet, *M. Clemenceau*, p. 94; and Geffroy, *Clemenceau*, p. 180. The book is in the Musée Clemenceau.

28. Wythe Williams, *The Tiger of France: Conversations with Clemenceau* (New York: Duell, Sloan & Pearce, 1949), p. 236.

29. Watson, *Georges Clemenceau*, p. 18.

30. The letter has been published in Wormser, *République de Clemenceau*, p. 475.

31. This is not to suggest that Clemenceau was ever secretly troubled by matters of the soul or that he ever wavered in his staunch atheism; he did not. The point is only that there was another side of his character in this respect. In Clemenceau's writings on the social question in the 1890s, particularly in *La Melée sociale*, there is an emphasis on personal compassion and altruism, which, as Watson has noted (*Georges Clemenceau*, pp. 141–42) has a close affinity to religious attitudes toward social and economic problems. Samuel Isaac Applebaum's "Clemenceau, Thinker and Writer" (Ph.D. diss., Columbia University, 1948), p. 45, points out that while Clemenceau detested organized religion and its doctrines of rewards and punishment after death, he admired Jesus for His mercy and compassion. As a young man, Clemenceau wrote to a friend: "I really doubt that there is another atheist who regrets as much as

I the absence of Providence. I would abandon everything to His supreme justice, and that would relieve me of hate. But it is sad to think that all the evil men slumber under the same sun as the good" (Treich, *Vie et mort de Clemenceau,* pp. 64–65). As an old man, he once said to Martet: "God! God! Can you stick God up on a wall? One of these days you are going to see me becoming a believer in God just to show them how He should be loved" (Martet, *Silence de Clemenceau,* p. 81).

32. *Travail,* February 2, 1862, in Clemenceau's review of volume 14 of Jules Michelet's *Histoire de France.*
33. Martet, *M. Clemenceau,* p. 188.
34. Ibid., pp. 181, 183.
35. *Travail,* February 2 and 16, 1862.
36. For Clemenceau's own impressions of the lycée experience see Martet, *M. Clemenceau,* pp. 181–82.
37. Erikson, *Identity,* pp. 120–21.
38. Martet, *M. Clemenceau,* pp. 146–47.
39. Ibid., p. 183. Benjamin's words apparently made a deep impression on the boy. He related the story on several occasions toward the end of his life. See, for example, Williams's *Tiger of France,* p. 16.
40. Martet, *M. Clemenceau,* p. 184.
41. Erikson, "Problem of Ego Identity." See also Jacobson, *Self and the Object World,* pp. 68, 170–71, 194–95, 200.
42. Anna Freud, *Ego and the Mechanisms of Defence,* pp. 117–31.
43. Jacobson, *Self and the Object World,* p. 146.
44. Ibid., pp. 64–69.
45. Martet, *M. Clemenceau,* p. 189.
46. Erikson, *Childhood and Society,* pp. 263–66, and "Problem of Ego Identity," p. 122 n.
47. On Clemenceau's medical studies see Charles Coutela, "Georges Clemenceau, la médicine and les médecins," *Presse Medicale,* no. 24 (May 15, 1965), pp. 1435–38; and Gaston Cordier and André Soubiran, "La Thèse d'une étudiant en médecine hors série: Georges Clemenceau (13 mai 1865)," ibid., no. 52 (December 4, 1965), pp. 3029–34.
48. Martet, *M. Clemenceau,* p. 208.
49. *Travail,* February 16, 1862.
50. Ibid., February 2 and 9, 1862.

51. Ibid., February 9, 1862.
52. Ibid.
53. Ibid., February 22, 1862.
54. Watson, *Georges Clemenceau*, p. 144 n.
55. A description of Clemenceau's stay at Mazas is given in his *Grand Pan* (Fasquelle, 1919), pp. 296–97.
56. Letter published in Wormser, *République de Clemenceau*, pp. 475–76.
57. See *Temps*, April 6, 12, and 13, May 18 and 26, 1862.
58. *Matin*, June 29, 1862.
59. Auguste Scheurer-Kestner, *Souvenirs de jeunesse* (Fasquelle, 1905), p. 65.
60. Clemenceau, writing in *Le Journal*, November 27, 1896.
61. Clemenceau, *Au Fil des jours*, pp. 193–201.
62. These events are related in Maurice Dommanget's *Blanqui et l'opposition révolutionnaire à la fin du Second Empire* (A. Colin, 1960), pp. 51–53.
63. Clemenceau to Scheurer-Kestner, February 2, 1863, Bib. Nat., NAF, 24409, no. 8.
64. Clemenceau to Scheurer-Kestner, August 30, 1863, Bib. Nat., NAF, 24409, no. 11.
65. Letters from Jourdan to Clemenceau, September 10 and November 11, 1865, published in Martet, *M. Clemenceau*, pp. 221–29. Martet includes (on pp. 221–32) three letters from Jourdan that Clemenceau saved when he burned his personal papers toward the end of his life.
66. Albert Krebs, "Le Secret de Clemenceau, révélé par les souvenirs d'Auguste Scheurer-Kestner," *Bulletin de la Société industrielle de Mulhouse*, no. 735 (1969), pp. 67–86. Krebs includes those letters referring to the Hortense affair from the Clemenceau–Scheurer-Kestner correspondence that has been cited above. He also includes the comments of Scheurer-Kestner, which may be found in his unpublished journal, Bib. Nat., NAF, 12704–11.
67. Clemenceau to Arago, January 4, 1864, which is included in the letter of Arago to Scheurer-Kestner, January, 1864, Bib. Nat., NAF, 24409, no. 15.
68. Ibid.
69. Arago to Scheurer-Kestner, January 13, 1864, Bib. Nat., NAF, 24409, no. 16.
70. Clemenceau to Scheurer-Kestner, February 9, 1864, Bib. Nat., NAF, 24409, no. 17.

71. Clemenceau to Scheurer-Kestner, February 14, 1864, Bib. Nat., NAF, 24409, no. 18.
72. Martet, *M. Clemenceau*, p. 222.
73. These lines were written after Clemenceau's defeat in 1893. See Krebs, "Secret de Clemenceau, révelé par les souvenirs d'Auguste Scheurer-Kestner."
74. Clemenceau to Scheurer-Kestner, April 20 and May 9, 1864, Bib. Nat., NAF, 24409, nos. 22 and 24.
75. Clemenceau to Scheurer-Kestner, May 16, 1864, Bib. Nat., NAF, 24409, no. 25; and *Temps*, March 22, 1865.
76. Robin appears to have had an important influence on many young medical students of Clemenceau's generation. Born in 1821 in the Ain, he had received his medical degree in 1846; a year later, he had been named an *agrégé* at the Faculty of Medicine of Paris. A chair of histology was created for him in 1862. Later on, he and Émile Littré created the Société de sociologie, whose aim was the application of the principles of Auguste Comte to the study of society. Robin was elected to the Senate for the Ain in 1876. I am grateful to Mlle. Catherine Moureux, archivist of the Faculty of Medicine of the University of Paris, for allowing me to examine Robin's dossier as well as that of Clemenceau. For background information on medical studies during this period see Erwin Heinz Ackerknecht, *Medicine at the Paris Hospital, 1794–1848* (Baltimore, Md.: Johns Hopkins Press, 1967), and J. Leonard, "Les Études médicales en France entre 1815 et 1848," *Revue d'histoire moderne et contemporaine* 13 (January–March, 1966): 87–94.
77. Roger L. Williams, *The World of Napoleon III, 1851–1870* (New York: Free Press, 1965), pp. 152–72.
78. Clemenceau, *De la génération des éléments anatomiques* (J. B. Baillière et Fils, 1865), foreword.
79. Ibid., pp. 89–90, 106–9.
80. In the thesis, p. 221 n, Clemenceau said that he did not count himself "among those who believe with the Positivist school that science cannot furnish us with information about the origin of things. . . . To ignore questions is to suppress them." See also Donald G. Charlton, *Positivist Thought in France during the Second Empire, 1852–1870* (Oxford: Clarendon Press, 1959), pp. 7–8, 10, 32; and Walter M. Simon, *European Positivism in the Nineteenth*

Century (Ithaca, N.Y.: Cornell University Press, 1963), p. 157 n. For a different point of view see David Robin Watson, "A Note on Clemenceau, Comte and Positivism," *Historical Journal* 14 (1971): 201–4. Watson argues that "there is a sense in which Comtean positivism was an important influence on Clemenceau, and in this he was typical of his generation, . . . even if he incorporated it into a materialist outlook which could be said to be strictly incompatible with a rigorous definition of positivism." Watson is correct in stressing that Clemenceau was indebted to certain ideas derived from Comte, especially the latter's biological theories. My main concern has been to show that Clemenceau's republican and materialist beliefs, which were more akin to a metaphysical dogma than to a scientific system of thought, sprang from the early influence of his father, who in turn had himself been influenced by Comtean ideas during his own studies.

81. The *procés-verbal* of the examination shows that Clemenceau was given a high pass, the examiners having been "*extrêmement satisfaits*" with his performance. His dossier reveals that he had performed well on the five examinations that he had had to take prior to defense of the thesis, earning a judgment of "*trés satisfait*" on three of them. These examinations, which he began to take in April, 1864, dealt with such subjects as anatomy, physiology, dissection, internal and external pathology, physical and medical chemistry, pharmacology, hygiene, legal medicine, and childbirth.

82. Martet, *M. Clemenceau*, pp. 93–94. See also Williams, *Tiger of France*, p. 17.

83. Arthur H. Schmale, Jr., in "Needs, Gratifications, and the Vicissitudes of the Self-Representation," stresses that if the sense of self is not firmly established, "there may be a giving up with feelings of helplessness or hopelessness." This point is also made by Jacobson's *Self and the Object World*, pp. 189–90, in calling attention to adolescent states of elation and depression, the latter being caused by guilt conflicts, failure to attain goals, or loss of sexual love. As I will show in the present study, there appear to be, in Clemenceau's early life, cycles of intense activity, followed by depression and withdrawal, which I think were related to his identity conflicts. These cycles are discussed in the

text, but they may be summarized as follows: 1860–65—intense activity; 1865–70—withdrawal; 1870–77—intense activity; 1877–80—withdrawal; 1880–85—intense activity; 1885–93—withdrawal.

84. Erikson, *Life History,* pp. 199–200.
85. Clemenceau to Scheurer-Kestner, February 10, 1865, Bib. Nat., NAF, 24409, no. 37.
86. See Jourdan's comments on Benjamin in Martet, *M. Clemenceau,* pp. 221–22.
87. Clemenceau to Scheurer-Kestner, December 27, 1867, Bib. Nat., NAF, 12704–11.
88. Clemenceau's letter to John Durand (in English), published in *Revue de littérature comparée* 12 (April, 1932): 420–22. See also a letter of recommendation for Clemenceau written by Durand's father, Asher-Brown, to the director of the Smithsonian Institute, in ibid. 13 (January, 1933): 186–87. Two articles from which some of the detail in this section is taken are Fernand Baldensperger's "L'Initiation américaine de Georges Clemenceau," *Revue de littérature comparée* 8 (January–March, 1928): 127–54; and Albert Kreb's "Le Mariage de Clemenceau," *Mercure de France,* August, 1955, pp. 634–50.
89. Clemenceau to Scheurer-Kestner, December 27, 1867, Bib. Nat., NAF, 12704–11.
90. Martet, *M. Clemenceau,* p. 224.
91. Clemenceau to Scheurer-Kestner, October 31, 1867. The original is in the private collection of Albert Krebs, conservateur à la Bibliothéque Nationale.
92. The bulk of Clemenceau's letters to *Le Temps* were collected and published by Fernand Baldensperger in *American Reconstruction, 1865–1870,* trans. Margaret MacVeagh (New York: Dial Press, 1928). A reprint of this edition is available, with a foreword and notes by Otto H. Olsen (New York: Da Capo Press, 1969). The following are Clemenceau's letters to *Le Temps* not included in Baldensperger's book: those of December 26, 1865; January 29, 1867; May 27 and 29, August 18, October 17 and 31, 1868; February 25, September 6, October 11, November 1 and 13, 1869; and February 4 and 28, March 9, April 1 and 14, May 7 and 19, June 16, August 1, 1870. Unless otherwise noted, all citations to these letters are by the date of the letter, the date of its appearance in *Le Temps,* and

the page numbers in Baldensperger where they may be read in English. Translations for all citations in Baldensperger are those of Margaret MacVeagh in the 1928 edition.

93. Martet, *M. Clemenceau*, pp. 231–32.
94. Note from Dana, in the William Henry Seward Collection, Rush Rhees Library, University of Rochester. In his letter to *Le Temps* of May 1, 1869, Clemenceau also mentions meeting Charles Sumner, the New England abolitionist and Republican senator. See also Clemenceau, *Lettres à une amie*, p. x.
95. Letter of September 28, 1865, in *Temps* on October 11, 1865 (Baldensperger, pp. 40–41).
96. Letters of November 6 and 18, 1865, in *Temps* on November 21 and December 2, 1865 (Baldensperger, pp. 42–49).
97. Letter of September 4, 1868, in *Temps* on September 23, 1868 (Baldensperger, pp. 239–45).
98. Wormser, *République de Clemenceau*, p. 476.
99. Letter of November 1, 1867, in *Temps* on November 15, 1867 (Baldensperger, pp. 129–32).
100. Letter of December 16, 1865, in *Temps* on January 3, 1866 (Baldensperger, pp. 54–59).
101. Watson, *Georges Clemenceau*, p. 31. In later years Clemenceau noted that he had found in the South a "remarkably refined society in which the selfish prejudice in favour of slavery was mingled with the most delicate sentiment. Almost every evening I found on my table some work in which it was proved that slavery was sanctioned in the Bible. The proof of that was not hard to furnish" (*In the Evening of My Thought*, trans. Charles Miner Thompson and John Heard, Jr., 2 vols. [Boston and New York: Houghton Mifflin, 1929], 2:399 n).
102. Letter of September 28, 1865, in *Temps* on October 11, 1865 (Baldensperger, pp. 35–42).
103. Letters of November 1, 1867, and September 28, 1865, in *Temps* on November 15, 1867, and October 11, 1865 (Baldensperger, pp. 129–33, 35–42).
104. Letters of March 3, 1869, September 28, 1865, and January 5, 1867, in *Temps* on March 15, 1869, October 11, 1865, and January 25, 1867 (Baldensperger, pp. 277–80, 35–42, and 74–78).
105. Letters of January 26, September 10, and October 18,

1867, and March 20, 1868, in *Temps* on February 8, September 25, and November 2, 1867, and April 3, 1868 (Baldensperger, pp. 82–87, 102–7, 125–26, and 165–69).

106. Letters of September 10, 1867, in *Temps* on September 25, 1867 (Baldensperger, pp. 102–7); and letter appearing in *Temps* on January 29, 1867 (not in Baldensperger).

107. Letter of August 20, 1868, in *Temps* on September 8, 1868 (Baldensperger, pp. 229–33).

108. For generations, the orthodox view in American historical circles held the Radicals in disrepute and pictured Andrew Johnson as the victim of vengeful men such as Stevens. When Clemenceau's letters first appeared in English in 1929, a reviewer for the *New York Times* (January 13, 1929) labeled them "a record of violent prejudices now thoroughly discredited." In the *Saturday Review of Literature* 5 (December, 1928): 426, Claude Bowers, author of *The Tragic Era*, found Clemenceau's account "immensely amusing in its misrepresentations and misinterpretations." The continuing agony over race in America has now shifted the balance, and in the works of such modern writers on Reconstruction as Kenneth Stamp, Eric L. McKitrick, and Lawanda Cox and John H. Cox one finds sympathy and support for many of Clemenceau's original insights and arguments.

109. During the debates over Egypt in 1882, for example, Clemenceau, responding to comments of opponents concerning the superiority of certain races, said: "Does anyone think that the inhabitants of Egypt are inferior to the Negro slaves of the American plantations? I have seen these men: they appeared to be absolutely incapable of being educated; and yet today, delivered from slavery, America has not been afraid to make them citizens. They are fulfilling with dignity their political functions and know how to make their rights respected." *JO, Chambre des Députés*, July 19, 1882.

110. Letter of November 3, 1869, in *Temps* on November 23, 1869 (Baldensperger, pp. 297–99).

111. Letter of August 6, 1869, in *Temps* on August 25, 1869 (Baldensperger, pp. 295–96).

112. Martet, *M. Clemenceau*, p. 207.

113. Dommanget, *Blanqui*, pp. 140–41.

114. Krebs, "Mariage de Clemenceau."

115. Part of this letter was published in Alexandre Zévaès, *Clemenceau* (Julliard, 1949), pp. 22–23. See also Treich, *Vie et mort de Clemenceau*, pp. 63–65.

116. See the letter of one of his pupils in Wormser, *République de Clemenceau*, pp. 99–100. Reminiscences of others are found in the Stamford (Conn.) *Advocate*, November 10, 13, 18, and 25, 1922, and November 26, 1929. It would be interesting to know Clemenceau's own reactions to his students and to the idea of education for women during this period, especially since John Stuart Mill had begun to argue for women's rights. Unfortunately, Clemenceau had little to say about this episode in his later writings, although at some time during his visit to America he drew up an outline for a book on women in which he intended to examine their place in the biological and social orders. In his notes he sketched an argument for the physical inferiority of the female sex in the biological world ("male flowers consume more oxygen than female flowers"). While he agreed with Mill that women ought to be given equality in both marriage and civil rights, he believed that women would be unable to cope with the rigors of political life. Clemenceau's antifeminism, which lasted all his life, was certainly characteristic of his times; but in his case, one perceives an exaggerated notion of the mental and physical delicacy of women in general. It is possible that this attitude had its origins in the tender relationships that he had with his mother and older sister during his early childhood, in contrast to the tough and manly attributes that he associated with his father. In his old age, for example, Clemenceau told Martet that women did not have the necessary qualities for engaging in political action and combat and that those who entertained such notions reminded him of "bearded women." He also said: "I would never be able to marry a woman doctor. Medicine presupposes a brutality and a harshness of heart that are not made for women." See Martet, *M. Clemenceau*, pp. 245, 257–69.

117. Krebs, "Secret de Clemenceau, révelé par les souvenirs d'Auguste Scheurer-Kestner."

118. Clemenceau to Scheurer-Kestner, October 13, 1868, in the private collection of Albert Krebs.

119. Martet, *Silence de M. Clemenceau*, pp. 311–14.

120. Krebs, "Secret de Clemenceau, révélé par les souvenirs d'Auguste Scheurer-Kestner."
121. Ibid.
122. Ibid.

CHAPTER TWO:

THE RADICAL OF MONTMARTE, 1870–1880

1. Stewart Edwards, *The Paris Commune, 1871* (London: Eyre & Spottiswoode, 1971), p. 50. For further background on developments within Paris see Roger L. Williams, *The French Revolution of 1870–1871* (New York: Norton, 1969). Additional secondary works consulted for this chapter include Alistair Horne, *The Fall of Paris: The Siege and the Commune, 1870–71* (Garden City, N.Y.: Doubleday Anchor Books, 1967); Denis W. Brogan, *The Development of Modern France, 1870–1939* (London: Hamish Hamilton, 1940); and Jacques Chastenet, *Histoire de la troisième république,* vol. 1: *L'Enfance de la troisième, 1870–1879* (Hachette, 1952).

2. *Journal officiel de la république française,* September 6, 1870, pp. 1529–30.

3. Edwards, *Paris Commune,* pp. 46–47, 68–72.

4. Edmond de Goncourt, *Paris under Siege, 1870–1871: From the Goncourt Journal,* ed. and trans. George J. Becker (Ithaca, N.Y.: Cornell University Press, 1969), p. 266.

5. On wall placards signed by Clemenceau see *Les Murailles politiques françaises: Depuis le 18 juillet 1870 jusqu'au 25 mai 1871,* 2 vols. (Chevalier, 1874), 1:428; and Martet, *M. Clemenceau,* pp. 165–66. On Blanqui's election see Geffroy, *Georges Clemenceau,* p. 31.

6. Testimony on petrol bombs is found in France, Assemblée Nationale, *Enquête parlementaire sur l'insurrection du 18 mars 1871,* 3 vols. (Versailles: Imprimeur de l'Assemblée Nationale, 1872), 2:322. Once during a midnight inspection of fortifications along rue André, he found guards asleep and artillery untended. He reprimanded the guilty, returned every three hours during the night, and submitted to General Trochu the names of battalions and

companies that had failed in their duty. See Archives de Paris, Départment de la Seine, 2 AZ 190.

7. Martet, *M. Clemenceau*, p. 166.
8. For details on these events see Edwards, *Paris Commune,* pp. 77–84.
9. Wormser, *République de Clemenceau,* p. 105.
10. See *Murailles françaises,* 1:222, 548; and Louise Michel, *La Commune* (P. V. Stock, 1898), p. 132. The circular to school directors can be found in Archives de Paris, Départment de la Seine, 3 AZ 322.
11. Part of this letter is on display at the Musée Clemenceau. The letter, which never reached his wife, has been published in its entirety by Stanley J. Pincetl, Jr., in *French Historical Studies* 2 (fall, 1962): 511–14.
12. Letter published by Martet, *M. Clemenceau,* p. 153.
13. The five groups that featured Clemenceau's name were the Republican Central Committee of the National Guard of the Seine (which also included such names as Louis Blanc, Victor Hugo, Henri Rochefort, Edgar Quinet, and Giuseppe Garibaldi, the old fighter for Italian unity); the Republicans of Good Sense, who also supported the mayors of the third, eleventh, fourteenth, and twentieth arrondissements because they had "constantly protested against the conduct of affairs"; a group that called itself the Radical Republican Committee of the Left Bank and Right Bank; the Radical Republican Committee of the Eleventh Arrondissement; and the Republican and Socialist Fusion, which also listed Auguste Blanqui and Félix Pyat. For full electoral lists see *Murailles françaises,* 1:857, 867, 873, 882, 889. In the Bordeaux assembly, republicans captured only 200 seats, the remainder of the 675 seats going to monarchists. See Williams, *French Revolution of 1870– 1871,* pp. 116–17.
14. *Journal officiel de la république française: Assemblée nationale: Compte rendu in extenso,* February 19 and March 4, 1871, pp. 113, 145.
15. Ibid., March 1, 1871, pp. 131–32.
16. Martet, *M. Clemenceau,* pp. 169–70.
17. *Enquête parlementaire sur l'insurrection,* 1:50.
18. Ibid., 1:52 and 2:434.
19. Clemenceau related these events in his speech to the National Assembly at Versailles on March 21, 1871. See

Journal officiel de la république française: Assemblée Nationale, March 22, 1871, p. 219. To the end of his life he maintained that Thiers had promised not to try to take the cannons by force. See Martet, *M. Clemenceau,* p. 249.

20. Martet, *Silence de M. Clemenceau,* p. 210.
21. Clemenceau's recollections of the events of March 18 can be found in ibid., pp. 269–99. Martet claims that this is only a part of an account of two hundred pages that deal with Clemenceau's role in the Commune. Martet never did keep his promise to publish the full account, which remains in the possession of his widow and has not been made available to scholars.
22. Michel, *Commune,* pp. 139–40.
23. *Enquête parlementaire sur l'insurrection,* 1:62. A good treatment of the events of March 18 may be found in Stewart, *Paris Commune,* pp. 134–52.
24. *Enquête parlementaire sur l'insurrection,* 2:518.
25. Valigranne's account has been published by Wormser, *République de Clemenceau,* pp. 481–83.
26. *Enquête parlementaire sur l'insurrection,* 1:68.
27. Ibid., 2:519; and *Journal officiel de la république française: Assemblée nationale,* March 21, 1871, p. 199.
28. *Journal officiel de la république française: Assemblée nationale,* March 21 and 22, 1871, pp. 195–96, 213–22.
29. *Murailles françaises,* 2:38.
30. *Journal officiel de la république française: Assemblée nationale,* March 25, 1871, p. 270.
31. Edwards, *Paris Commune,* pp. 181–86; and Williams, *French Revolution of 1870–1871,* pp. 131–32. A copy of the electoral decree that was signed by Clemenceau is found in Michel, *Commune,* pp. 155–56.
32. See *Temps,* April 4, 7, and 9, 1871. For a more detailed analysis of the activities of the Republican Union see Watson, *Georges Clemenceau,* pp. 51–53.
33. Léon Treich, *L'Esprit de Clemenceau* (Gallimard, 1925), pp. 102–3.
34. Clemenceau could never forgive the communards for launching "one of the maddest, most insane events in history." No one, he said later, "really knew what the Commune was. These people killed, committed arson, got themselves shot, often with great nobleness. But they never knew why." See Martet, *M. Clemenceau,* pp. 47, 154.

35. *Journal officiel de la république française: Assemblée nationale,* March 21, 1871, p. 195.

36. Watson, *Georges Clemenceau,* pp. 54–55. It should be noted that Floquet and Lockroy, both of whom would later occupy ministerial positions under the Third Republic, were also active in the Republican Union for the Rights of Paris. What made Clemenceau vulnerable was his role in the events leading to the murders of Lecomte and Thomas. As I show in chapter 3 of this book, however, the reasons for Clemenceau's failure to build a reform party in the 1880s were more complex than the popular perception of what he did or did not do in 1871.

37. Piers and Singer, *Shame and Guilt,* p. 16: "It is as if the loved parental images or the projected power and life sustaining sources of one's own omnipotence threaten to abandon the weakling who fails to reach them."

38. See *Temps,* November 10, 11, 12, 13, and 15, 1871.

39. Ernest Judet, *Le Véritable Clemenceau* (Berne, Switzerland: F. Wyss, 1920), pp. 53–63.

40. Watson, *Georges Clemenceau,* p. 55 n.

41. Samuel M. Osgood, *French Royalism under the Third and Fourth Republics* (The Hague: Nijhoff, 1960), p. 34. For further background on monarchism during this period see also Robert R. Locke, *French Legitimists and the Politics of Moral Order in the Early Third Republic* (Princeton, N.J.: Princeton University Press, 1974); and Réne Remond, *The Right-Wing in France from 1815 to De Gaulle,* trans. James M. Laux, 2d ed. (Philadelphia: University of Pennsylvania Press, 1969).

42. The standard history of the Paris Municipal Council is that of Pierre Bernheim, *Le Conseil municipal de Paris de 1789 à nos jours* (Presses modernes, 1937).

43. Information on Clemenceau's work is taken primarily from Conseil municipal de Paris, *Procès-verbaux,* 8 vols. (Typographie la hure, 1871–76).

44. Ibid., vol. 3, February 24 and March 18, 1872, nos. 6 and 14; vol. 4, December 12, 1872, no. 80; vol. 5, August 9, 1873, no. 40; and vol. 6, October 10, 1874, no. 41.

45. Ibid., vol. 3, February 26, 1872, no. 7; vol. 5, March 8, 13, and 15 and July 11, 1873, nos. 11, 12, 13, and 32; and vol. 6, January 29, June 4, and August 10, 1874, nos. 3, 22, and 36.

46. Ibid., vol. 3, March 2, 1872, no. 8. The report was published in *La République française,* November 25–28, 1874. See also the unsigned article "Clemenceau et les enfants-assistés," in *L'Hôpital et l'aide sociale à Paris,* no. 35 (1965), pp. 641–43.

47. Conseil municipal de Paris, *Procès-verbaux,* vol. 7, November 29, 1875, no. 62.

48. See the three letters that Louise Michel wrote to him in 1879 in Zévaès, *Clemenceau,* pp. 307–11. After her return to France in 1880, he continued to send her money, even after she was jailed again for political activities. See Édith Thomas, *Louise Michel: ou, La Velléda de l'anarchie* (Gallimard, 1971), pp. 211, 267, 277.

49. Arthur Ranc, *Souvenirs: Correspondance, 1831–1908* (Édouard Cornély, 1913), p. 213.

50. For detail on the working of the organic laws of 1875 see Ernest Lavisse, ed., *Histoire de France contemporaine,* vol. 8: Charles Seignobos, *L'Évolution de la 3ᵉ république (1875–1914)* (Hachette, 1921), pp. 1–8; and Roger H. Soltau, *French Parties and Politics, 1871–1921* (New York: Russell & Russell, 1965), pp. 9–19.

51. *Temps,* February 2 and 5, 1876. See also Georges Michon, *Clemenceau* (Rivière, 1931), p. 13; and Jean T. Joughin, *The Paris Commune in French Politics, 1871–1880* (Baltimore, Md.: Johns Hopkins Press, 1955), p. 92.

52. For a breakdown of the conservative majority in the Senate see Chapman, *The Third Republic of France,* p. 161, and Seignobos, *Évolution de la 3ᵉ république,* p. 5. For further background on the upper house during the early years of the Republic see J.-J. Chevallier, *Histoire des institutions politiques de la France moderne, 1789–1945* (Dalloz, 1958,) pp. 312–15; and Peter Campbell, *French Electoral Systems and Elections since 1789,* 2d ed. (Hamden, Conn.: Archon Books, 1965), pp. 139–40. Only about ten senators could be considered Radicals in 1876; these included Victor Hugo. For background on individual senators see Jules Clère, *Biographie complète des sénateurs* (Garnier frères, 1876). On the election of the Chamber see Seignobos, *Évolution de la 3ᵉ république,* pp. 6–8. On the Extreme Left see Kayser, *Grandes batailles du radicalisme,* pp. 94–95.

53. Zeldin, *France, 1848–1945,* 1:23.

54. For a breakdown on the percentage of Radical deputies who were lawyers and doctors see Kayser, *Grandes batailles du radicalisme,* p. 370. The medical men among the hard-core Radicals included, besides Clemenceau, Jules Bouquet, Charles Félix Frébault, Alfred Leconte, Paul Massot, Jean Moreau, Alfred Naquet, François-Vincent Raspail, Jean Turigny, and Émile Vernhes. The percentage of medical men for other political groups was as follows: Republican Union, 12.28%; Republican Left, 10.52%; Center Left, 3.48%. Of the forty-six medical men in the Chamber of 1876, only two sat on the Right. See Michel Bisault, "La Composition socio-professionelle de la Chambre des Députés de la IIIème république" (unpublished memoire for the diplome de science politique de la Faculté de Droit de Paris, 1960). For a study of those deputies who were trained in the law see also Yves-Henri Gaudemet, *Les Juristes et la vie politique de la IIIᵉ république* (Presses universitaires de France, 1970).

55. Kayser, *Grandes batailles du radicalisme,* p. 372; and Loubère, *Radicalism in Mediterranean France,* p. 110.

56. See Dora B. Weiner, *Raspail: Scientist and Reformer* (New York: Columbia University Press, 1968).

57. Sorlin, *Waldeck-Rousseau,* p. 184.

58. Naquet, who was born at Carpentras in 1834, had received his medical degree from the Paris Faculty in 1860 and had later become an *agrégé,* giving courses in chemistry in the late 1860s. His political activities soon got him into trouble with the school's administration, however, and he was compelled to leave the faculty, though according to his dossier, the dean regretted his leaving and called him "a very distinguished chemist." Naquet's book *Religion, propriété, famille,* which was published in 1869, spelled more trouble with the authorities, and he was forced to spend several months in Spain. Elected to the National Assembly for the Vaucluse in July, 1871, he sat with the Extreme Left and spoke frequently in debates, especially on issues involving medicine and public health. Another of his books, *La République radicale,* which appeared in 1873, contains a good statement of the early philosophy of radicalism. Naquet would later be the author of the divorce law.

59. Gambetta is supposed to have referred to Clemenceau,

Périn, and Lockroy as "the three musketeers." Louis Andrieux, one of Clemenceau's friends from their Latin Quarter days, later recalled that "bent on having their party
respected, perfectly trained in pistol-shooting and fencing,
ever ready to call out the parliamentary quarrels on
another ground, these three deputies never heard any challenge from the Right without at once taking it up"
("Georges Clemenceau," *North American Review*, February 15, 1907, pp. 371–82). See also the report by the
correspondent for the London *Times*, May 15, 1876.

60. Joughin, *Paris Commune in French Politics*, p. 105.
61. *Temps*, March 14, 1876.
62. *JO, Chambre des Députés*, May 17, 1876, pp. 3332–41.
63. Joughin, *Paris Commune in French Politics*, pp. 119–20.
64. *Temps*, May 13, 1877.
65. The best study on the events of *seize-mai* is that of Fres-
    nette Pisani-Ferry, *Le Coup d'état manqué du 16 mai 1877*
    (Lafont, 1965).
66. See Clemenceau's somewhat humorous recollections of the
    committee, in Martet, *M. Clemenceau*, pp. 209–12. See
    also the exchange of letters between Clemenceau and
    Antonin Proust on the affair, in *La Justice*, February 14,
    16, 19, 20, and 26, 1884.
67. Pisani-Ferry, *Coup d'état manqué du 16 mai*, pp. 301–2,
    notes that, according to the memoirs of General de Wimp-
    fen, there was also a plan to sever telegraphic lines be-
    tween Versailles and the provinces and to proclaim a
    National Assembly of republican deputies in Paris.
68. *Justice*, February 26, 1884.
69. Clemenceau's only significant parliamentary activity in
    1878 was in helping to prepare reports that invalidated the
    elections of some of the seventy-eight monarchists who
    were subsequently expelled from the Chamber. These in-
    cluded the comte d'Aulon of Nyons, Alfred Leroux of
    Fontenay-le-Comte in the Vendée, de Puibernéau of Roche-
    sur-Yon, Barcilon of Carpentras, La Rochefoucauld, the
    duke of Bisaccia, and the comte de Prunières of Embrun.
    See *JO, Chambre des Députés*, February 8 and 14, pp.
    1279–80, 1878; and March 5 and 21, pp. 2458, 5519–20.
70. Wormser, *République de Clemenceau*, pp. 137–41.
71. Erikson, *Life History*, p. 20, and *Identity*, p. 23.
72. Camille Pelletan, *Georges Clemenceau* (A. Quantin, 1883),

p. 5; Geffroy, *Clemenceau*, p. 18; Andrieux, "Clemenceau"; Léon Daudet, *Flammés: Polémique et polémistes: Proudhon—les Châtiments—Rochefort et Vallès—Bloy—Clemenceau* (Grasset, 1930), p. 190; and *Temps*, March 5, 1879.

73. *JO, Chambre des Députés*, May 17, 1876, pp. 3332–41 (during his speech on amnesty).

74. *Justice*, July 29 and 30, 1883.

75. New York *World*, March 14, 1892.

76. Georges Gatineau-Clemenceau, *Des Pattes du Tigre aux griffes du destin* (Presses du mail, 1961), pp. 26–29, 34–37, 54–57.

77. New York *World*, March 14, 1892.

78. Martet, *Silence de M. Clemenceau*, pp. 212–13.

79. W. T. Stead, "Georges Clémenceau, the Warwick of French Politics," *Review of Reviews*, June, 1906, pp. 677–78.

80. Brandes, "M. Georges Clemenceau."

81. Judet, *Véritable Clemenceau*, p. 3.

82. A duel between Clemenceau and a man named Paul Foucher in 1887 resulted in no injuries; the same was true for Clemenceau's more famous duel with Déroulède in 1893. Many others would not accept his challenges: Cassagnac in 1876, Mitchell in 1877, the editor of the *Petit méridional* in 1881. A challenge from a deputy named Duchesne was settled peacefully in 1886. Clemenceau served as a second for many others, including Gambetta, Rochefort, Pelletan, and Floquet. He strictly adhered to the unwritten code of honor in these matters. When Baron Harden-Hickey sent his seconds to Clemenceau, Clemenceau disdainfully refused, saying: "If I had judged that a duel could resolve the question pending between us, it is I who would have sent my witnesses to him." See *Justice*, October 2, 1886.

83. Erikson, *Childhood and Society*, pp. 263–66.

84. Louis Guitard, in "Georges Clemenceau et Léon Daudet: Deux enfants terribles de la troisième république," *Oeuvres libres*, no. 25 (July, 1948), pp. 245–82, notes that Alphonse Daudet and his son Léon often visited Clemenceau at the offices of *La Justice* and that Alphonse, in the event of his death, had entrusted to Clemenceau the care of Léon. Guitard says that Clemenceau wept at the death of Alphonse in 1897. Manet began to paint Clemenceau's portrait in the early 1880s, but neither of the two works

that he started was ever completely finished. The more
famous of the two—which was eventually to hang in the
Jeu de Paume at the Louvre—was executed in oil on
canvas and is a good example of early Impressionism.
Manet had also begun a pastel portrait of Mary Plummer
before his death; this, along with the two other works,
Manet's widow gave to Clemenceau. Clemenceau eventually sold the two portraits of himself. See Georges
Bataille, *Manet* (New York: Skira, 1955), pp. 14–15, 19;
Adolphe Tabarant, *Manet et ses oeuvres* (Gallimard, 1947),
pp. 358–59; and Pierre Schneider, *The World of Manet,
1832–1883* (New York: Time-Life Books, 1968), p. 63.

85. Wormser, *République de Clemenceau*, p. 35.
86. An English translation of the full letter may be found in
Historical Journal 16 (September, 1973): 604–15, with an
introduction by Maurice Paz. Paz's comments on the significance of this letter are misleading, however, and one
should consult David Robin Watson's "Clemenceau and
Blanqui: A Reply to M. Paz," in ibid. 21 (June, 1978):
387–97.
87. *JO, Chambre des Députés*, February 22, 1879, pp. 1310–13.
88. Joughin, *Paris Commune in French Politics*, pp. 243–44.
89. *JO, Chambre des Députés*, March 4, 1879, pp. 1644–48.
90. There are accounts that just after MacMahon's resignation,
Clemenceau called on Gambetta and asked him to run
for the presidency. Gambetta refused, denying Clemenceau's suggestion that he was now afraid of political
combat. "Are you tired?" asked Clemenceau. "Perhaps,"
Gambetta answered. This is related in Chapman, *Third
Republic of France*, p. 197. For a comparison of the dif-
fering attitudes of Gambetta and Clemenceau see John
Roberts, "Clemenceau the Politician," *History Today* 6
(September, 1956): 581–91.
91. *Temps,* May 13, 1879.
92. *JO, Chambre des Députés,* May 28, 1879, pp. 4381–84.
93. "It is the enormous power that the state gives to the
Church," he said at the cirque Fernando in 1880, "that
accounts for the fact that in this struggle the state is always
vanquished." See *Justice,* April 13, 1880. In a later speech
given there, he argued for a concept of national sovereignty
in which France would no longer be "the property of any
man, sect, or coterie." See ibid., November 1, 1882.

94. *Temps,* May 13, 1879.
95. Watson, *Georges Clemenceau,* p. 68, notes that this sum may have represented the bulk of Clemenceau's inheritance.
96. Geoffroy, *Georges Clemenceau,* p. 56; and Zévaès, *Clemenceau,* p. 317.
97. *JO, Chambre des Députés,* December 17, 1879, pp. 11217–22. For a breakdown of the voting pattern on Lockroy's motion of no confidence see *Le Temps,* December 18, 1879. Six days later, the newspaper noted that Waddington had given "personal reasons" for his resignation. But the fact that he had been severely weakened on December 16 by the great number of abstentions on the confidence motion that finally passed (only 289 had voted) was the real reason for his resignation.
98. See the report of the meeting with Constans in *La Justice,* May 29, 1880.
99. *JO, Chambre des Députés,* May 29, 1880, pp. 5808–13.
100. *Justice,* June 5 and 6, 1880.
101. Bernard H. Moss, in *The Origins of the French Labor Movement, 1830–1914* (Berkeley: University of California Press, 1976), p. 89, argues that Gambetta's tendency to compromise with the bourgeoisie on the matter of amnesty was an important event leading to the formation of a labor movement that would seek to protect its own interests.
102. In his famous speech at Salernes in 1893, he called the achievement of amnesty the "first victory" of *La Justice.* See *Justice,* August 10, 1893.
103. Erikson, *Childhood and Society,* p. 267.

CHAPTER THREE:

THE CREATOR & THE DESTROYER, 1880–1885

1. Zeldin, *France, 1848–1945,* 1:698–706; Chapman, *Third Republic of France,* p. 241; Jacques Chastenet, *Histoire de la troisième république,* vol. 2: *La République de républicains, 1879–1893* (Hachette, 1954), p. 116; Maurice Baumont, *Gloires et tragédies de la IIIᵉ république* (Hachette, 1956), pp. 180, 184–85; Chevallier, *Histoire des institutions politiques de la France moderne,* p. 433; Maurice

Reclus, *Jules Ferry, 1832–1893* (Flammarion, 1947), p. 342; and Watson, *Georges Clemenceau,* p. 137. Zeldin notes that Clemenceau's nickname of "The Tiger" "conveyed his wild destructiveness but it should not mislead into suggesting that he was a mass of strength. He was a small man and after middle age fat as well as short, undistinguished. He was extremely nervous and given to the most profound depression, which he relieved by violent outbursts of rage." Baumont adds that "with a reputation for terror, this perpetual opposer was the *enfant terrible* of the Republic." Chevallier calls Clemenceau a "ferocious Wrecker of Ministries" and compares him to Robespierre in his "defiance toward all government."

2. Lynd, *On Shame,* pp. 132–40.
3. Alexander, *Fundamentals of Psychoanalysis,* p. 108.
4. Lynd, *On Shame,* p. 92.
5. Jacobson, *Self and the Object World,* pp. 153–54, 200–201.
6. L. Arthur Minnich, Jr., "The Third Force, 1870–1896," in Edward Mead Earle, ed., *Modern France: Problems of the Third and Fourth Republics* (Princeton, N.J.: Princeton University Press, 1951), pp. 109–36.
7. See Antoine Prost and Christian Rosenzveig, "La Chambre des Députés (1881–1885): Analyses factorielle des scrutins," *Revue française de science politique* 21 (January–June, 1971): 5–49. See also François Goguel-Nyegaard, *La Politique des partis sous la IIIe république,* 3d ed. (Seuil, 1958), pp. 25–29, 37–43.
8. Mattei Dogan, "La Stabilité du personnel parlementaire sous la troisième république," *Revue française de science politique* 3 (April–June, 1953): 319–48. Dogan also points out that there was a remarkable stability of parliamentary personnel as measured by its slow turnover. Of the 4,892 deputies elected under the Third Republic, 2,621 were elected for at least two terms, 2,066 of the latter for consecutive terms.
9. Bisault, "Composition socio-professionelle," pp. 11–15.
10. An example was his speech at Marseilles in October, 1880. Attacking Gambetta for his failure to prevent the succession of weak cabinets, he said: "What was the Waddington ministry if not the Dufaure ministry minus Dufaure? What was the Freycinet ministry if not the Waddington ministry minus Waddington? And finally, what is the

Ferry ministry if not the Freycinet ministry minus Freycinet?" See *Justice,* November 1, 1880.

11. See the session of March 6, 1883, in *JO, Chambre des
Députés,* where, during a debate over constitutional revision, Ferry accused Clemenceau of being responsible for
destroying two cabinets thus far. Clemenceau answered
that he could easily demonstrate that he had "never overthrown any cabinets and that we have never witnessed
anything but cabinets committing suicide and overthrowing themselves." Later, in the same speech, he stressed
that the Radicals had, in fact, never gained anything from
the frequent fall of ministries, "because even though ministries have been overthrown, the policies of all these
cabinets have remained the same. The men have changed,
but the policies have remained the same." See also his
speech at Salernes, in *La Justice,* August 10, 1893, where
he defended himself against the charge of being a "systematic opposer."

12. Zévaès, *Clemenceau,* p. 319.

13. These included Waddington (February to December,
1879), who resigned for "personal reasons" but who, as
pointed out earlier, had been weakened by Radical attacks
and the abstentions of Gambetta's group on confidence
motions; first Freycinet (December, 1879, to September,
1880), whose fall was caused by dissent within the cabinet,
especially between Freycinet and Ferry, over the move
against unauthorized teaching congregations; Eugène Duclerc (August, 1882, to January, 1883), who claimed that
he was ill and who also suffered from dissension within
his cabinet over a proposal by Floquet to ban from French
soil the members of former ruling families; Armand Fal-
lières (January to February, 1883), who was weak from
the start and became essentially a casualty of Ferry's successful effort to create a new majority for himself by
negotiating with the followers of the now-deceased Gambetta; Henri Brisson (April to December, 1885), whose
cabinet was really a caretaker government during the elections of 1885; and finally the earlier ministry of Dufaure
(December, 1877, to February, 1879), who set the prece-
dent of resigning upon the election of a new president of
the Republic.

14. Chapman, in *Third Republic of France,* p. 273, claims that

Clemenceau "had been responsible for the fall of Ferry, Brisson, Freycinet, and Goblet, four cabinets in two years." Henry Louis Dubly's *La Vie ardente de Georges Clemenceau*, 2 vols. (Lille: Mercure de Flandre, 1930), 1:242, speaking of the fall of Freycinet in 1886, of Goblet in 1887, of Rouvier in 1887, and of Tirard in 1890, says that "it was always Clemenceau who was the architect of their fall." Geoffrey Bruun, in his *Clemenceau* (Cambridge, Mass.: Harvard University Press, 1943), has an entire chapter entitled "Wrecker of Ministries," yet he neglects to give precise examples of exactly which ministries Clemenceau was responsible for destroying. Ernest Judet, on the other hand, in his *Véritable Clemenceau,* p. 10, blames Clemenceau for the fall of Ferry in 1881, of Gambetta in 1882, of Freycinet in 1882, of Ferry in 1885, of Brisson in 1885, of Freycinet again in 1886, and of Goblet in 1887.

15. Michelle Perrot, *Les Ouvriers en grève: France, 1871–1890,* 2 vols. (Mouton, 1974), p. 90. Perrot shows that the consolidation of the Republic created high hopes among workers. In 1878, she notes, miners attributed their low salary levels to the anger of the big companies, which were "furious over the results of the elections of October 1877." Miners at Montceau, at Decazeville, and in the Allier believed afterwards that they could expect some real material improvement in their lives as a result of their faithfulness to the Republic.

16. Moss, *Origins of the French Labor Movement,* pp. 4–5, 156–57.

17. Clemenceau believed that a postponement of reform and a cowering before the conservative elements in France were the real dangers to republican unity. "In trying to accommodate oneself to circumstances," he told a rally at Montmartre in 1881, "one ends up being the slave of circumstances." See *Justice,* August 13, 1881.

18. Sanford Elwitt, *The Making of the Third Republic: Class and Politics in France, 1868–1884* (Baton Rouge: Louisiana State University Press, 1975), pp. 19–21, 27.

19. John B. Christopher, "The Desiccation of the Bourgeois Spirit," in Earle, ed., *Modern France,* pp. 44–57.

20. Minnich, "Third Force"; and Sorlin, *Waldeck-Rousseau,* p. 243. See also Weill, *Histoire du mouvement sociale en*

France, p. 241; and Édouard Doléans, *Histoire du mouvement ouvrier,* vol. 2: *1871–1936* (Colin, 1939), pp. 17–18. Weill points out that moderate republicans generally rejected state intervention in economic affairs and held to the view that liberty and education would be enough to solve any social problems. For a good treatment of a typical representative of this attitude see Martin E. Schmidt, *Alexandre Ribot: Odyssey of a Liberal in the Third Republic* (The Hague: Nijhoff, 1974). On the political attitudes of lawyers see Gaudement, *Juristes et la vie politique,* p. 32.

21. Despite all that has been written concerning the political obstructionism of Clemenceau and the Extreme Left, the Radicals usually voted *for* reform legislation that was sponsored by Opportunist cabinets after Radical amendments had been defeated. This pattern was especially apparent in laws relating to education. Radicals, for example, supported such bills as the following: normal schools for training lay teachers (*JO, Chambre des Députés,* March 21, 1879, p. 2297); government control of the administration of charity (ibid., July 31, 1879, p. 7833); the whole of Ferry's anticlerical legislation, including article seven (ibid., July 10, 1879, pp. 6433–34); exclusion of the clergy from higher councils of public education (ibid., July 10, 1879, p. 7071); secondary education for girls (ibid., January 21, 1880, pp. 582–83); free primary education (ibid., November 30, 1880, p. 11729); and compulsory primary education (ibid., December 25, 1880, pp. 12879–80).

22. Loubère, "French Left-Wing Radicals: Their Economic and Social Program since 1870"; *Radicalism in Mediterranean France,* pp. xv, 35–36, 61 n; and *Louis Blanc: His Life and His Contribution to the Rise of French Jacobin-Socialism* (Evanston, Ill.: Northwestern University Press, 1961), pp. 15–21. See also Nordmann, *Histoire des radicaux,* p. 45; and Kayser, *Grandes batailles du radicalisme,* pp. 25–26.

23. Moss, *Origins of the French Labor Movement,* p. 29.

24. See ibid., p. 73; Perrot, *Ouvriers en grève,* 1:196–97; and Minnich, "Third Force."

25. Loubère, "French Left-Wing Radicals: Their Views on Trade Unionism" and "French Left-Wing Radicals: Their Economic and Social Program since 1870."

26. Chapman, *Third Republic of France*, p. 340.
27. A glance at voting patterns on defeated pieces of social legislation indicates that, despite the conservatism of the majority, there did exist a genuine reformist sentiment in the Chamber that included deputies to the right of the Extreme Left, most of them belonging to the advanced wing of Gambetta's group. See note 126 of this chapter.
28. See Prost and Rosenzveig, "Chambre des Députés," and William Morton Fullerton, "Georges Clemenceau." In his *Georges Clemenceau*, pp. 5–7, Pelletan wrote that "M. Clemenceau's words are like cold, sharp, well-tempered steel, and his speeches resemble fencing matches in which his direct lunges pierce his adversaries."
29. *JO, Chambre des Députés*, February 2, 1881, p. 120.
30. Henry Mayers Hyndman, *The Record of an Adventurous Life* (New York: Macmillan, 1911), pp. 314–29. My italics.
31. "Political reformation is the instrument of social reformation," he said at the cirque Fernando, "we must have republican institutions in order to have social reform." See *Justice*, April 13, 1880. Nordmann, in *Histoire des radicaux*, p. 33, stresses that Radicals had long recognized the intrinsic relationship between control of the public powers and social reform.
32. In December of 1882 he charged the local governments that were dominated by monarchists of encouraging the faithful not to send their children to state schools. He urged that payments be made to parents in order to encourage them to send their children to school and thus to guarantee to the child a free intellectual development. See *JO, Chambre des Députés*, December 24, 1882, pp. 2175–76.
33. The Opportunists shared Clemenceau's view that many judges who undermined educational laws were monarchists or leftovers from the Empire. In February of 1882 a bill was brought in to "purify" the bench. It passed the next year, but not before Clemenceau had consumed two whole sessions trying to prove that the views of the great men of the Revolution supported the concept of election of judges. See ibid., January 23, 1883, pp. 102–10, and January 24, 1883, pp. 113–23.
34. Speech at Marseilles, October, 1880, in *Justice*, November 1, 1880. Ferry's proposals to ban unauthorized teaching

had failed in the Senate in March, 1880; and the government had therefore decided to press forward by enforcing the existing laws. All unauthorized congregations had to apply for authorization within three months or be closed down. In the spring of 1879 Ferry wrote to Scheurer-Kestner regarding Clemenceau's hostility to Ferry's anticlerical proposals: "This puzzling fickleness, this impatient demagoguery, this complete and naïve absence of political morality, are bound to play a disastrous role in the destinies of the Republic." Quoted in Reclus, *Jules Ferry*, p. 155.

35. See *Temps*, February 2 and 5, 1876.
36. Perrot, *Ouvriers en grève*, 1:150–51. Claude Willard, in *Les Guesdistes: Le Mouvement socialiste en France, 1893–1905* (Éditions Sociales, 1965), p. 33 n, points out that figures on unemployment in the 1880s fail to take into account additional workers who were partially unemployed. Perrot speaks of somewhere between 200,000 and 300,000 unemployed during the worst period of the depression. See also Moss, *Origins of the French Labor Movement*, p. 15.
37. Edward Shorter and Charles Tilly, *Strikes in France, 1830–1968* (London: Cambridge University Press, 1974), p. 75.
38. Detailed statistics on the absolute number of strikes and strikers in France during the 1880s are available in both ibid., pp. 360–61, and in Perrot, *Ouvriers en grève*, 1:80–93. Perrot shows that in the year 1880 there was a 115.9% increase over the previous year in the number of strikes. Perrot also notes that the "years of catastrophe" were 1884 and 1885, the rate of failure for strikes during these two years approaching 71% and 72% respectively.
39. Shorter and Tilly, *Strikes in France*, p. 147. This figure represented 0.7% of the nonagricultural population.
40. Willard, *Guesdistes*, pp. 18–20.
41. Moss, *Origins of the French Labor Movement*, pp. 4–5, 66, 95. See also Georges Lefranc, *Le Mouvement syndical sous la troisième république* (Payot, 1967), pp. 13–27, for a general survey of the labor movement between 1871 and 1876.
42. Joughin, *Paris Commune in French Politics*, p. 314 n.
43. *Justice*, April 13, 1880. Examples of other speeches during which Clemenceau was heckled by collectivists may be found in ibid., August 13, 1881, November 1, 1882, and

May 1, 1883. See also Hyndman, *Record of an Adventurous Life,* p. 316.

44. Hyndman, *Record of an Adventurous Life,* pp. 314–29.

45. Speech at cirque Fernando, May 25, 1884, in *Justice,* May 26 and 27, 1884.

46. Ibid., August 13, 1881.

47. *JO, Chambre des Députés,* March 20, 1883, pp. 657–59, and June 20, 1883, pp. 1359–60. See also *Justice,* May 26 and 27, 1884.

48. *Justice,* November 1, 1880. In his speech to the Chamber of January 31, 1884, on the general economic situation, Clemenceau observed that since 1848 the republicans had demanded that the railroads be repurchased. He accused the directors of the railroads of creating their own companies, which were then favored with low tariff rates. In his speech at the cirque Fernando the following May, he argued that the high costs of railroad transport for all other companies were crippling French industry and workers and that the railroads' financial oligarchy was so powerful that the repurchasing of the railroads was impossible. See *JO, Chambre des Députés,* February 1, 1884, pp. 249–63; and *Justice,* May 26 and 27, 1884.

49. Willard, in *Guesdistes,* pp. 20–21, stresses that from the elections of 1881 on, when Radicals began to "borrow" points from the Guesdist program, Guesde was concerned over the absorption of the proletarian party by the Radicals, which he considered to be the "most dangerous bourgeois party." Willard also notes that Guesde's attacks against Radical leaders were often personal and false.

50. See *Justice,* January 9 and 10, 1881, and *Temps,* May 3, 1884. Watson, *Georges Clemenceau,* p. 71 n, points out that the Alliance socialiste républicaine was often mentioned in police reports and that Clemenceau clearly played the dominant role in the organization.

51. The *cahiers des électeurs* may be found in Seignobos, *Évolution de la 3ᵉ république,* pp. 81–82. See also *Justice,* August 13, 1881. Hecklers ridiculed Clemenceau as being nothing more than a "parliamentary athlete." He protested, in turn, that the social question was not "the monopoly of any caste or sect."

52. On Clemenceau's campaign see *Justice,* August 16, 17, 18,

19, 20, and 21, 1881. See also Willard, *Guesdistes*, p. 20; and Seignobos, *Évolution de la 3ᵉ république*, p. 82.

53. *Justice*, June 24 and November 1, 1880.

54. See S. A. Ashley, "The Failure of Gambetta's *Grand Ministère*," *French Historical Studies* 9 (spring, 1975): 105–24.

55. Perrot, *Ouvriers en grève*, p. 191.

56. Sorlin, *Waldeck-Rousseau*, pp. 243, 253–55. On *barberettisme* see also Moss, *Origins of the French Labor Movement*, pp. 95–97.

57. Sorlin, *Waldeck-Rousseau*, pp. 253–54, 258, 259.

58. *JO, Chambre des Députés*, February 1, 1884, p. 256.

59. *Justice*, November 1, 1882.

60. *JO, Chambre des Députés*, April 9, 1884, pp. 1081–85.

61. These proposals are treated in detail, with a summary of debates and votes, in Loubère, "French Left-Wing Radicals: Their Economic and Social Program since 1870."

62. *JO, Chambre des Députés*, April 29, 1883, pp. 797–805.

63. Loubère, "French Left-Wing Radicals: Their Economic and Social Program since 1870."

64. *Justice*, November 1, 1880 (from his Marseilles speech of October 29, 1880).

65. *JO, Chambre des Députés*, July 25, 1884, p. 1839.

66. On Clemenceau's actions regarding the Marseilles epidemic see *La Justice*, July 25, 28, 29, 30, and 31 and August 4, 1884.

67. *JO, Chambre des Députés*, July 27, 1876, pp. 5600–5601.

68. Ibid., May 18, 1871, pp. 917–32. Madier de Montjau was among the Radicals who opposed the Cantagrel amendment.

69. Loubère, "French Left-Wing Radicals: Their Views on Trade Unionism."

70. Sorlin, *Waldeck-Rousseau*, p. 296. Though Waldeck-Rousseau is sometimes referred to as the father of the law of 1884, he, as Sorlin shows, intervened in the Senate only at the last moment and in response to a plea for help from the *barberettistes* "in order to save a law that he judged had been badly prepared."

71. *JO, Chambre des Députés*, February 1, 1884, pp. 249–63, and March 14, 1884, pp. 741–42. During the latter session, Ferry interrupted Clemenceau's speech to ask him what was wrong with trade-union leaders having to give their

names to the police. Clemenceau answered: "What is so wrong with this, you ask? There is certainly little danger in it for politicians, who occupy themselves with politics at its risk and peril. But the danger is considerable for a man who labors everyday at the workshop and who often finds himself in a struggle with the bosses and who, very often in these struggles, finds the state not on his side but on the side of the bosses."

72. Moss, *Origins of the French Labor Movement*, p. 100.
73. *Justice*, February 3 and 23, 1882.
74. *JO, Chambre des Députés*, March 10, 1882, pp. 270–76.
75. Shorter and Tilly, *Strikes in France*, p. 378 n.
76. Clemenceau's speech at the cirque Fernando, in *Justice*, November 1, 1882.
77. *Justice*, January 17, 1884.
78. *JO, Chambre des Députés*, February 1, 1884, pp. 249–63. Clemenceau's concern over the absence of statistical data regarding the condition of the working classes touched on a significant problem during the early Third Republic. Perrot's *Ouvriers en grève*, 1:19–22, points out that it was only with the creation of the Office du Travail in 1891 that labor research and the keeping of social statistics in a systematic fashion received any real impetus. Since 1860, prefects had had the responsibility of providing information on labor organization and movements, but the prefects had often been negligent in their duties. See also Weill, *Histoire du mouvement sociale en France*, pp. 249–50, which stresses France's need for economic education in the 1880s.
79. *La Justice* for March 11, 1884, includes a typical report of the complaints of gas fitters and lamp makers, who protested against a slump in the construction trades and wage rates, which had fallen to fifty-five centimes an hour. As to the London trip, except for taking some tours of working-class areas, Clemenceau appears to have accomplished little; he spent much of his time in the company of various political figures such as Lord Granville. It should be noted, however, that, like many French Radicals, he admired several aspects of English society, especially its freedom of the press, assembly, and association. Over the years he had developed a wide range of English friends and acquaintances, including an admiral named Frederick Au-

gustus Maxse, whose daughter, Violet, the future Lady Milner, became one of his favorite protégées. There was also Joseph Chamberlain, who in the 1880s served as president of the Board of Trade and as a member of Gladstone's cabinet. Chamberlain himself had a reputation as a reformer in such areas as labor legislation and municipal planning; and on occasion, as in his speech at the cirque Fernando of May 25, 1884, Clemenceau referred to Chamberlain's ideas while he was discussing the housing crisis in Paris. See James L. Garvin, *The Life of Joseph Chamberlain* (London: Macmillan, 1932), vol. 1, pp. 239, 501; John Morley, Viscount, *Recollections* (New York: Macmillan, 1917), vol. 1, pp. 161–62; and Lady Milner, "Clemenceau intime," *Revue des deux mondes,* no. 4 (1953), pp. 611–19.

80. *Justice,* April 6 and 25 and May 26 and 27, 1884.

81. Ibid., March 11, 1884.

82. *JO, Chambre des Députés,* April 9, 1884, pp. 1081–82.

83. *Justice,* November 11, 1885.

84. Loubère, "French Left-Wing Radicals: Their Views on Trade Unionism."

85. Shorter and Tilly, *Strikes in France,* p. 49; and Perrot, *Ouvriers en grève,* 1:194–95.

86. Moss, *Origins of the French Labor Movement,* p. 95.

87. See, for example, Stephen H. Roberts, *History of French Colonial Policy (1870–1925)* (London: P. S. King, 1929), p. 428; Reclus, *Jules Ferry,* pp. 342–43; and James J. Cooke, *New French Imperialism, 1880–1910: The Third Republic and Colonial Expansion* (Hamden, Conn.: Archon Books, 1973), pp. 10, 12, 172–73.

88. On the idea of prestige see John F. Cady, *The Roots of French Imperialism in Eastern Asia* (Ithaca, N.Y.: Cornell University Press, 1954), and Jean Ganiage, *L'Expansion coloniale de la France sous la troisième république, 1871–1914* (Payot, 1968). On economic motives see John Laffey, "Les Racines de l'impérialisme française en extrême-orient à propos des thèses de J.-F. Cady," *Revue d'histoire moderne et contemporaine* 16 (April–June, 1969): 282–99. Laffey demonstrates the long-standing economic interest in East Asia that had been evident in Lyons, especially in the area of raw silk for the Lyons silk industry. In the

1880s there were great hopes that the acquisition of Tonkin would bring economic advantages to this city.

89. Charles-Robert Ageron, "Gambetta et la reprise de l'expansion coloniale," *Revue française d'histoire d'outre-mer* 59 (April–June, 1972): 165–204; and Elwitt, *Making of the Third Republic,* pp. 277, 279, 280.

90. Charles-Robert Ageron, *L'Anticolonialisme en France de 1871 à 1914* (Presses universitaires de France, 1973), pp. 12–16, 54–64. Ageron also treats the very important tradition of anticolonialism on the Right.

91. *JO, Chambre des Députés,* November 28, 1884, p. 2501.

92. Cooke, in *New French Imperialism,* pp. 10, 13, 31, mistakenly portrays Clemenceau in the 1880s as being one of the leaders of the *revanchards* and says that revenge against Germany was his main motive in opposing colonialism.

93. *JO, Chambre des Députés,* November 1, 1883, p. 2202.

94. Ageron's "Gambetta et la reprise de l'expansion coloniale" shows that while Gambetta opposed Ferry in 1881, it was Gambetta who had "the initial responsibility for the French intervention in Tunisia." Ageron also argues that during the Egyptian crisis of 1882, Gambetta would have intervened militarily had he been in power and that he contributed to the fall of Freycinet because of the latter's halfway measures in Egypt.

95. *JO, Chambre des Députés,* March 6, 1881, pp. 405–12.

96. Ibid., May 24, 1881, p. 982.

97. *JO, Chambre des Députés,* November 10, 1881, pp. 1967–75.

98. See the exchange between Clemenceau and Gambetta on June 1, 1882, in ibid., June 2, 1882, pp. 762–63.

99. *Justice,* July 12 and 13, 1882.

100. *JO, Chambre des Députés,* July 19, 1882, p. 1319.

101. Ibid., July 20, 1882, pp. 1325–31.

102. Ibid., July 30, 1882, pp. 1505–9.

103. Charles de Freycinet, *Souvenirs, 1878–1893* (Delagrave, 1913), pp. 238–39.

104. *La Justice* of January 17, 1884, for example, describes a meeting of the Extreme Left, which received a delegation of trade unionists who had a petition that they requested be read in the Chamber of Deputies. The petition denounced the waste in both the budget for religion and the

budget for Tonkin: "This latter budget is used to kill men. It would be better used to make them live."

105. *JO, Chambre des Députés,* July 4, 1883, pp. 1570–71.

106. Ibid., November 1, 1883, pp. 2202–6.

107. Ibid., pp. 2177–84.

108. Ibid., November 30, 1883, pp. 2549–50, and December 11, 1883, pp. 2741–44.

109. *Justice,* October 23 and 24, 1884.

110. *JO, Chambre des Députés,* November 22, 1884, p. 2405.

111. Ibid., November 29, 1884, pp. 2495–2503. Clemenceau long remembered this exchange as a good example of Ferry's incompetence. How could one trust the judgment of ministers on major issues when they were ignorant of their own maps? See Martet, *M. Clemenceau,* pp. 149–50.

112. *JO, Chambre des Députés,* March 29, 1885, pp. 692–95.

113. Seignobos, *Évolution de la 3ᵉ république,* p. 111.

114. *Times* (London), March 31, 1885.

115. *JO, Chambre des Députés,* March 31, 1885, pp. 704–5.

116. Ibid., July 7 and December 25, 1885, pp. 1335–37, 376–98. The vote was 273 to 267, with most Radicals opposing. Clemenceau accused the Opportunitists of being "timid in domestic policy and adventurous in foreign policy. Our approach is to be vigorous in domestic policy and cautious in foreign policy." See Eric Schmieder, "La Chambre de 1885–1889 et les affaires du Tonkin," *Revue française d'histoire d'outre-mer* 53 (July–December, 1966): 153–214.

117. Henri Brunschwig, *Mythes et réalités de l'impérialisme colonial français, 1871–1914* (A. Colin, 1960), pp. 98–101, 157–71. Raoul Girardet's *L'Idée coloniale en France de 1871 à 1962* (Table ronde, 1972), p. 82, points out that the budget for the colonies rose from 42,652,000 francs in 1885 to 116,000,000 in 1902, even though colonial commerce in the total volume of French commerce accounted for only 7.81% of imports and 9.84% of exports for the period 1896 to 1900. Girardet also notes that in 1900 the colonies accounted for only 5.3% of French investment abroad. For further discussion on the economic aspects of the empire see Jean Bouvier, "Les Traits majeurs de l'imperialisme français avant 1914," in Jean Bouvier and René Girault, eds., *L'Impérialisme français d'avant 1914* (Mouton, 1976), pp. 305–33; and David K. Fieldhouse, *Economics and*

Empire, 1830–1914 (Ithaca, N.Y.: Cornell University Press, 1973), pp. 3–62, 84–87.

118. *JO, Chambre des Députés,* July 29, 1885, pp. 1659–71.
119. Ibid., July 31, 1885, pp. 1677–86.
120. "The policy of Jules Ferry has borne its fruit," he told an interviewer from *Le Matin,* after the monarchists had made gains on the first ballot in 1885. See *Justice,* October 13, 1885. See also Martet, *M. Clemenceau,* pp. 149–50.
121. Paul Cambon, *Correspondance, 1870–1924* (Grasset, 1940), vol. 1, pp. 272–73.
122. *Justice,* July 21, 1885.
123. David Stafford, in his *From Anarchism to Reformism: A Study of the Political Activities of Paul Brousse within the First International and the French Socialist Movement, 1870–1890* (Toronto: University of Toronto Press, 1971), pp. 209–13, notes that while Brousse represented the *possibilist* strain of French socialism and opposed the revolutionary ideology of Guesde, there was enmity and competition for working-class votes between the Broussists and the Radicals. The two cooperated only once— and that for a brief time—in forming the Société des droits de l'homme in 1888 in order to combat Boulangism. Thus there were serious obstacles to any systematic collaboration between the Radicals and the moderate Socialists.
124. Kayser, *Grandes batailles du radicalisme,* pp. 366–67.
125. Loubère, "French Left-Wing Radicals: Their Views on Trade Unionism."
126. The following are examples of votes on these issues; they can be found in *JO, Chambre des Députés* for the dates indicated: total amnesty, 114 votes (February 13, 1880, pp. 1677–78); the prosecution of officials who had been involved in the *seize-mai* affair, 159 votes (March 14, 1879, p. 2013); abolishing the irremovability of judges, 199 votes (November 21, 1880, p. 11329); the protection of railroad workers, 210 votes (March 4, 1881, pp. 401–2); the ten-hour day, 133 votes (March 30, 1881, pp. 692–93); a liberal trade-union law (legalization of unions without the obligation to register), 163 votes (May 18, 1881, pp. 931–32); and revision of the constitution, 184 votes (June 1, 1881, p. 1094).
127. Just before each legislative election, *La Justice* published

the voting records of outgoing deputies who were candidates for a new term. The bills and orders of the day that were selected as examples reflected the legislative goals of the Radicals. As is evident from the above examples, these bills were invariably defeated.

128. Prost and Rosenzveig, "Chambre des Députés."
129. Although republicans had captured control of the Senate in 1879, it continued to be an extremely conservative body that was capable of frustrating the intentions of the lower house on a variety of issues—from liberal trade-union laws to the income tax. See Minnich, "Third Force."
130. *Justice*, January 23 and 24, 1883.
131. Kayser, *Grandes batailles du radicalisme*, p. 119.
132. *Temps*, December 18, 1881. Those who sided with Clemenceau included Barodet, Blanc, Brousse, Courmeaux, Cantagrel, Datas, Desmons, Maurel, Benjamin Raspail, Révillon, Roque de Filliol, Pelletan, and Vernhes. See also Kayser, *Grand batailles du radicalisme*, p. 117.
133. *Temps*, December 15, 16, and 24, 1881, May 7 and November 19 and 24, 1882. Eight of the twelve had been inscribed in the Extreme Left in the previous legislature, including Ballue (Rhône), Casse (Seine), Chavanne (Rhône), Floquet (Seine), Leconte (Indre), Lockroy (Seine), Naquet (Vaucluse), and Saint-Martin (Vaucluse).
134. *Temps*, November 4, 1881, and July 22, 1884.
135. Ibid., July 9 and 22, 1884.
136. Loubère, *Radicalism in Mediterranean France*, pp. 1–3; and Kayser, *Grandes batailles du radicalisme*, pp. 372–75.
137. Clemenceau's 1885 victory reflected strong Radical organization in these areas. Radicals owned three major newspapers and controlled most of the cantonal capitals. See Loubère, *Radicalism in Mediterranean France*, pp. 118, 167, 179. Watson, in *Georges Clemenceau*, pp. 99–100, points out the change of emphasis in Clemenceau's program of 1889, as compared to that of 1885. The program of 1889 contained a clause calling for high tariffs in favor of agriculture. Clemenceau's "Manifesto to the Electors of Draguignan (19 September 1885)" is published in Kayser, *Grandes batailles du radicalisme*, p. 337.
138. *JO, Chambre des Députés*, August 2, 1883, pp. 2060–61.
139. *Justice*, April 13, 1880.

140. *JO, Chambre des Députés,* June 1, 1881, pp. 1078–84.
141. See Clemenceau's 1883 speech at Lille in *La Justice,* May 1, 1883.
142. *JO, Chambre des Députés,* January 15, 1882, pp. 8–12.
143. Ibid., November 15, 1881, pp. 2029–32.
144. Ibid., March 6, 1883, p. 465. Around 97% of the Radicals had included constitutional revision in their programs during the elections of 1881. See Kayser, *Grandes batailles du radicalisme,* p. 371.
145. *Justice,* January 23, 1882.
146. *JO, Chambre des Députés,* January 27, 1882, p. 57. See also Ashley, "Failure of Gambetta's *Grand ministère.*"
147. *JO, Chambre des Députés,* March 7, 1883, pp. 500–513.
148. *Justice,* March 9, 17, 22, 23, and 24, 1883.
149. Ibid., March 16 and 24 and June 16, 1883.
150. Ibid., May 24, 1883. Other speeches were delivered by Barodet at Lyons, by Pelletan at Agen, and by Lefévre at Lille. See ibid., April 19 and 28 and July 4, 1883.
151. Ibid., March 12, 17, and 23, April 11, and June 17 and 22, 1883, and February 14, 1884.
152. *Justice,* April 20, 1884.
153. *JO, Chambre des Députés,* July 4, 1884, pp. 1574–75, 1580–81.
154. *Justice,* August 2, 1884.
155. Ibid., August 14, 1884.
156. *JO, Chambre des Députés,* June 1, 1881, pp. 1078–84.
157. Michon, *Clemenceau,* p. 39.
158. *Times* (London), August 14, 1884.
159. Ibid., April 6, 1885.
160. *Justice,* September 17, 1885.
161. Ibid., June 21, 1885.
162. Ibid., September 11, 12, 19, 22, 26, and 27, 1885.
163. See ibid., September 19, 1885, for a description of a typical rally during the campaign at the town of Lons-le-Saunier.
164. Ibid., October 13, 1885.
165. Cambon, *Correspondance,* 1:253, 260, 268–69.

CHAPTER FOUR:

SUFFERING & EXPIATION, 1885–1893

1. Watson, *Georges Clemenceau,* p. 101.

2. Piers and Singer, *Shame and Guilt,* pp. 28–29.
3. Erikson, *Childhood and Society,* pp. 268–69. Here Erikson defines this stage as "the ego's accrued assurance of its proclivity for order and meaning. . . . It is the acceptance of one's one and only life cycle as something that had to be and that, by necessity, permitted of no substitutions: it thus means a new, a different love of one's parents." Erikson defines the opposite of accrued ego integration as despair, which "expresses the feeling that the time is now short, too short for the attempt to start another life and to try out alternate roads to integrity. Disgust hides despair."
4. Wormser, *République de Clemenceau,* p. 151.
5. Victor Henri Rochefort-Luçay, *Les Aventures de ma vie* (Dupont, 1896–97), vol. 5, p. 242.
6. *Justice,* December 25, 1892, and March 11, 1893. See also Rochefort-Luçay, *Aventures de ma vie,* 5:254–56.
7. Geffroy, *Georges Clemenceau,* p. 70.
8. Wormser, *République de Clemenceau,* p. 22 n. On Michel see Gatineau-Clemenceau, *Des Pattes du Tigre,* p. 35.
9. Geffroy, *Georges Clemenceau,* pp. 70–72.
10. See, for example, the views of the deputy Jules Siegfried, in André Siegfried, "Une crise ministérielle en 1887 d'après le journal de mon père," in *Hommes et mondes* 11 (1950): 477–50.
11. Edmond de Goncourt, *Pages from the Goncourt Journal,* ed. and trans. Robert Baldick (London: Oxford University Press, 1962), p. 391. See also Gatineau-Clemenceau, *Des Pattes du Tigre,* p. 27.
12. Gatineau-Clemenceau, *Des Pattes du Tigre,* pp. 26–29.
13. *Justice,* January 4, 1886.
14. *Times* (London), April 6, 1885. My italics.
15. Wormser, *République de Clemenceau,* pp. 161–62.
16. On the vote of confidence that toppled the Goblet cabinet in May, 1887, seventy members of the Union des gauches voted for Goblet. On the vote of confidence that brought down Floquet in February, 1889, forty members of the Union des gauches voted for Floquet. In the latter case a vote for Floquet was a vote in favor of discussing constitutional revision. See *Temps,* May 19, 1887, and February 16, 1889. The point here is that the leftist faction of the Union des gauches offered possibilities for a legis-

lative coalition with moderate Radicals had Clemenceau been able or willing to exploit them.

17. See *Le Temps,* November 23, 1887, and *La Justice,* November 21, 1887, for an account of this caucus.
18. *JO, Chambre des Députés,* March 31, 1888, p. 1231.
19. *Temps,* April 1, 1888.
20. The best study of Boulangism is Frederic H. Seager's *The Boulanger Affair: Political Crossroad of France, 1886–1889* (Ithaca, N.Y.: Cornell University Press, 1969). The older study by Adrien Dansette, *Du Boulangisme à la révolution dreyfusienne: Le Boulangisme, 1886–1890* (Perrin, 1938), is still useful. An insider's view is provided by Gabriel Terrail [Mermeix], *Les Coulisses du boulangisme* (Cerf, 1890).
21. See *Justice* of December 29, 1882, January 30, 1883, and February 24, 1884.
22. Freycinet, *Souvenirs,* pp. 328–33; and Terrail, *Coulisses du boulangisme,* p. 4.
23. Dansette, *Boulangisme,* p. 24.
24. See Cambon, *Correspondance,* p. 253; Charles de Mazade, "Chronique de la quinzaine," *Revue des deux mondes* 70 (August 15, 1885): 944–55; and Charles Benoist [Sybil], *Croquis parlementaires* (Perrin, 1891), pp. 54–55.
25. David B. Ralston, *The Army of the Republic: The Place of the Military in the Political Evolution of France, 1871–1914* (Cambridge, Mass.: M.I.T. Press, 1967), pp. 46, 76–77.
26. *JO, Chambre des Députés,* December 17, 1879, p. 11219; and *Justice,* January 5, 1882.
27. Ralston, *Army of the Republic,* p. 96.,
28. *JO, Chambre des Députés,* June 12, 1887, pp. 1198–99.
29. Rochefort-Luçay, *Aventures de ma vie,* 4:380.
30. Cambon, *Correspondance,* pp. 245, 272–73.
31. *JO, Chambre des Députés,* February 12 and March 14, 1886, pp. 192, 441.
32. Ralston, *Army of the Republic,* pp. 102–3.
33. See Clemenceau's comments in *JO, Chambre des Députés,* July 12, 1887, p. 1662.
34. Ibid., June 27, 1886, pp. 1203–4.
35. Terrail, *Coulisses du boulangisme,* pp. 8–9.
36. Ibid., p. 5; and Rochefort-Luçay, *Aventures de ma vie,* 5:32–33.

37. The debate on the budget, which began on November 4, 1886, lasted for seven sessions. Clemenceau took little part in this debate. The most important speeches were those by the Radical Camille Dreyfus on November 5, in support of an income tax, and by Sadi Carnot on November 15, in defense of his budget, which was based on governmental economies. The vote of 262 that overthrew Freycinet included 173 members of the Right, 67 of the Extreme Left, 16 of the Gauche radicale, and 6 independent republicans. There were 44 abstentions on the vote, most on the part of the Gauche radicale. See *Temps,* December 5, 1886.

38. Ibid., December 7, 1886. See also Pelletan's comments in *La Justice,* December 4, 1886.

39. *Temps,* December 7 and 8, 1886.

40. Ibid., December 10, 1886.

41. *JO, Chambre des Députés,* December 14, 1886, p. 2150, and March 31, 1887, p. 888.

42. This epigram was first attributed to Clemenceau by his biographer Georges Suarez (see his article "Georges Clemenceau, Cornélius Herz et le Général Boulanger," in *Annales politiques et litteraires* 94 (February, 1930): 111–15. I have been unable to find any other contemporary references to the remark, but it summed up concisely a view that Clemenceau had expressed on other occasions. See, for example, his comments on generals and politics in the Tonkin debate in the Chamber on November 27, 1884.

43. According to *Le Temps,* May 19, 1887, those who voted against Goblet on a motion of confidence, which was presented by Anatole de la Forge, included 165 members of the Right, 58 from the Union des gauches, 37 from the Extreme Left (including Clemenceau and Pelletan), 6 from the Gauche radicale, and 13 Independents. Those who supported Goblet included 40 members of the Extreme Left, 60 from the Gauche radicale, 70 from the Union des gauches, and a scattering of Independents. A very feeble defense of the vote against Goblet was presented by Édouard Durranc in *La Justice* of May 18, 1887. In subsequent articles by Pelletan and Millerand on May 19 and 20, mention is first made of an "Opportunist plot" against Goblet, though Pelletan still stressed that he was not sorry to have voted with the Right.

44. Terrail, *Coulisses du boulangisme*, pp. 34–35.
45. *JO, Chambre des députés*, July 12, 1887, pp. 1658–64.
46. See the comments of the correspondent for the London *Times* of July 13, 1887.
47. *JO, Chambre des Députés*, February 1, 1889, pp. 265–67.
48. On the Boulangist appeal among certain sectors of the industrial working force see Perrot, *Ouvriers en grève*, 2:438; and Patrick H. Hutton, "The Impact of the Boulangist Crisis upon the Guesdist Party at Bordeaux," *French Historical Studies* 7 (fall, 1971): 226–44.
49. *Justice*, November 1 and 3, 1887.
50. *JO, Chambre des Députés*, November 20, 1887, pp. 2066–67.
51. Adrien Dansette, *L'Affaire Wilson et la chute du Président Grévy* (Perrin, 1936), pp. 135–36.
52. Ibid., pp. 136–44, 157.
53. Clemenceau told a journalist for the London *Times* that had Ferry become president, popular violence might have followed. "I did not want to have a spot of blood on our Republic," he said. See *Times* (London), December 20, 1887. There was, in fact, intense opposition to Ferry on the part of many Parisians, who remembered him from the days of the siege as "Famine Ferry." Blanquists and other Socialist factions, including some members of the Municipal Council, shared the Radicals' hatred for Ferry.
54. The account of the "historic nights" given here is based on Terrail, *Coulisses du boulangisme*, pp. 206–29; Rochefort-Luçay, *Aventures de ma vie*, 5:103–6; and Dansette, *Affaire Wilson*, pp. 176–98.
55. Dansette, *Affaire Wilson*, pp. 176–98.
56. Rochefort-Luçay, *Aventures de ma vie*, 5:103–6.
57. Terrail, *Coulisses du boulangisme*, p. 22.
58. Rochefort-Luçay, *Aventures de ma vie*, 5:108. For a detailed account of Clemenceau's role in the election of Carnot see Terrail, *Coulisses du boulangisme*, pp. 70–73.
59. *Times* (London), December 20, 1887.
60. Dansette, *Affaire Wilson*, p. 228.
61. Seager, in *Boulanger Affair*, pp. 80–84, 115–17, 133–40, and 249–57, describes these seemingly contradictory elements on which Boulangists of both the Right and the Left were in accord.
62. *Justice*, March 20, 1888.

63. *JO, Chambre des Députés,* March 21, 1888, pp. 1100–1102.
64. See ibid., March 31, 1888, p. 1230, for Clemenceau's remarks. When he stated that the constitution of 1875 was responsible for France's current disorders, the deputy Lefèvre-Pontalis answered: "It's you who has thrown the country into disorder!" The vote that overthrew Tirard was 268 to 232, the majority including 84 members of the Extreme Left, 35 from the Gauche radicale, 9 Independents, 4 Socialists, and 136 of the Right. See *Temps,* April 1, 1888.
65. The alleged incident is supposed to have involved Clemenceau's public exposure of Michou for the latter's habit of stuffing his pockets with sandwiches from the buffet of the Chamber and enjoying them later at his seat. Humiliated at the laughter, Michou cast his vote for Méline, although he had earlier planned to vote for Clemenceau. The incident is related in Gatineau-Clemenceau, *Des Pattes du Tigre,* p. 127. It is also alluded to in a few other sources, including Fullerton's "Georges Clemenceau, Prime Minister of France," which was cited earlier. *Le Temps,* April 6, 1888, on the other hand, does not mention the incident and notes that some deputies were saying that the abstention by the Socialist Félix Pyat was the crucial factor in Clemenceau's loss.
66. Freycinet, *Souvenirs,* p. 394.
67. Quoted in *Times* (London), April 5, 1888.
68. *Justice,* May 23, 1888.
69. For a detailed analysis of the work of the society see Seager, *Boulanger Affair,* pp. 158–62.
70. *JO, Chambre des Députés,* June 5, 1888, pp. 1627-39.
71. Seager, *Boulanger Affair,* pp. 150–58.
72. *Justice,* August 22 and 23, 1888. Laguerre explained apologetically that he would never "allow political motives to betray old friendships."
73. Speech at Barjols of October 10, 1888, in ibid., October 13, 1888. See also the issues of October 10, 12, and 14.
74. Seager, *Boulanger Affair,* pp. 203–10.
75. *JO, Chambre des Députés,* February 1, 1889, pp. 265–67. During this speech, Clemenceau refused to engage in any disputes from the podium with Laguerre, whom he chided for placing a man above the Republic. "I don't recognize you anymore," Clemenceau said to his former "colt."

76. *Justice,* January 6, 1889; and *JO, Chambre des Députés,* February 12, 1889, pp. 377–97. Clemenceau and 41 other members of the Extreme Left voted against the return to single-member constituencies, while 27 members voted for it. Figures for the Gauche radicale were 20 against and 58 for.

77. Ibid., February 15, 1889, pp. 400–404. The vote against Floquet was 307 to 218, with the majority comprising 157 members of the Right, 137 members of the Union des gauches, including some Independents, and 13 deputies who called themselves Boulangists. See *Temps,* February 16, 1889.

78. *JO, Chambre des Députés,* January 29, 1891, p. 156.

79. The comments by *La Cocarde* were published by *La Justice,* May 31, 1889.

80. On the election campaign in the Var see *La Justice,* August 24, September 12, 16, 19, and 24, and October 7, 1889. See also Seignobos, *Évolution de la 3ᵉ république,* p. 145.

81. *Temps,* February 16, 1889.

82. Quoted in Geffroy, *Georges Clemenceau,* p. 189.

83. Benoist, *Croquis parlementaires,* pp. 35–36, 40.

84. The moderate majority of about 200 was usually supported by a Center Left of around 40. The Radicals themselves began to tone down their demands for constitutional revision and an income tax. See Seignobos, *Évolution de la 3ᵉ république,* p. 147.

85. *JO, Chambre des Députés,* January 30, 1891, pp. 155–56.

86. Ibid., February 19, 1892, pp. 136–43. The vote against Freycinet was 282 to 210, the majority being composed of 148 members of the Right, 29 Boulangists, and 105 members of the Left. Only 13 Radicals supported Freycinet. See *Temps,* February 20, 1892.

87. Perrot, *Ouvriers en grève,* 1:195.

88. *JO, Chambre des Députés,* May 9, 1891, pp. 814–16.

89. On Clemenceau's role in the Carmaux strike see *La Justice,* October 23 and 27 and November 1, 1892. For greater detail on the Carmaux strike see Harvey Goldberg, *The Life of Jean Jaurès* (Madison: University of Wisconsin Press, 1962), pp. 97–107.

90. Goldberg, *Life of Jean Jaurès,* p. 105.

91. *JO, Chambre des Députés,* December 10, 1891, pp. 2534–36, and July 5, 1892, pp. 1045–46.
92. Ibid., November 1, 1883, p. 2202.
93. Garvin, *Life of Joseph Chamberlain,* 2:456–62
94. Wormser, *République de Clemenceau,* pp. 487–89.
95. Ibid.
96. *Justice,* September 5 and 12, 1892.
97. See the deposition of Clemenceau before the parliamentary commission of investigation into the Panama affair of March 10, 1893, in *La Justice,* March 11. Deliberations and depositions of others are found in Chambre des Députés, *Commission d'enquête sur les affaires de Panama,* 3 vols. (Imprimerie de la Chambre des Députés, 1893). Adrien Dansette's *Les Affaires de Panama* (Perrin, 1934) offers a general treatment of the scandal. For an anti-Clemenceau view see Ernest Judet's *Le Véritable Clemenceau* and Maurice Barrès's *Leurs figures* (Émile-Paul frères, 1917), especially pp. 76–106, 155–66.
98. Dansette, in *Affaires de Panama,* p. 88, discusses the mysterious nature of Herz's domination over Reinach.
99. Clemenceau's deposition before the parliamentary commission of March 10, 1893, in *Justice,* March 11. Testimony of Charles de Lesseps at his own trial in ibid., March 9, 1893. See also the article "Au *Figaro,*" by Clemenceau, in ibid., March 2, 1893.
100. Barrès, *Leurs figures,* pp. 77–79, 92–100; and Judet, *Véritable Clemenceau,* pp. 159–63.
101. Clemenceau's deposition of March 10, 1893, in *Justice,* March 11.
102. Ibid., August 10, 1893.
103. Comment of de Lesseps during Clemenceau's deposition of March 10, 1893, in ibid., March 11.
104. Ibid.
105. Clemenceau's account of the meeting, in ibid., December 13, 1892. He repeated the same version before the parliamentary commission the next day.
106. Wormser, *République de Clemenceau,* p. 171.
107. Clemenceau's testimony before the parliamentary commission of December 14, 1892, in *Justice,* December 15.
108. *JO, Chambre des députés,* December 16, 1892, p. 1827.
109. Ibid., December 21, 1892, pp. 1886–90.
110. In the words of Barrès, who was there, "The general an-

guish found its deliverance." See his account in *Leurs figures,* pp. 155–66.

111. On the Clemenceau-Déroulède duel see accounts in the London *Times* and the *New York Times* issues of December 23, 1892.
112. Wormser, *République de Clemenceau,* p. 171.
113. *Justice, January* 16, 1893.
114. Ibid., January 24, 1893.
115. *JO, Chambre des Députés,* June 20, 1893, pp. 1764–66.
116. Ibid., June 23, 1893, pp. 1767–94.
117. *Justice,* August 6 and 7, 1893.
118. For details of the Var campaign of 1893 see *La Justice,* August 10 to September 5, 1893. See also Francis Varenne, "La Défaite de Georges Clemenceau à Draguignan, en 1893," *Revue politique et parlementaire,* no. 646 (1955), pp. 255–59, from which some of the background for this chapter was taken.
119. *Justice,* August 10, 1893.
120. Ibid., August 11, 15, and 17, 1893.
121. Ibid., September 1, 1893.
122. Ibid., September 5, 1893.
123. For a synopsis of press reaction to Clemenceau's defeat see Michon, *Clemenceau,* pp. 63–65.
124. Wormser, *République de Clemenceau,* p. 175.
125. Zévaès, *Clemenceau,* p. 153.

CHAPTER FIVE:

APPRAISAL OF CLEMENCEAU'S LATER YEARS
IN THE LIGHT OF HIS IDENTITY CONFLICTS

1. Quoted in Michon, *Clemenceau,* pp. 63–65.
2. Prost and Rosenzveig, "Chambre des Députés."
3. Christopher, "Desiccation of the Bourgeois Spirit."
4. Minnich, "Third Force."
5. Michon, *Clemenceau,* p. 278.
6. For a discussion of these measures see Zeldin, *France, 1848–1945,* 1:665–71.
7. See Alexander, *Fundamentals of Psychoanalysis,* p. 119.
8. Quoted in Watson, *Clemenceau,* p. 142.

9. For a detailed analysis of the literary aspects of his writings see Applebaum, "Clemenceau."

10. Watson, *Clemenceau*, pp. 140–44.

11. *Justice*, October 3, 1893.

12. Watson, *Clemenceau*, p. 40; and Applebaum, "Clemenceau," pp. 33–46.

13. Applebaum, "Clemenceau," pp. 56–57.

14. Ernest Dimnet, "M. Clemenceau as Writer and Philosopher," *Nineteenth Century* 61 (April, 1907): 611–17.

15. For examples of these see Applebaum, "Clemenceau," pp. 79, 99.

16. According to Gatineau-Clemenceau, Michel was expelled from school in Paris and in 1894 was sent to study at the Institut agronomique in Zurich. He later worked in sugar-refining in Hungary and married a Hungarian, whom he divorced (he was married three times). For several years after 1905, apparently until the war, Michel and his father were not on speaking terms as a result of the former's involvement in a business scandal that involved government contracts. The husband of Clemenceau's daughter Thérèse abandoned her. Madeleine's husband, a lawyer who was twenty years her senior named Numa Jacquemaire, shot himself in her presence after he found her committing adultery with a friend of his in 1902. See *Des Pattes du Tigre*, pp. 28–29, 35–37.

17. Quoted in Watson, *Clemenceau*, p. 144.

18. Applebaum, "Clemenceau," pp. 85–88.

19. These books include *L'Iniquité* (1899), *Vers la réparation* (1899), *Contre la justice* (1900), *Des Juges* (1901), *Justice militaire* (1901), *Injustice militaire* (1902), and *La Honte* (1903).

20. Watson, *Clemenceau*, pp. 182, 139.

21. See the excellent study by David Sowle Newhall, "Georges Clemenceau, 1902–1906: 'An Old Beginner'" (Ph.D. diss., Harvard University, 1963).

22. *Justice*, July 25, 1897.

23. Geffroy, *Georges Clemenceau*, p. 72.

24. Quoted in Milner, "Clemenceau intime."

25. See *Justice*, April 30, 1896.

26. Quoted in Geffroy, *Georges Clemenceau*, p. 11.

27. Watson, *Clemenceau*, pp. 169–70, 175–76, 192.

28. Loubère, *Radicalism in Mediterranean France*, pp. 209, 230.
29. Watson, *Clemenceau*, p. 252.
30. Martet, *M. Clemenceau*, pp. 127, 314.
31. The will was published in *L'Illustration*, November 30, 1929, p. 42.

Bibliography

Shortly before his death, Clemenceau burned most of the letters that he had received throughout his career. The letters that he himself wrote have never been collected and published as a whole. The Musée Clemenceau, which is at 8, rue Franklin in Paris, has on file a number of Clemenceau's letters pertaining to the pre-1893 period; these include one letter written to his father from Mazas in March, 1862, and photocopies of eight letters written to Madame Jourdan between 1867 and 1872. There are also a great number of letters written to the comte d'Aunay, to Admiral Maxse, and the latter's daughter Violet, many of which fall within the pre-1893 period. These letters, however, were not available to researchers. In a conversation with Georges Wormser, who controlled access to these materials, I was denied permission to consult them. Madame Boilot and her staff at the Musée Clemenceau were most helpful in other ways, however. The museum contains Clemenceau's newspapers, printed copies of many of his speeches, books and articles by and about Clemenceau, and bibliographies. There is an enormous literature on the life of Clemenceau, though much of it is of doubtful quality. The following list presents primary sources as well as a selective list of books and articles that I have used in gathering material relevant to his pre-1893 career.

Publications of the French Government

Assemblée nationale. *Enquête parlementaire sur l'insurrection du 18 mars.* 3 vols. Versailles: Imprimeur de l'Assemblée nationale, 1872.

Chambre des députés. *Commission d'enquête sur les affaires de Panama.* 3 vols. Paris: Imprimerie de la Chambre des députés, 1893.

Journal officiel de la république française. September, 1870, to February, 1871.

251

Journal officiel de la république française: Assemblée nationale: Comte rendu in extenso. February to March, 1871.

Journal officiel de la république française: Débats parlementaire, Chambre des députés. March, 1876, to June, 1893.

Paris. Conseil municipal. *Procès-verbaux.* 8 vols. Paris: Typographie la hure, 1871–76.

CLEMENCEAU'S SPEECHES

NATIONAL ASSEMBLY AT VERSAILLES, 1871

1871: March 20, proposes creation of Paris Municipal Council
March 23, 24, urges conciliation toward Paris

MUNICIPAL COUNCIL OF PARIS, 1871–76

1875: November 29, assumes presidency of this body

CHAMBER OF DEPUTIES, 1876–93

1876: May 16, asks amnesty for Communards

1877: March 24, defends election of deputy Mestreau

1879: February 21, condemns limited amnesty
March 3, attacks de Marcère
May 27, defends election of Blanqui

1880: May 28, attacks police handling of Père-Lachaise demonstration
November 11, condemns lack of enforcement of anticlerical laws

1881: March 5, condemns sending arms to Greece
May 23, condemns Tunisian expedition
May 31, proposes constitutional revision
November 9, on Tunisia

1882: March 9, defends strikers of Grand'Comb
June 30, opposes building of Sacre-Coeur
July 2, proposes reform of magistracy
July 19, attacks Freycinet over Egypt
July 21, supports compensation for victims of December 2, 1851
July 23, 24, on magistracy

July 29, attacks Freycinet over Egypt
August 9, attacks new Duclerc ministry
November 18, condemns ecclesiastical pensions
December 24, 25, urges building of schoolhouses

1883: January 23, on magistracy
March 6, on revision of the constitution
March 20, defends strikers of Montceau-les-mines
April 28, condemns measure on criminal recidivists
May 1, on revision of the constitution
August 2, attacks Senate
October 31, condemns Tonkin expedition
November 29, on Tonkin
December 10, on Tonkin

1884: January 31, speaks on social and economic situation
March 26, on Tonkin
April 8, defends strikers of Anzin
July 4, on revision of the constitution
July 24, urges investigation of Marseilles epidemic
August 2, on Marseilles epidemic
August 5, 14, on revision of the constitution
November 21, 27, on Tonkin

1885: March 28, on Tonkin
March 30, attacks Ferry
July 30, answers Ferry's defense of colonial policies

1886: February 11, supports strikers of Decazeville

1887: June 11, supports military service law
July 11, condemns demonstrations for Boulanger at the
    Gard de Lyon
November 19, denounces Wilson scandal; Rouvier over-
    thrown

1888: March 20, speaks on Boulangist threats
June 4, responds to Boulanger

1889: January 31, speaks on Paris victory of Boulanger
June 8, responds to de Mun

1891: January 29, condemns Sardou's *Thermidor*
May 8, defends strikers of Fourmies
December 10, urges modern naval armament

1892: February 18, attacks Freycinet over teaching orders
July 4, on naval armaments
December 20, responds to Déroulède's attack

1893: January 28, on naval armaments
June 19, supports electoral reform
June 22, answers Norton forgeries

SPEECHES TO HIS ELECTORS OF MONTMARTRE AT THE
CIRQUE FERNANDO, 1879–84

> May 11, 1879
> April 12, 1880
> April 12, 1881
> August 13, 1881
> October 29, 1882
> November 1, 1882
> May 1, 1883
> May 25, 1884

SPEECHES IN OTHER PLACES

> Marseilles, October 29, 1880
> Lille, May 23, 1883
> Bordeaux, July 19, 1885
> Draguignan, September 13, 1885
> Toulon, October 22, 1887
> Paris (Grand-Orient), May 23, 1888
> Toulon, October 9, 1888
> Paris (Court of Assizes), August 6, 1893
> Salernes, August 8, 1893

NEWSPAPER WRITINGS

Le Travail, 1861–62

1861: December 22, "Un Feuilleton de M. About"

1862: January 5, "Chronique dramatique"
January 12, "Causerie"
February 2, "Histoire de France de M. Michelet"
February 9, "Chronique dramatique"
February 9, "Un Lettre de M. About"
February 16, "Causerie"
February 22, "Les Martyrs de l'histoire"

Le Matin, 1862

> *1862: June 29, "Les Bleus et les blancs,* par Étienne Arago"

Le Temps, 1865–70

> Most of Clemenceau's letters to *Le Temps* have been translated in Baldensperger's *American Reconstruction;* a more recent edition, with a new introduction by the American scholar Otto H. Olson, has been published by Da Capo Press (New York, 1969). For other letters to *Le Temps* that are not included in these two see note 92 of chapter 1.

La Justice, 1880–93

> *1880: January 16,* "A Nos lecteurs"
> *February 15,* "L'Opposition"
> *April 19,* "Concordat"
> *May 14,* "L'Election du Rhône"
> *June 6,* "L'Election de Lyon"
> *June 22,* "L'Amnistie"
> *June 24,* "Le Maître du pouvoir"
> *July 9,* "L'Amnistie et le sénat"
> *July 11,* "La Chambre des conflits"
> *September 24,* "Dernier expedient"
> *November 24,* Brief entry on the Newspaper *Voltaire*
> *1881: February 1,* "Signe des temps"
> *June 12,* "Revision"
> *1884: February 12–19,* Exchange with Antonin Proust over the *seize-mai* affair
> *1886: January 22,* Brief note on Boulanger
> *1887: May 24,* Note to newspaper *Le Matin*
> *November 1, 3,* Note on a conversation with Jules Ferry
> *December 21,* Note on an interview with the London *Times*
> *1888: August 23, 24,* Response to newspaper *La Presse*
> *December 9,* "Dépêche fausse"
> *1889: September 28,* Letter to electors of Draguignan
> *1890: September 4, 5,* Response to Joseph de Reinach
> *September 6,* Reply to Henri Rochefort
> *1892: September 12,* Letter to Baron de Mohrenheim
> *December 13,* Responses to charges of *Figaro*

1893: *January 16,* Response to rumors concerning himself
January 26, "Encore une lettre que je n'ai pas reçue"
March 2, "Au *Figaro*"
March 12, 13, Brief entries on his relations with Charles de Lesseps
July 24, "Disqualifié"
August 17, 20, 26, Appeals to the electors of Draguignan
September 2, "Les Faussaires"
September 5, "M. Clemenceau à ses electeurs"

LETTERS AND ARCHIVAL MATERIALS

BIBLIOTHÈQUE NATIONALE

Correspondance Clemenceau–Auguste Scheurer-Kestner, MSS Nouvelles acquisitions françaises, 24409, nos. 8–37.
Journal de Auguste Scheurer-Kestner, MSS Nouvelles acquisitions françaises, 12704–11.

ARCHIVES DE PARIS, DEPARTMENT DE LA SEINE

Circular to school directors of Montmartre of October 26, 1870, forbidding compulsory attendance at mass. V.D. 6, 2454, no. 1.
Instructions to mayors of Paris (1870–71) from the mayor of Paris and the minister of the interior. V.D. 6, 715, no. 19; V.D. 6, 2452, nos. 2, 3, 4.
Letter of Clemenceau of October 24, 1870, to a teacher concerning attendance of students at mass. 3 AZ 322.
Report submitted by Captain Prudhomme and citizen Clemenceau to General Trochu. No date. 2 AZ 190.

OTHER WRITINGS BY CLEMENCEAU RELATING TO PRE–1893 PERIOD

Au fil des jours. Paris: Fasquelle, 1900.
Auguste Comte et le positivisme. Trans. by Clemenceau from the work by John Stuart Mill. Paris: G. Ballière, 1868.
De la génération des éléments anatomiques. Paris: J.-B. Ballière, 1865.
Figures de Vendée. Paris: Librairie Plon, 1930.
Les Plus forts. Paris: Charpentier, 1898.

Rapport présenté par M. Clemenceau, au nom de la 3e commission du conseil général, sur le service des enfants-assistés, in *La République française,* November 25, 26, 27, and 28, 1874.

INTERVIEWS WITH CLEMENCEAU

Abensour, Léon. *Clemenceau intime.* Paris: Éditions Radot, 1928.
Martet, Jean. *M. Clemenceau peint par lui-même.* Paris: Albin Michel, 1929.
————. *Le Silence de M. Clemenceau.* Paris: Albin Michel, 1929.
————. *Le Tigre.* Paris: Albin Michel, 1930.
Neuray, Fernand. *Entretiens avec Clemenceau.* Paris: Éditions Prométhée, 1930.
Villiers, Adam de. *Clemenceau parle.* Paris: Éditions Tallandier, 1931.
Williams, Wythe. *The Tiger of France: Conversations with Clemenceau.* New York: Duell, Sloan & Pearce, 1949.

MEMOIRS, DIARIES, CORRESPONDENCE, CONTEMPORARY WRITINGS

"A Sketch of M. Clemenceau, by an Anglo-Parisian Friend." *Eclectic Magazine of Foreign Literature* n.s. 39 (May, 1884): 676–79.
Barrés, Maurice. *L'Appel au soldat.* Paris: Juven, 1911.
————. *Leurs figures.* Paris: Émile-Paul frères, 1917.
Benoist, Charles [Sybil]. *Croquis parlementaires.* Paris: Perrin et cie., 1891.
Cambon, Paul. *Correspondance, 1870–1924.* 3 vols. Paris: Éditions Bernard Grasset, 1940–46.
Drumont, Édouard. *La Fin d'un monde.* Paris: Savine, 1889.
————. *La France juive.* 2 vols. Paris: C. Marpon & E. Flammarion, 1886.
Freycinet, Charles de. *Souvenirs, 1878–1893.* Paris: Delagrave, 1913.
Goncourt, Edmond de. *Pages from the Goncourt Journal.* Edited and translated by Robert Baldick. London: Oxford University Press, 1962.

Hyndman, Henry Mayers. *The Record of an Adventurous Life*. New York: Macmillan Co., 1911.

Lissagaray, Prosper Olivier. *Histoire de la Commune de 1871*. Brussels: H. Kistemaeckers, 1876.

Mazade, Charles de. "Chronique de la quinzaine." *Revue des deux mondes* 70 (August 15, 1885): 944–55.

Michel, Louise. *La Commune*. Paris: P. V. Stock, 1898.

Morley, John, Viscount. *Recollections*. 2 vols. New York: Macmillan Co., 1917.

Les Murailles politiques françaises: Depuis le 18 juillet 1870 jusqu'au 25 mai 1871. 2 vols. Paris: Chevalier, 1874.

Paul-Boncour, Joseph. *Entre deux guerres: Souvenirs sur la IIIᵉ république*. Vol. 1: *Les Lettres républicaines, 1877–1918*. New York: Brentano's, Inc., 1946.

Pelletan, Camille. *Georges Clemenceau*. Paris: A. Quantin, 1883.

Ranc, Arthur. *Souvenirs: Correspondance, 1831–1908*. Paris: Édouard Cornély, 1913.

Rochefort-Luçay, Henri. "The Boulangist Movement." *Fortnightly Review* 44 (July, 1888): 10–23.

————. *Les Aventures de ma vie*. 5 vols. Paris: Dupont, 1896–97.

Scheurer-Kestner, Auguste. *Souvenirs de jeunesse*. Paris: Fasquelle, 1905.

Siegfried, André. "Une crise ministérielle en 1887 d'après le journal de mon père." *Hommes et Mondes* 11 (1950): 477–500.

Le Temps, 1876–1893.

Terrail, Gabriel [Mermeix]. *Les Coulisses du boulangisme*. Paris: Leopold Cerf, 1890.

Washburne, Elihu Benjamin. *Recollections of a Minister to France*. 2 vols. New York: Charles Scribner & Sons, 1887.

SELECT LIST OF BOOKS AND ARTICLES ON CLEMENCEAU

Abensour, Léon. "Pensées inédites de Georges Clemenceau." *Grand Revue* 131 (February, 1930): 529–50.

Adam, George. *The Tiger: Georges Clemenceau, 1841–1929*. London: Jonathan Cape, 1930.

Ajalbert, Jean. *Clemenceau*. Paris: Gallimard, 1931.

Applebaum, Samuel Isaac. "Clemenceau, Thinker and Writer." Ph.D. dissertation, Columbia University, 1948.

Baldensperger, Fernand. "L'Initiation américaine de Georges Clemenceau." *Revue de littérature comparée* 8 (January–March, 1928): 127–54.

Bédé, Jean-Albert. "Paris et Clemenceau." *Renaissance* 1 (July–September, 1943): 391–406.

Brandes, Georg. "M. Georges Clemenceau." *Contemporary Review* 84 (November, 1903): 656–74.

Brown, Alice F. "The Love Story of Georges Clemenceau." *Mentor,* October, 1928, pp. 17–19.

Bruun, Geoffroy. *Clemenceau.* Cambridge, Mass.: Harvard University Press, 1943.

Coutela, Charles. "Georges Clemenceau, la médicine et les médecins." *Presse medical,* no. 24 (May 15, 1965), pp. 1435–38.

Daudet, Léon. *La Vie orageuse de Clemenceau.* Paris: Michel, 1938.

Dimnet, Ernest. "M. Clemenceau as Writer and Philosopher." *Nineteenth Century* 61 (April, 1907): 611–17.

Dubly, Henry Louis. *La Vie ardente de Georges Clemenceau.* 2 vols. Lille: Mercure de Flandre, 1930.

Erlanger, Philippe. *Clemenceau.* Paris: Grasset, Paris-Match, 1968.

Gatineau-Clemenceau, Georges. *Des Pattes du Tigre aux griffes du destin.* Paris: Presses du mail, 1961.

Geoffroy, Gustave. *Georges Clemenceau, sa vie, son oeuvre.* Paris: Larousse, 1932.

Guitard, Louis. "Georges Clemenceau et Léon Daudet: Deux enfants terribles de la troisième république." *Oeuvres libres,* no. 25 (July, 1948), pp. 251–52.

Helle, Marie-Antoine de. "Clemenceau journaliste." *Revue politique et parlementaire,* no. 765 (1966), pp. 55–67.

Hyndmann, Henry Mayers. *Clemenceau: The Man and His Time.* New York: Frederick A. Stokes Co., 1919.

Jackson, John Hampden. *Clemenceau and the Third Republic.* New York: Macmillan Co., 1948.

Judet, Ernest. *Le Véritable Clemenceau.* Berne, Switzerland: F. Wyss, 1920.

Krebs, Albert. "Le Mariage de Clemenceau." *Mercure de France,* August, 1955, pp. 634–50.

.

————. "Le Secret de Clemenceau." *Miroir de l'histoire,* no. 106 (1958), pp. 426–34.

————. "Le Secret de Clemenceau, révélé par les souvenirs d'Auguste Scheurer-Kestner." *Bulletin de la Société industrielle de Mulhouse,* no. 735 (1969), pp. 67–86.

Lacombe, Pierre. "The Enigma of Clemenceau." *Psychoanalytic Review* 33 (April, 1946): 165–76.

Lucchini, Pierre [Pièrre Dominique]. *Clemenceau.* Paris: Hachette, 1963.

Michon, Georges. *Clemenceau.* Paris: M. Rivière, 1931.

Milner, Lady. "Clemenceau intime." *Revue des deux mondes,* no. 4 (1953), pp. 611–19.

Monnerville, Gaston. *Clemenceau.* Paris: Fayard, 1968.

Morel, Adolphe. *Clemenceau, médecin et philosophe.* Paris: Maison du livre français, 1930.

Pearce, Howard J. "Georges Clemenceau: Chronicler of American Politics." *South Atlantic Quarterly* 29 (October, 1930): 394–401.

Pratt, Julius W. "Clemenceau and Gambetta: A Study in Political Philosophy." *South Atlantic Quarterly* 20 (April, 1921): 96–104.

Ratinaud, Jean. *Clemenceau: ou, La Colère et la gloire.* Paris: Fayard, 1958.

Rieux, Calixte de. "Clemenceau et le parti radical." *Cahiers de la république,* no. 8 (1957), 93–108.

Roberts, John. "Clemenceau the Politician." *History Today* 6 (September, 1956): 581–91.

Robuchon, Jean. *Les Grandes heures de Georges Clemenceau.* Fontenay-le-Comte: Lussaud frères, 1967.

Sorre, Maurice. "Clemenceau: Notes sur l'empirisme radical." *Cahiers de la république,* no. 1 (1956), pp. 43–47.

Suarez, Georges. *La Vie orgueilleuse de Clemenceau.* Paris: Éditions de France, 1930.

Talvart, Hector. *La Vendée de Clemenceau.* La Rochelle: Raymond Bergevin, 1931.

Treich, Léon. *L'Esprit de Clemenceau.* Paris: Gallimard, 1925.

————. *Vie et mort de Clemenceau.* Paris: Édition de Portiques, 1929.

Varenne, Francis. "La Défaite de Georges Clemenceau à Draguignan, en 1893." *Revue politique et parlementaire,* no. 646 (1955), pp. 255–59.

Watson, David Robin. *Georges Clemenceau: A Political Biography*. New York: David McKay Co., Inc., 1976.

Wormser, Georges. *La République de Clemenceau*. Paris: Presses universitaires de France, 1961.

Zévaès, Alexandre. *Clemenceau*. Paris: René Julliard, 1949.

Index